LEE, MYSELF & I

WYNDHAM WALLACE

INSIDE THE VERY SPECIAL WORLD OF LEE HAZLEWOOD

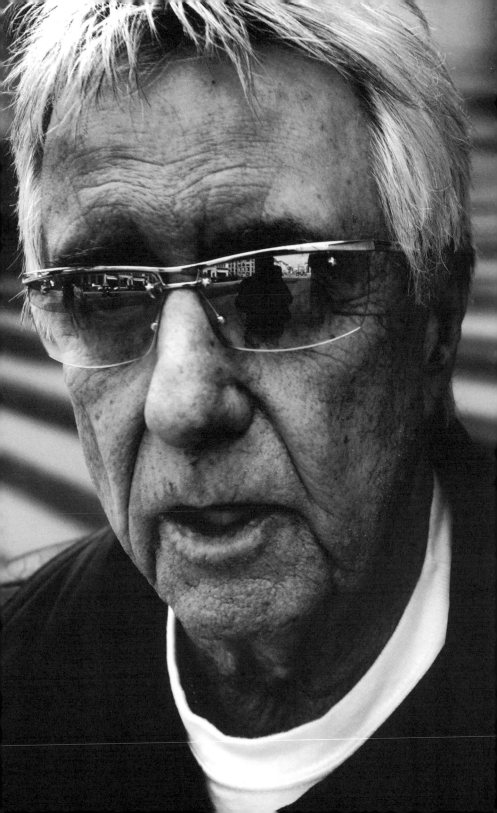

LEE, MYSELF & I
INSIDE THE VERY SPECIAL WORLD OF LEE HAZLEWOOD
WYNDHAM WALLACE

Dedicated to the memory of Granny Panda.

A Jawbone book
First edition 2015
Published in the UK and the USA by
Jawbone Press
2a Union Court,
20–22 Union Road,
London SW4 6JP,
England
www.jawbonepress.com

ISBN 978-1-908279-72-9

EDITOR Tom Seabrook
JACKET DESIGN Stefan Kassel

Printed in the Czech Republic by PB Print UK

1 2 3 4 5 19 18 17 16 15

CONTENTS

FOREWORD

BY STEWART LEE | 6

INTRODUCTION

| 10

SIDE A

CHAPTER 1 *I AM A PART* | 16

CHAPTER 2 *GOT IT TOGETHER* | 59

CHAPTER 3 *NOT THE LOVING KIND* | 79

CHAPTER 4 *THE PERFORMER* | 82

SIDE B

CHAPTER 5 *MY AUTUMN'S DONE COME* | 112

CHAPTER 6 *WE ALL MAKE THE LITTLE FLOWERS GROW* | 175

CHAPTER 7 *CAKE OR DEATH* | 184

CHAPTER 8 *I'LL LIVE YESTERDAYS* | 211

AUTHOR'S NOTE

DIRTNAP STORIES | 231

HAZLEWOOD 101

AN INEVITABLY INCOMPLETE GUIDE TO THE VOCAL RECORDINGS OF LEE HAZLEWOOD | 233

ACKNOWLEDGEMENTS

| 244

FOREWORD
BY STEWART LEE

All writing is, to some extent, autobiography. It's an especially egoless writer who can remove all traces of themselves, their own hopes, their own agenda, entirely from their work. In the late 80s, working as a botanical fact-checker, I read Mao-era Chinese plant directories whose pedagogic compilers had made even the natural processes of flowering shrubs fit their own views on the social order.

Wyndham Wallace's book about the American singer-songwriter Lee Hazlewood, *Lee, Myself & I*, acknowledges the role of the subjective writer in its very title, as he inserts himself, Boswell-style, into the final act of the story of a more significant figure. From the outset, Wallace admits that the observer and the observed are, in his tale, inextricably intertwined.

Who, then, was Lee Hazlewood? If you were a mainstream pop consumer of the 60s and 70s, maybe you noticed his name as a writing credit on Nancy Sinatra's ageless 'These Boots Are Made For Walkin'', a staple of Ed 'Stewpot' Stewart's Saturday morning requests show. If you were an underground indie-rock consumer of the 80s and 90s then you'd have seen that same writing credit attached to a slowly resurfacing song called 'Some Velvet Morning', covered by Thin White Rope, Lydia Lunch, and Primal Scream.

But you'd rarely have been able to hear Hazlewood's originals, their holy dirty realist visions suffused with a sexual mysticism and fatalistic humour none of the interpreters' versions come close to. More revered rock names would plunder Hazlewood's back catalogue—The Fall, Nick Cave,

Megadeth—but in the pre-internet days it remained impossible to simply google your way to enlightenment. Then, gradually, the silver-disc reissues of Hazlewood's own work began creeping out, and the man himself finally emerged from the cloud of unknowing, a ludicrous, absurd, brilliant Tin Pan Alley genius.

And who then, is Wyndham Wallace? I met Wyndham once or twice in the pre-Britpop era, when I was writing record reviews for a Sunday newspaper, and when he was acting as some kind of publicist for arty American post-rock bands, and then never met him again. But from what I remember, Wallace was a man clearly cut from rather too cultured a cloth to be slumming nightly in Camden dive bars, but nonetheless distinguished himself by his genuine and persuasive enthusiasm for his clients' work.

My initial prejudices, it appears, upon reading his book, were correct. Wallace is a virtual aristocrat, expensively educated at boarding school, born and bred to rule alongside Cameron and Osborne. A disappointment to his ancient military lineage, he chose to go to London to chase childhood dreams of working in rock'n'roll, only to find himself sleeping in a converted garage, in which he is woken by the sound of men urinating only inches from his head. Like a good performer, Wyndham selects his clown—he is the innocent abroad in a wicked world—and embodies it.

And why Lee Hazlewood and Wyndham Wallace? It appears these two travellers' paths crossed at the perfect point. Today, nearly a decade after his death, few who know his work would hesitate in declaring Lee Hazlewood an artist. He was a writer and performer of exceptional talent, who found a depth and density in the pop format few have ever equalled, but Hazlewood himself seemed reluctant to accept any accolades.

An invisible man, Hazlewood hid behind comedic alter egos when DJing, behind other singers' voices when writing, behind a moustache, and behind gnomic anecdotes and sayings when in conversation, and his former studio intern, Phil Spector, made off with the unmarked plans from which he went on to build his own Wall of Sound.

Hazlewood was, it appeared, a journeyman, a songwriter and producer for hire, second fiddle to the famous star he duetted with on his own mighty compositions, a satellite of the Rat Pack, a lounge lizard and barfly wit, more likely to talk percentages and publishing deals than be drawn into a discussion of meaning or metaphor or the creative process.

I'm a stand-up comedian. I spend a lot of time trying to convince myself, and others, that I am an artist, that I have some sense of worth. The comedian Frank Skinner says comedians are never artists, merely service providers, and that they should be happy to be service providers. Hazlewood, I expect, would have related to this, even though all the evidence shows that he transcended the limits of the formats he worked within to create a timeless body of work. Thankfully for Hazlewood, and also for us, someone arrived in his twilight years who was looking for a sense of purpose, and the critical rehabilitation of Lee Hazlewood would do just fine.

Hearing the then unheralded Hazlewood on an old vinyl slab on a cheap stereo in someone else's bedsit in the early 90s, Wallace fell quickly and heavily for the voice in question and eventually ended up as the reclusive singer-songwriter's de-facto European manager, overseeing re-releases and new releases and possible live dates. Wallace and Hazlewood's journey, recalled by the writer as peppered with bon mots and good dinners, leads to a performance at London's Royal Festival Hall, a spindle on which the story turns.

Hazlewood's appearance before the Liberal Intelligentsia, a guest in Nick Cave's 1999 Meltdown, while not even as lucrative as a B-side he might have tossed off for someone else in the mid-60s, nonetheless moves the Texan troubadour through the tradesmen's entrance and squarely into the Salon Des Arts. I suspect, though it's never made entirely explicit in the text, that the experience offered these two very different personalities a similar taste of self-respect.

Wallace confesses, modestly, that he feels his attempt to reposition Hazlewood in the star-spangled firmament alongside other great American archetypes failed, and it's true that the whisky-voiced auteur is still not a household name. But Wallace helped shift quality physical media product bearing Hazlewood's name, in the dying days before everything went virtual, paved the way for further reissue programmes, and, above all, left us with this document of Lee Hazelwood's own reluctant attempts to reconcile his life and his legend, a process through which Wallace himself found a kind of redemption.

Stewart Lee,
Writer/clown,
December 2014

INTRODUCTION

As I worked on this book, people would sometimes ask me what I was writing about.

'Lee Hazlewood,' I'd say.

'Who's he?' most would reply.

'The man who wrote "These Boots Are Made For Walkin'" for Nancy Sinatra,' I'd explain.

'Oh!' they'd claim. 'I've heard of him.'

But usually they hadn't. Though the general public might be familiar with the global hits—and these also include 'Summer Wine', 'Sugar Town', 'Houston', and 'Some Velvet Morning'—few recognise Lee as the man behind these classics, especially the ones on which he avoided the microphone. Fewer still are aware of his solo work, and even now his influence upon generations of musicians is only slowly being acknowledged. Furthermore, his chequered career as a music mogul, radio DJ, record producer, and filmmaker remains a secret to all but the most curious of fans.

Such ignorance is forgivable, and understandable. Recognition for one's work in the arts is hard to gain at the best of times, and, frequently, it's ephemeral anyway. Lee, moreover, vigorously shunned it. Perhaps this wasn't always true: having been born almost exactly forty-two years later than Lee, I'm far too young to insist upon this. But the facts point towards someone distinctly uncomfortable with uninvited attention.

Lee grew up with a stutter, and his later, obstinate exterior hid a sensitive, troubled personality. When, in his late thirties, he wrote prophetically of his old age in 'My Autumn's Done Come', he reserved his pithiest delivery for the line 'Leave me alone, damn it, let me do as I please'. At his memorial party, I learned that early in his life he'd been treated with lithium to overcome depression, and after he chose to disdain this medication, because he believed it numbed his creative spirit, he was sometimes forced to remove himself from the family he'd fathered, on occasion for days at a time. As he'd realised all too soon, such moods would haunt him all his life. The spotlight was never going to be his friend.

Nonetheless, in his glory days, Lee moved in rarefied circles. He didn't seek celebrity society—in fact, he often preferred to spend time with those who had few, if any, connections to his work—but his endeavours led him to encounter a roll call of figures as implausible as it was impressive, spread across multiple fields, many of whom remain household names to this day: Jack Nicholson, Mick Jagger, Richard Pryor, Frank Sinatra, Joan Collins, Björn Borg, Rod Stewart, ABBA, Ingrid Bergman, Peter Sellers, Jacqueline Bisset, and of course the members of The Rat Pack were all names that tumbled freely from his tongue, often with a gentle tone of disbelief.

His songs, too, found him in illustrious company: quite apart from the monster hits he enjoyed with Nancy Sinatra—and 'Boots' was a transatlantic #1—his compositions were recorded during his heyday by the likes of Diana Ross & The Supremes, B.B. King, Dusty Springfield, Elvis Presley, Dean Martin, Frank Sinatra, and Loretta Lynn, while his magnetic appeal to musicians has rarely declined since. Over the last couple of decades, his catalogue has been plundered by a dizzyingly varied selection of acts, including Beck, Lana Del Rey, Marc Almond, The Fall, Einstürzende Neubauten, Jarvis Cocker and Richard Hawley, The Corrs with Bono, The Jesus & Mary Chain, Tracey Thorn, Frank Black (of the Pixies), Primal Scream with Kate Moss, Nick Cave, and even Megadeth, though Lee successfully—and gleefully—sued the latter for infantile alterations to his lyrics.

Right from the outset, Lee steered clear of scrutiny by choosing to write songs rather than record them. Even that left him exposed: he once told me how as a young man he'd take the Greyhound bus from Phoenix to Los

Angeles to visit music publishers who 'were kind enough to listen to [my songs] and tell me how bad they were, which would bring a tear to your eye when you're in your early twenties'. So, instead of standing behind a microphone to begin his career, he sat behind one as a DJ, and even there he regularly employed different personae to conceal himself. In fact, having finally stepped sideways into the music business, he still released records performed by others—albeit sometimes written by him, another sure-fire way to avoid the limelight while nonetheless enacting his ambitions—before becoming a record producer out of necessity, almost by accident rather than design. This was a happy accident, of course: among other achievements, he'd later end up responsible for another American and British #1, Frank and Nancy Sinatra's evergreen version of 'Somethin' Stupid'.

The seemingly haphazard route he pursued was similarly discernible in his career as a singer: though it's true he recorded a few solo singles while still in his twenties, he employed a pseudonym, Mark Robinson. Additionally, his later duets with Nancy were only recorded because she grew so fond of his 'whisky voice' as he sang them to her that she rejected the idea of other musical partners. Even his first solo album, *Trouble Is A Lonesome Town*, was cut with his own voice—intended purely as a demo—simply because 'it saved me a lot of time. I would have had to teach somebody how I wanted it narrated, how I wanted it sung'.

Since his regular demo singers, he informed me, included Glen Campbell, it's evident that Lee had a very strong sense of his goals. This, perhaps, was another reason that he was never embraced by the mainstream: compromise was never on his agenda, either artistically or financially. Such inflexibility, coupled with his habit of shielding his vulnerability behind an irascible personality, and what became known as a legendarily fierce temper, meant his unsuitability for the glare of mainstream pop was indisputable.

And yet he left his mark all over the place—occasionally conspicuously, but more frequently unnoticed beside the more prominent names of those with whom he worked. As a DJ, he hosted a popular morning show and introduced Elvis Presley to Arizona. As a label entrepreneur, he earned a reputation as an indomitable businessman, and was later chosen by Lester Sill to be his partner following the departure of former colleagues Jerry Leiber and Mike Stoller, the songwriting heavyweights behind Presley's 'Hound Dog' and 'Jailhouse Rock'. As a studio guru, he hit the big time in 1956 producing Sanford Clark's 'The Fool', before collaborating with Duane Eddy and changing the way people played guitar.

Little of this is celebrated by the world at large. In fact, it's only known to me because, growing up, I developed the kind of habits familiar to those who sometimes find more comfort in music than in company. Lee Hazlewood provided one of the most exciting journeys available to a twenty-one-year-old youth in the early 90s. Though comebacks by forgotten or little-known artists, whether in the flesh or on vinyl, weren't unheard of—Nick Drake's profile, for instance, had grown during my last years at school in the mid-to-late 80s, as had The Velvet Underground's—learning about Lee Hazlewood presented a real test. Apart from his most established work—and at times including even that—it was almost impossible to purchase copies of the records upon which he appeared.

But what rewards the efforts reaped. Just to hear his voice was a joy, albeit a double-edged joy, given the manner in which his voice veered from a swooning croon to a foreboding snarl. To admire his lyrics, too, was to revel in layers of forbidden meaning often hidden beneath an artless, almost childlike sincerity. And to revel in the sound of his records—so innovative as to be spine-tingling; at times lushly orchestrated, at others barren and sepulchral—felt almost like a sin. To become his friend, however? That, naturally, was an inconceivable ambition.

Just as Lee's voice had thrilled and threatened me on vinyl, so it did in real life. I've always been equally attracted to and intimidated by charismatic, dominant figures whose affection is hard earned but fleeting, and Lee was no exception. The fear his legend provoked in me only subsided because I grew to love him, and it never entirely disappeared: however close we became, he always remained just out of reach, part human, part myth, a figure to file—but still yet to be filed—in the catalogue of great American idols alongside

Lee Marvin, John Wayne, Clint Eastwood, Robert Duvall, James Coburn, and Robert Mitchum. That these are all actors is no coincidence: at times my existence around him seemed so far removed from the reality with which I'd grown up that I felt like I was indeed in a movie.

Today, Lee Hazlewood's name remains undiscovered on any grand scale, despite my attempts, from 1999 until a year or so after his death in 2007, to re-establish what I consider to be his rightful place in the musical firmament, and a second, laudable undertaking in recent years by the Seattle-based independent label Light In The Attic to reissue a number of his records. This may be partially due to the failure of my efforts, but it's also a symptom of Lee's own relationship with success and fame, as well as, perhaps, the eccentric nature of his output. Whatever the cause, it's something that saddens me. His praises deserve to be sung as much as his songs.

SIDE A

My father, Gabe Hazlewood, was a teller
of stories, as was my grandfather, Ed
Robinson. They told great stories.

   Some of my first memories were their
stories. At the end of the story I'd question
them. 'Are they true?'

   My father's reply was always, 'That's not
important. Good stories need to be told.'

   I didn't understand then.

   I think I do now.

LEE HAZLEWOOD

I AM A PART

It's mid-afternoon on a sunny springtime Friday as I stroll back and forth in front of hotel lobby elevators, the confusingly autumnal light of New York's Grand Hyatt reflected in their golden doors. Tourists flood check-in desks while nearby, in plush chairs and on elegant sofas, businessmen and women try to wrap up meetings so they can head to the bar. I, however, am nervously awaiting the entrance of a man whose reputation precedes him with such ferocity that my hands are clammy and trembling. No one knows where he's been, or what he's been doing. Hardly anyone's seen him for years. Why I've been selected for this privilege remains puzzling.

A polite chime announces another lift's arrival, but as I wipe my palms on ragged Levi's, all that greets me is a fresh set of anonymous faces. I look around to see if anyone is watching, conscious that I resemble a stalker who's slipped past security. These people can afford to stay here, while I, on my salary, barely dare ask the price of water. Still, despite these luxury surroundings, I remain unnoticed, dwarfed beneath a high ceiling, with only my trainers, which squeak on polished floors, drawing attention to my presence. I wonder if I'll remain invisible to the man I'm supposed to meet.

I have every right to be here, but my presence in the lavish setting of this Manhattan hotel only serves to emphasise the differences between the two of us. My night was spent in a windowless Brooklyn basement, sharing a narrow bed with the only person I know who can accommodate me for free. The master I am hoping to encounter probably has a suite upstairs on a private floor with a view of 42nd Street.

This man—a hero of mine for the best part of a decade—surely expects to find a veteran of the music industry waiting for him. The least he'll anticipate is someone well accustomed to classy hotels, steak dinners, vintage whisky, gold discs on the wall, the popping of flashbulbs, the scent of celebrity. It won't take long for him to recognise that I'm incapable of providing the kind of service with which he's undoubtedly familiar. After all, the musicians for whom I work are—relative to his accomplishments— marginal at best. Even the most successful of them still sands floors for a living. But this gentleman? He's been employed by Frank Sinatra, written for Dean Martin, hung out with Elvis, and given the world one of the most instantly recognisable pop songs it's ever known. Coming here was a stupid, stupid idea.

I slump down into one of the few vacant armchairs, apprehensive about what I'm sure will soon unfold. I pull my frayed red James Dean jacket around me, trying to conceal myself from view, and watch as the elevator doors slide open once again.

It's too late to hide. At long last he emerges, dressed all in black: a black leather jacket, loose black jeans, and a black cotton shirt with a sagging pocket over the breast. His face is shaded by a cheap baseball cap pulled down over greying hair, his eyes hidden by expensive sunglasses. He's shorter and stockier than I expected, but he's still built like a former fighter who, once his moustache was softened with whisky, probably sent more than a few men to the floor.

As it happens, the trademark handlebar he sported in the 60s is gone, his jawline and upper lip instead stubbled with lazy white whiskers. In fact, he looks more like a suntanned pensioner clinging to his youth on a visit to see the grandchildren than a reclusive, fabled singer, songwriter, producer, and music Svengali. But I know it's him immediately, even if he remains invisible to everyone else but me.

It's time to get this over. Leaping to attention, I clear my throat and step forward politely towards him.

'Lee Hazlewood?' I ask.

'Wyndham Wallace?' he smiles.

'Hi,' I say, holding out a shaking hand. 'It's a pleasure to meet you.'

He looks me up and down, amused yet suspicious. While I'm barely more underdressed than he is for the environment, I'm immediately embarrassed by my shabby charity-store clothes, my uncontrollably curly hair, my evident youth and inexperience. I'm mere shit on his shoes.

It's April 1999. I'm twenty-seven years old and live by one of London's toughest streets in a roughly converted garage, its wood-panelled door still installed on my bedroom's outer wall. Sometimes I'm awoken by the sound of men pissing inches from my head.

Lee Hazlewood is sixty-nine years old and lives in Kissimmee, Florida, where an alligator eyes him every day as he drinks Chivas Regal by his pool.

I spent ten years in a red brick boarding school that cost my parents thousands of pounds every term. He wrote one song, 'These Boots Are Made For Walkin'', that could have paid for me to study there all my life.

I once kissed a woman after she was seduced by 'Some Velvet Morning', Lee's hallucinatory duet with Nancy Sinatra, which I played on a tinny car stereo. Lee once seduced the whole of America performing 'Some Velvet Morning' on a national TV special.

I own battered copies of his albums on vinyl that I tirelessly hunted down. He wrote, produced, and recorded those albums and saw them advertised on Sunset Strip.

I've never worked for an act that's sold more than 15,000 records in the UK. He's worked with artists who sold that many records in a day.

His handshake is firm. His face is inscrutable. He turns to the crop-haired blonde accompanying him, then back to me.

'How the fuck old are you? Thirteen?'

I'm not even shit on his shoes.

* * *

Twenty-one years old, unruly hair tied up in a ponytail that sprouts from my head like broccoli, I wander past soggy, suitably dog-eared posters for

Quentin Tarantino's *Reservoir Dogs*. Rain pricks my face and numbs my fingers as I read the tagline: *'Every dog has his day.'* They probably don't mean today. A suit like the ones in the picture might help, but I'm sick of suits: when you start wearing them at the age of eight you build up a little resentment towards them.

In any case, this is no place for a suit. Exhaust fumes from double-parked delivery trucks linger in the moist, grey air while their drivers haul caged trolleys laden with goods into waiting stores, the clatter of metal on concrete as ugly as a hangover. The fruit racked out in front of a nearby grocery store appears terminally pale, as if covered by a thick film of dust. It's a weekday morning in early 1993 on London's Golborne Road, a parochial, black-and-white setting far from Tarantino's Los Angeles. The only suits appropriate here are for funerals. This is England, my England.

London on this crucial day—full of filthy buildings, filthy pigeons, and filthy mouths—is stunning in its squalor, thrilling in its danger. The capital's grime enfolds us: its gutters are a rusty dun, its walls stained with piss, its sky pasty like an English holiday. These monochrome streets are so dirty that one's shoes stick to the tarmac, unlike the polite, well-kept roads of Exeter, the city where I'm currently studying, or the perfectly strimmed paths of Radley College, my earlier alma mater.

I love it here. It's a million miles removed from the polished corridors of the schools where I spent a decade that still haunts me; a million miles from that gloomy, oak-panelled dining room, with its oil portraits of former headmasters, and the grand, high-ceilinged chapel with wooden pews, wheezing organ, and rare reredos. This street—this scummy road with its graffiti-covered walls, discarded food wrappers, and patches of chewing gum like dried phlegm—lies instead at the heart of a world I've come to love through some of my favourite music. London is the capital of a land that my mind inhabits, one filtered through the records of artists I adore. It's a strange place, for it also boasts Manchester, Minneapolis, Liverpool, New York, Glasgow, and Melbourne. It's been built by Talk Talk, The Smiths, Prince, and Frankie Goes To Hollywood, and decorated by Sonic Youth,

The Blue Nile, and The Go-Betweens. I've barely seen it, but I'm lost anywhere else.

I'm also lost in music, just as I'd be lost without it. Sister Sledge made the point with more style and panache, but music is my salvation. Try as I might, I just don't fit in where I belong—probably because I've spent half my life wishing I were somewhere else. Heirloom carriage clocks, leather-bound bibles, and gold signet rings can never provide any of the comfort that my rattling cassette collection represents. Songs speak to me—certainly more than most kids my own age do. Play that indie music, white boy.

All the same, the music that will make this occasion one of the most significant of my life is still just out of earshot, until now unheard. All music obsessives have days they'll never forget, but they designate them as such from the moment the apparently recognisable, life-changing incident occurs: the minute they heard Kurt Cobain had shot himself, for instance.

This is not one of those days. I won't recognise the repercussions of what is about to happen for some time. It will instead be distinguished by an absence of information, and what will make it extraordinary years down the line is that this space will in time, in the most unlikely fashion, be filled.

Right now, the day's significance lies in the fact that in eighteen months I'll leave university. The one thing I want to do is work in the music business, and the only way to work in the business is to make friends with people who do just that. My ambition, I suspect, is a forlorn hope, a no doubt elusive dream; self-confidence isn't my strength, and it seems unlikely that I'll stand a chance in the competitive world of the music industry. Still, hope sings eternal.

I've not made it this far alone. Strolling beside me is Drew, my co-editor at the university magazine that has provided the excuse for our presence in London. He calls me 'Indie Wyndy', and is, typically, completely unruffled by the prospect of the meetings ahead. His cocksure charm is impervious—it's one of the reasons I've befriended him—and he's also a shield behind which I can retreat. My Queen's English betrays me, and my stonewashed jeans and cheap red denim jacket can't camouflage the Little Lord Fauntleroy I once was. With casually greasy hair, a flowery, vintage shirt, and brown, corduroy flares, Drew is a man of confidence, brash and hip, and has no problem at all taking charge.

It's Drew who set up this first of the day's engagements. Though I'm grateful, I also fear he'll dominate it. He knows the guy from the phone, whereas I just know him from *Melody Maker*, the music paper I buy obsessively every week: the man played in Loop, a band its journalists championed. One Sunday I even saw them perform on the main stage at Reading Festival. It's true they played third on the bill that afternoon, and actually I hadn't liked them—though naturally I pretended I did—but to me he's a rock star all the same. I can afford to make neither a bad impression nor a timid one on any of the people we're here to meet, and these are things at which I'm expert. The fact that there are more of these meetings to come over the course of the next forty-eight hours—and that some of them are appointments I've set up—does nothing to reassure me.

'*Every dog has his day*,' the poster warned, and I might only get this one chance. I push open a spattered glass door before Drew leads me to a Formica-topped table under the fluorescent lights of this greasy spoon café. I settle down beside him and pick up a stained, plastic-laminated menu, studying it closely in silence before tossing it to Drew, who soon places our order at the till.

Honestly, this is the most exciting place I could be in the world. I just might die with a smile on my face after all. On the other side of the road, in a glass-fronted, ground-floor office that is now tantalisingly close, I can see the headquarters of Rough Trade Records, a company that stands for much of the independent label aesthetic that I've come to admire.

Any moment now, one of their publicists, James Endeacott, will join us at this table. Drew and I are, of course, acquainted with concert promoters back in Exeter, but up until now no one in London's music industry has considered us worthy of personal time. While Drew perhaps couldn't care less, I appreciate what this development symbolises. London is where it all happens. Exeter is … well, Exeter's in Devon.

I have to work in music. There's nothing else I can imagine doing. True musicians are, to me, untouchable, capable of provoking a magical response through nothing so much as vibrating air. To manoeuvre myself into a place where I can associate with them, just as the man about to meet us has already done, is the only future I can envisage that might genuinely fulfil me. If I could, I'd make music myself, obviously, but that's out of the question. You should have heard the bands I was in; each one changed its name after every show.

No, performing is inconceivable. I've got to make it in the biz.

James bustles in, a mass of hair bursting from his head in an even more mutinous fashion than my own, though worn with enviably more swagger. He confirms our identities, orders a coffee, then sits down and pushes a seven-inch vinyl record across the ring-stained table towards us. It's part of what's called the Rough Trade Singles Club, and though I've heard of the band—Tindersticks—its content excites me less than the implications of the action, which feel like a secret initiation. This is a limited-edition release, one that only a restricted number of people will own, and we've been deemed worthy of a copy. One between two of us, true, but it's the gesture that matters, and maybe Drew won't want it anyway.

I let my colleague examine it first, hoping to hide my girlish enthusiasm. After only a cursory scan of its cover, he passes it on for inspection. The sleeve's design is generic, a logo like a postage stamp in the top right-hand corner and the band's name justified to the left. Only the central image has been selected by the band, and they've chosen a black-and-white illustration of a moustachioed man, his mouth open slightly, as though lost deep in thought. One dark, sleepy eye stares, yearning, towards some undisclosed object out of sight. The other is lost in shadow.

It's a quietly dramatic sketch, the sympathetic face of an old man remembering his childhood, or perhaps the weather-beaten face of a rugged gunslinger watching his life leave him. It's a face I've known for years.

'Who's that?' I ask.

'Lee Hazlewood,' James replies.

I nod knowledgeably, though I've certainly never seen him before. If I recognise the name it's only from a few interviews I've read with artists who—as far as I can recall—suggested he was a forgotten country singer. While the tinkle of teaspoons and café chatter continue around us, I scrutinise the portrait, the way the moustache droops despondently towards the jawline; the longing betrayed in those mysterious eyes. I'm impatient to know why this man is on the cover of a single with which he's got no obvious connection.

'My parents have some of his records,' Drew informs us proudly.

Though I hope I appear nonchalant, I start to take mental notes.

'Yeah, he did a lot more than "These Boots Are Made For Walkin'",' James replies, his tone to me like a bullshit detector waiting to sound an alarm.

I'm confused: I always thought 'These Boots Are Made For Walkin'' was bubble-gum, kitschy girl pop, but the man on this record looks like an outlaw. I must be mixing something up. Curiosity coaxes me out of my shell.

'Wasn't that sung by a woman?' I ask shyly, praying I'm not mistaken. If you're going to talk cult heroes to experts, you need to know your subject.

'Yeah,' James confirms, slightly impatiently. 'Nancy.'

He fails to see any flicker of recognition in my eyes.

'Nancy Sinatra,' he clarifies. 'Frank's daughter.'

I feel a little stupid, but James is kind enough not to notice. I try to ignore the noise around me: the hiss of steam and crackle of bacon behind the counter, the buzz of a scooter passing trucks outside. I've got to keep up with him.

'He did a lot of stuff with her,' James continues, 'wrote it and produced it, sometimes even sang with her. But the solo records are the best. The records he made in Sweden in the 70s: that's the shit you've got to get.'

'Yeah, I know,' Drew boasts decisively. 'But that stuff's hard to find.'

He's bullshitting, surely, but convincing nevertheless.

'I've noticed his name around,' I say, trying to claw back credibility. 'I've seen him mentioned in *Melody Maker*.'

'True,' James interrupts,' but I don't think many people know much about him. No one really knows where he is. One time I heard he joined a monastery.'

'A monastery?' Drew splurts, surprised at last. Even a pro couldn't have held that one in.

'Yeah,' James laughs. 'Another story I heard is he got chased out of America because he was having an affair with Nancy. Ol' Blue Eyes didn't like that, so Lee ran away to Sweden. It's probably bollocks, but you never know: no one's heard much from him since. So maybe he is in a monastery. Or maybe Frank got to him. You know what Frank could do …'

Drew chuckles, but what Frank could do is a mystery to me. So, with my companions' voices fading like an old pop song, I pick up the sleeve to inspect the credits, before turning it over to examine the picture once more, as if it will offer clues. There's something about this Lee Hazlewood character that has taken me elsewhere. Where his music should now be there are only empty grooves waiting to be filled. It's their prevailing silence—the sound of his mysterious absence—I hear rather than the on-going discussion, and by the time we stub out our cigarettes to leave, I'm no longer present at all. I'm already in record stores, in charity shops, in musty, dark basements, my fingers dirty, my eyes tortured by faint print, my nostrils dry with the dust of a thousand lives buried in oily black vinyl.

* * *

'Well, come on then,' Lee Hazlewood barks, looking around at the Grand Hyatt's busy lobby, already impatient. 'Why stand 'round talking here when there's a bar?'

He turns on his heels and speeds away across the marble floor towards the front of the building, where bow-tied men in pressed white shirts and immaculate waistcoats stand before a row of spotless bottles, preparing drinks for businessmen wielding bulky mobile phones like remote controls. Raven-haired businesswomen in power suits, their stockinged legs hanging from barstools, sip Martinis beside them. It doesn't look like I'm going to feel any more comfortable over there.

'Hi,' I say weakly, as Lee strides off into the distance. 'You must be Jeane. Nice to meet you at last.'

'Hi,' she replies, smiling welcomingly back at me. 'Nice to meet you, too.'

We catch up with Lee and seat ourselves around a table on plush red-leather benches, our silhouettes reflected in the windows that separate us from yellow taxicabs sneaking along the tarmac beneath. Despite the bustle below, it's quiet in the bar, as though we're observing animal behaviour through glass.

'What do you drink?' Lee asks.

'I'm a lager man,' I tell him.

'A lager man,' he smirks, turning to Jeane and enjoying the sound of an English accent. 'Guess we got ourselves a Brit!'

'That's true,' I laugh nervously. 'That's definitely true.'

'Well, I don't know if they have *lager*'—he says the word with inverted commas—'but I'm sure you can find something to suit your tastes. Unless you feel more adventurous …'

I rub a finger nervously along the edge of the table. There's a hint of a challenge to his tone.

'What are you having?' I enquire.

'I always drink the same thing: Scotch,' he says. 'Chivas on the rocks.'

He pronounces it 'Shee-vas', I notice, not 'Shivers'.

'And you?' I ask Jeane. She's sliding around on her seat, like a child making herself comfy. She looks happy, even excited. She's dressed in jeans as plain as mine and a golden sweater, its price admittedly unlikely to reflect its colour, and is obviously younger than Lee, her short, fair hair framing a round face with a smile that so far appears permanent.

'I'll just have a Coke,' she says. 'I don't really drink.'

'Well, what can you recommend?' I ask. I'm British, but not inflexible.

'Well, what do you like?' she replies.

'I don't really drink much apart from beer, though I quite like a gin and tonic. And Margaritas,' I remember. 'I like a good Margarita. Though I'm not sure I've drunk enough Margaritas to know what a good one tastes like.'

'Well, then,' Lee decides on my behalf, 'I think you'd better have a good Margarita. Here you go, baby'—he slips Jeane a wad of cash—'go get me a Chivas and Wyndham Wallace a Margarita. And whatever you want. Otherwise we'll be here all day waiting to get served.'

Jeane slides off her seat.

'Sure thing, honey.'

She skips to the bar.

There's silence at the table now that the drinks are decided, and, for a second or two, the reality of whom I'm with smacks me hard across a peach-fuzzed cheek. This is the man who made Nancy Sinatra a star, delivering her to the top of the charts with songs so beloved they could start playing in this bar any moment. He recorded under-appreciated but outstanding albums of his own, too—records so eccentric that they rarely penetrated the mainstream but nonetheless so good they more than justify the commitment, energy, and substantial cash it now takes to track them down. He discovered and produced Duane Eddy, 'The Titan of Twang', so named because of the resonant sound the two of them coaxed from Duane's guitar, and also ran record labels, instigating the career of other influentials, including Gram Parsons, who'd gone on to join The Byrds, and Phil Spector, whose 'Wall of Sound' was arguably a refinement of techniques he'd witnessed Lee using while working as his apprentice.

Merely a handful of these facts should have guaranteed his spot in the Rock and Roll Hall of Fame, and yet here he is, unrecognised, sitting so close that I can see the nostril hair poking from his nose. His girlfriend, meanwhile, is buying me a Margarita with money plucked from his very pocket. No wonder he's looking at me, head slightly cocked, as though he's waiting for me—or even daring me—to speak.

'So,' I panic, 'how's the trip been so far?'

'Oh, fine, fine,' he replies, pulling a cigarette from his packet, immune to the banality of the question. 'We've just been seeing a few people, wandering around. We're going for steaks with Sonic Youth later.'

There's a trace of adolescent pride in this last statement, as if he's a long-term fan of this celebrated New York band. As Jeane returns, he names the restaurant, as though this underlines the honour.

'Your Margarita is coming,' Jeane announces gaily, sinking back down beside her older companion. 'I told them to salt it. That's how you're meant to drink them.'

The waiter arrives soon afterwards. My Margarita is huge, with giant rocks of salt clinging like frosted jewels to the rim of a glass the size of a mediaeval goblet.

'Go on, then, try it,' Jeane says impatiently. 'How is it?'

I lean over the table and suck on a straw that dangles from the pastel green slush.

'That's good,' I wince. 'That's really good.'

It's actually acutely sour and cold enough to crack my teeth, but I hoist my glass over the table.

'Cheers,' I say.

Lee raises his Chivas warily for the toast, keen to make sure no salt falls into his drink. Jeane's less fussy and bangs her glass carelessly against ours.

'Cheers,' she laughs, caricaturing my accent. 'Enjoy your Margarita.'

Muzak plays gently in the background. Voices bounce off the ceiling. I wonder how much my drink cost.

* * *

One rainy night later, Drew and I stagger along uneven pavements, skipping and tripping over split bin-liners and discarded beer cans, at last reaching a heavy wooden door that opens onto a cramped, poorly lit hallway. In front of us, traipsing up a dirty staircase, are members of a band called The Rockingbirds, who we met earlier over the pool table at a nearby venue. I left

Drew to charm them, barely uttering a single word. I'm Andrew Ridgeley to his George Michael.

We make our way into the living room and find space to sit.

'Beer, anyone?' our host calls.

'Naturally,' Drew laughs.

'Yes, please,' I reply. 'If you don't mind.'

My mother would be proud of my manners. A six-pack of warm Red Stripe appears, and we pluck cans from its plastic rings.

A couple of hours earlier, we'd attended a solo show by Mark Eitzel, whose band, American Music Club, have been a favourite of mine for some years. I'd hoped to shake Mark's hand afterwards—his publicists, also in attendance, had put us on the guest list after we'd squeezed time out of them that morning—but Mark is a notoriously troubled, sensitive performer. He left the stage of the Camden Falcon halfway through the gig, visibly troubled by a particularly blunt heckler. We learned later that Eitzel had walked straight out of the venue into a taxi; in distress, we heard elsewhere. To me, this confirmed his genuine artistic credentials, but Drew saw things differently.

'Never try to meet your heroes,' he reminded me. 'It always ends in tears.'

In actual fact, it had led to more beer, sloppy games of pool, and an invitation to a nearby flat. The Rockingbirds are definitely not my heroes, but they're signed to Heavenly Records, another successful indie label that I've read about time and time again. What the band's music is like is of little interest: I'm bound to enjoy it now they've invited Drew and me to their sanctuary. It's turned out to be a grubby, damp squat of a sanctuary, but that's the Camden of my student dreams.

'You want a smoke?' our host asks as he settles down into an armchair.

'Sure,' I respond, blushing when I realise he doesn't mean a cigarette, and then adding, possibly a little overeagerly, 'Definitely.'

London is certainly being kind to me: I've already watched one of my favourite musicians storm impulsively offstage. Now I'm about to smoke a joint with an up-and-coming band in colourful Western shirts whom both Drew and *Melody Maker* insist I should like. I've truly arrived in indie rock's inner sanctum, a promised land where mottled walls are lined with shelves of records; where threadbare, red wine-stained carpets are speckled with spilt ashtrays.

The man in the armchair beside me requests a cigarette. I throw my packet over. He pulls one out and licks its length, picking it carefully open and pouring the tobacco into a rolling paper. Tossing the pack back, he softens an impressive lump of hash with his lighter, before crumbling it into the Rizla. Drew is busy chatting elsewhere, so I watch this expert surreptitiously, keen to pick up tips.

The chair is uncomfortable, its springs poking me from underneath, foam spilling from its arms like toes from an old shoe. A siren in the distance prompts my neighbour to pass the joint my way so he can step up to the record player, where he slides an LP from the shelves. Placing the vinyl respectfully onto the turntable, he lifts the tone arm and lowers the needle. A lone cello chugs out a simple melody.

I draw on the joint, sucking hot smoke into my lungs. Its flowery perfume clings to my tonsils, making me want to gag. I sheepishly choke into my lap before taking a swig of Red Stripe to cool my throat, and then tap the ash into a nearby can. The next drag is a little gentler, and as I repeat the exercise I become accustomed to the flavour.

'Don't hog that, mate!' Drew reprimands me from shadows almost out of reach of the only light, a scuffed 1970s standard lamp. 'Leave some for us.'

'Sorry,' I stutter, and pass it on hurriedly, then sink further into my seat. I can never tell when he's serious.

My head tips back against the headrest as the cannabis dances with the night's alcohol. I stare up at the ceiling, where there's further discolouration spoiling what was once elaborate stucco. Closing my eyes and opening my ears seems preferable to facing my surroundings, and soon I find myself listening to a country song delivered in a voice as dark as the night outside: a tale of prison, of convicts who '*checked out in a casket*', the rhythm beaten out by the chip of hammer on stone. After a while I recognise in it a curious, comic absurdity, the hint of a hick accent in the voice increasingly ludicrous as—much like Travis Bickle committing to getting '*organised*'—he laments his '*ten thousand more breakfastses to go*'. Then, without warning, the tone shifts disarmingly to tender thoughts of Mama.

Perhaps it's the drugs, but I've never heard anything quite like this. In the past, I've winced at 'Jolene' and cringed at *Smokey & The Bandit*. I've been tortured by Kenny Rogers and endured 'American Pie'. If forced, I'll admit to having liked *The Dukes Of Hazzard*, but that theme tune, with a banjo that sounds like a plucked elastic band, is really best forgotten. As for 'Achy Breaky Heart' and its mulleted immortality, it's done no one but Billy Ray Cyrus any favours. Where I come from, unless they mean hunting horns, that's what they call country music.

This song, though, is something else. This song is rhinestone-free. I need to ask who it is, but as so often I don't dare appear unsophisticated. The music industry, the last forty-eight hours have warned me, is full of people trying to flaunt their knowledge while monitoring its lack in others. So I keep my mouth shut, and as the cello brings the song to a sedate conclusion, I slide further into my wrecked armchair. The record snaps, crackles, and pops.

A softly plucked guitar opens the next tune, a simple arpeggio that rolls by four times before the voice is back, lazy, seemingly as stoned as I now feel, echoing as though floating along damp granite corridors from a far-off prison cell.

'*Leather and lace,*' it intones, all distant and cavernous, '*hanging in place*'—now soft and loving—'*and the fire was as warm as the wine …*'

A drowsy oboe awakes, stirring the mist to rouse a solitary chord played on the strings of virgin-white violins. Things are definitely better with my eyes closed.

'*The leather was hot,*' it continues, '*the lace it was not*'—impossibly slowly—'*so she left my side for a time.*'

The pace picks up, the tune sweet enough for *Little House On The*

Prairie, though its lyrics—sung with relish, dragging just behind the beat— suggest otherwise. A female voice takes over, so sultry and indecently sexy that it tickles the hair on the back of my neck and almost makes me cross my legs. The strings are like veins swelling with blood—slowly at first, then increasingly uninhibited. A hint of horn and a tease of oboe offer brief flashes of bare skin, the melody floating over its surface. The song suddenly shifts up a key, and I gasp: it's like we've reached the peak of a treacherous mountain, and now, below us, as clouds part, we've discovered at last hidden hillsides and dark, unknown forests. I'm entering Freudian territory. Man, I really am stoned.

The male, more urgent now, lasciviously takes the lead, but the melody is swiftly snatched back by his foil, a suggestive, Scandinavian cadence nudging at the edge of her delivery. He grabs the song from her impatiently:

The leather was hot. (Saliva smacks in his mouth.)

The lace it was not. (Her again: proud, self-deluding.)

So she left my side for a time. (Him: sad but velvet smooth.)

Then I ran into town … (She throws a hand to her brow.)

Leaving my gown … (Her lip quivers.)

With a face like the red lace I wore … (I can almost smell the regret.)

Now the leather and lace still hangs in place … (Him again, defiant that he never needed more anyway.)

But I never see him anymore … (Her, one last time, regret now undeniable, as clear as her eyes are swollen.)

Almost imperceptibly, there's a final sigh from the cowboy: whether it's resigned or satisfied is hard to say. Next, the flutter of a heart: this time it's the strings. And, last, a chord that spreads and fades like a single drop of sweat on a shadowy, silken sheet: almost invisible, then gone.

This is the best fucking joint of my life.

I open my eyes and exhale, staring into the darkness on the other side of the window. It takes me a while to return to the room itself. Finally the spell is broken by the noise of conversation. I turn once more to our host.

'Who the fuck … ?' I stammer, unable to help myself, wide-eyed and immediately ashamed of my vulgarity in the light of this romance. 'Who the hell was that?'

'Lee Hazlewood,' our toking DJ answers. 'Do you know him?'

OK, I think, *that's weird. That's really, really weird.*

'Not yet,' I shake my head, still marvelling. 'I'm going to have to do something about that ...'

* * *

'So how long have you been doing this?' Lee asks.

'Oh,' I stammer. 'Erm ... five years or so.'

'That long, huh?' he grins. 'I bet you've seen some things ...'

Is he laughing at me already?

'Well, I run the UK office of a German record label, so I have a bit of experience,' I reply, hiding behind my Margarita. 'Though none of our artists are of quite the same stature as you.'

That was unnecessary. There's no need to kiss his arse.

'Yeah, well,' he replies, 'I'm not sure what kind of stature you think I have, but there are dwarves with more than me. Sorry: *little people.*'

Jeane laughs. I start to relax. The alcohol helps.

'I'm certainly not a man of stature,' he continues. 'I'm just an old cowboy who wrote a few songs, and God help anyone who thinks I'm going to make them rich. No, you'll do just fine.'

His eyes shine, a moist film covering irises that look like they absorb light.

'So, how does a guy with a name like Wyndham Wallace end up doing this? Are your folks in the biz?'

'No, actually my father's in the army,' I explain. 'I don't think this is what they had in mind for me.'

'Is that so?' Lee mulls this over slowly, and then grins mischievously. 'Don't they like cowboys?'

'That's not what I meant,' I hurriedly assure him. 'They just expected me to follow my dad. My grandfather was a soldier, and my great grandfather, too. I think I was the first in at least three generations not to sign up.'

'And what did your father think of that?'

'Oh, he was all right about it. He just asked me what I'd do instead.'

'And what did you say?'

'I told him I wanted to work in advertising or journalism.'

I'd not dared say music. Back then I may not have even dared think it.

'Journalism, eh?'

'Yeah, that's pretty much what he said,' I laugh, mimicking my father's voice fondly. "'*Journalism? Dirty raincoat job!*"

'Ha!' Lee spits, amused. 'I think I'd like your pa.'

He teases another cigarette from his packet and pushes it into the corner of his mouth. His upper lip, I notice, is barely visible, just a thin snake of pale red. There's a surprisingly significant gap between this and his nose, which is far from bulbous but nevertheless more prominent than expected. Perhaps he wore the celebrated droopy moustache to disguise the space between.

'He's right, of course,' he continues, blowing smoke across the table. 'As you know, I'm not a fan of journalists. They're proof that not all horse's asses are on horses.'

'Well,' I laugh, 'you should try dealing with them every day for a living.'

'You could offer me all the pussy in the world,' he says, 'and I wouldn't like critics any more.'

He's warming to his theme, though I suspect he's issuing a warning, too.

'The problem with critics is they think they know it all. But those goddamned snivelling little motherfuckers don't know shit. You spend months making a record, or you make a hundred-million-dollar movie, then they write four goddamn sentences and that's it. You're fucked. And they don't know their ass from their elbow. Half of them aren't even out of diapers. You can smell them coming. Shit always stinks. There's a couple over on your island that, if I ever see, I'm gonna break their nose.'

Jeane tries to distract him before this sudden, darker disposition takes hold.

'You ready for another drink, honey?'

'I'm talking,' Lee snaps back. He doesn't raise his voice, but his eyes, angled towards her momentarily, pinch for a second as he takes a deep drag off his cigarette. He shifts his gaze to examine its tip as he blows smoke out dismissively, then taps it carefully over the ashtray, twisting the end gently left and right against the glass bottom until he's sharpened it to a point.

This unexpected mood swing confirms how our meeting still has the potential to turn into an ordeal. I envy Lee's soft pack of Marlboro Reds: I was once a smoker, and now I badly need something to calm me. I've fantasised about coming face to face with him for a long while, but since the opportunity was confirmed I've lain awake at night. Now that he's actually opposite me, I'm so nervous that afterwards it'll seem like a dream.

Nine years later, almost to the day, Jeane will stand with me by the very same elevators in the very same hotel and point excitedly to chairs in the lobby.

'So, do you remember?' she'll ask. 'This is where we waited for you. We were sitting there when you came out of the elevator.'

I'll look around, confused.

'Come on,' she'll squeal, and take my arm as I try to align what she's just said with my own memories of the afternoon.

'This is where we sat drinking,' she'll continue as she pulls me towards the bar. 'I assume you'll have a Margarita? For old time's sake?'

'Of course,' I'll nod numbly. But there will be no tall tables with plush, red leather benches, no bar staff with bow ties and waistcoats, no businessmen with mobile phones nor businesswomen with elegant legs. Instead there will be a series of dark, empty diner booths and two olive green leather banquettes facing one another over tables with scant view of the street below. The bar itself will face back into the lobby, its bottles shielded by a steel grille.

'Damn it!' Jeane will grumble. 'It's closed. That sucks.'

'Are you sure this is where we were?' The unfamiliarity will feel genuinely upsetting.

'Of course!' she'll answer, looking at me with a bemused smile. 'We sat right over there. Don't you remember?'

'Have they renovated?' I'll persist.

'I don't think so,' Jeane will reply. 'No, this is exactly how it was.'

'Wow,' I'll say quietly. 'It's not how I remember things at all.'

* * *

Lee's words had lain, tongue-like, curling from the fax machine behind my desk. When I saw the bold letters of his name at the top of the page, I tore the paper impatiently from the machine, and without even sitting down I read its contents as fast as I could. Then I read the whole thing again, and one more time, slowly, just to be sure I'd not misunderstood. Finally I burst out laughing. Making people laugh, I'd soon learn, was something at which Lee Hazlewood excelled.

It was six years since I'd first heard him sing in that dingy Camden bedsit. My attempts that week to inveigle my way into the music industry had not been wholly in vain; seeds had been planted, though they took a while to flourish. Upon graduation, my initial attempts to become a music journalist were frustrated when the magazine that took me on as a freelancer went bankrupt. Shortly afterwards, however, I'd called to speak to a helpful publicist who regularly sent me promotional records, only to be told by her boss that she'd left the company. I volunteered myself as her replacement.

After almost two and a half years, in the summer of 1996, I was offered a job as PR for the UK office of a notable Berlin-based record label called City Slang. I joined one solitary employee who ran the business out of a cramped, stuffy room in a ramshackle Clapham business centre, and when, some months later, she announced her intention to leave, the owner gave me the choice of finding a new job or taking over her position. I agonised over whether I was capable of handling such responsibility, but doubted anyone would ever be foolish enough to offer such an opportunity again.

City Slang, I soon learned, wasn't selling enough records in the UK for my job to be entirely secure. In order to help make ends meet, I took on freelance projects as a publicist, channelling the money back into the company. Some merely helped pay bills, but others were more creatively satisfying and justified the longer hours. And it wasn't just devotion to my work that kept me sitting in front of the computer: most of the people I'd known in my youth might be making more money, but the appeal of their labour seemed elusive since their jobs didn't offer free music and T-shirts or compulsory hangovers most mornings.

Late one evening in June 1998, I found myself backstage at London's Shepherds Bush Empire, where the wife of a former colleague had played in the opening band. Mike, the man who'd once occupied a desk at the furthest corner of our office, was talking to his friend Steve Shelley, the drummer of Sonic Youth, who'd headlined the show. Their album, *Daydream Nation*, had excited me so much, ten years earlier, that I'd made the effort to hand-draw its cover on the inlay card of the cassette onto which I'd copied it. Mike and Steve were discussing a Nick Cave bootleg that, if I understood correctly, included a version of 'These Boots Are Made For Walkin''.

I hesitantly eased myself into the conversation, confessing that I was a Lee Hazlewood fan of some years.

'I'm talking to Lee,' Steve revealed, once he'd established I actually had half a right to be in the room, 'about reissuing some of his albums.'

I was overjoyed to find myself speaking with Steve, but even more excited to discover that someone had actually tracked Lee down.

'If you ever need a publicist, I'm well up for it,' I rapidly informed him, remembering how he ran a label, Smells Like Records.

'I'll bear that in mind,' Steve said, but soon turned away from me.

I hovered on the edges of the conversation, calculating whether or not I should grab another beer before the fridge nearby was emptied. Since it seemed I was unworthy of further attention, I settled for another drink. I'm not sure I even had the chance to tell Steve my name.

Though I soon forgot our brief exchange backstage, Steve proved true to his word. He reached out some months later to reveal that his deal with Lee was done. I was deeply flattered that he recalled my enthusiasm, especially since, as a member of a band I admired and whose career I'd seen celebrated in TV documentaries, he could secure the talents of more respectable publicists. This meant little, though, compared to the opportunity he was offering: to help revive the career of a man whose music had, in just a few years, come to mean a great deal to me.

Lee Hazlewood's name remained unfamiliar to most of those with whom I'd grown up. He'd been forgotten even by many of those who'd once known him. But to a small handful of people, some of whom I'd met through my work over recent years—people for whom his name had become shorthand for a deep understanding of true, instinctive craft—his accomplishments were unsurpassed. These connoisseurs traded cassettes and secrets, recommending in hushed voices the stores where, occasionally, illicit bootlegs or vintage vinyl emerged. Their alliance was evidence of a secret society into which I'd been admitted, and our love for Lee's music was like an old school tie that we wore with pride, even if few others recognised its import. Steve's decision therefore felt like an affirmation—a promotion from the rank of pupil to the role of school prefect. Though his budget was limited, and he himself seemed pretty intimidated by the man—he warned me, for starters, not to expect direct contact—to be associated with the legend was enough.

It seemed inevitable to me that, as soon as I announced the news of the forthcoming re-release of five of Lee's rarest but finest albums— alongside a new one, defiantly titled *Farmisht Flatulence, Origami, Arf!!! And Me*—I'd find myself unusually popular with journalists seeking copies. I underestimated just what an effect the announcement would have, however: Lee appeared to be even more appreciated by people of influence than I'd guessed, and my phone—which had previously, often fruitlessly, been used to harass journalists about instrumental post-rock acts and eccentric country collectives—started ringing off the hook.

There were, I discovered, plenty more fans out there as enthusiastic as Steve and I were. Like eager kids raising their hands before a question was posed, these critics were hungry to share their knowledge. All they'd needed was an excuse to celebrate Lee, and that was what we now provided. To be among the first to tell his tale would undoubtedly earn them kudos. For music journalists, showing off can sometimes be a key motivation, and retelling a remarkable yet forgotten story is always less risky than establishing a new one.

Lee wasn't planning to make my job easy, however. Acutely distrustful of the media, he'd refused Steve's previous requests for him to talk to journalists, so persuading him to undertake a single interview was likely to be a task. With no contact to the man, and unwilling to hazard an attempt—everything I'd learned, and the manner in which Steve had described him, suggested he could be an ogre—I left Steve to propose an exclusive chat with *Mojo*, which we considered the most suitable publication. The magazine's editor had already responded positively to my tentative suggestion of a feature, and they had an international reputation and wide circulation that might make Lee reconsider his stance. Predictably, however, they qualified their support: if I arranged a meeting for their writer they'd offer five pages of coverage. A phone interview would earn only two.

Steve, sensibly, was prepared to invest in sending a journalist to the US for those extra three sides. Via fax, he passed on the relevant information in gentle terms to Lee, who, I gathered, was recovering from painful dental surgery, a further reason to be prudent. I hoped Lee would see that such a prominent piece of publicity was worth his valuable time, but nonetheless I prepared myself for rejection. In fact, I wondered whether we should anticipate a riposte so furious that it might derail the entire campaign. Lee, in his post-op agony, might choose to interpret *Mojo's* demands as disrespectful, and frankly I'd sympathise with that reaction: in my opinion, he was long overdue his five pages just by continuing to breathe at all.

When I saw the reply Steve subsequently received and forwarded overnight, I was grateful that I'd played no part in the exchange. The man was indeed an ogre.

Dear Steve,

Remember as you read this—it's not about you—it's about your PR firm (and I hope it's not about them), it's most probably about that fuckin' Brit rag—MOJO.

So what is it with these people—Don't they know how much I dislike interviews (not quite as much as I hate interviewers). They have the balls to tell me they'll only give us 1 or 2 pages if I do the interview on the phone. But they'll give us 5 or 6 pages if I let some northern, frozen-ass writer have a 3 day vacation in sunny Florida—so he can talk to my swollen face. I get penalized 75% if I don't do the interview in person? Tell MOJO to P--- O--(piss off—that's about 75%—huh?)

OK, I'm only doing this for you Steve and here are my rules:

1. Tell them to send someone who has heard of me—not some frozen-ass, northern writer who thinks I'm Capt. Hazelwood (notice the spelling) of the ship Valdez that spilled ½ the oil in Alaska and killed off the fish and the animals.

2. 75% of the interview will be about the new CD and the re-releases.

3. I'll spend all the time they want, talking about my songs, (hits or no hits). But, no time talking about the bunch of old loser artists (who sell no records today—and never will again), that I produced in the 50s, 60s, 70s, 80s, even 90s, in the US and Europe.

So, (for you Steve) tell them to send that frozen-ass, northern writer on down to Florida for a 3 day vacation. I won't take up much of his time, especially if he starts asking the wrong questions.

Again, I wish Sonic Youth and you a very successful and profitable tour.

Regards,

Lee Hazlewood

PS You are more than welcome to show this fax to PR folks or MOJO. LH

His grudging cooperation surprised me, but not nearly as much as his ferocity shocked me. The repetition of the words 'frozen-ass, northern writer' exhibited a deep-seated resentment of the press, and that footnote suggested that Lee was utterly without fear as to how he might be perceived. His apparent 'I don't give a fuck' attitude had always been part of the man's appeal, but I had little desire to find myself at the sharp end of it.

Mojo sent their journalist over to Florida for a weekend during which I jumped every time my phone rang, anxious for news, fearful that Lee might have pulled out at the last moment or raged at the journalist for asking 'the wrong questions', something many critics pride themselves on doing. But when the writer returned, he seemed more than content. He shared unforeseen tales of sandwiches prepared by Jeane, and of entertaining anecdotes accumulated by the pool, where Lee's beloved alligator had eyed them up. Lee, too, seemed to have found the writer's company amenable, and the interview's success encouraged me to ask Steve whether it might be acceptable at last to make direct contact, since requests of a similarly high profile were piling up all around me. Steve reluctantly wished me luck.

I could tell—from Lee's lyrics and the earlier faxes Steve had shared— that, fierce as he undoubtedly was, the man with an alligator was also one with a playful sense of humour. My only hope of a breakthrough was to strike the right balance of reverence, professionalism and, with a little luck, wit. I worked late again that night, carefully honing my message. Proud though I was of the result, I knew that, if my approach was ill judged, it was most likely the last fax I'd send him.

Fortunately, it prompted the first of many that Lee would start sending to me.

February 14, 1999

Dear Wyndham Wallace,

If I had a name like Wyndham Wallace I would not associate or correspond with anyone with a simple name like mine. However, since you have lowered yourself to such depths, how can my old Indian heart (west not east) not respond favorably.

Now that the B.S. is out of the way, I enjoyed your fax very much. So, as you wrote, I am not the biggest fan of interviews (in fact I may be the smallest fan of interviews). The English press has never been kind to Jerry Lee Lewis, Prince Philip or me. But I've made more and done more than all of 'em with the exception of the Prince. So, you, Steve Shelley and little ole me will forget our grudges and pretend this is virgin territory we are prepared to let attack us.

My trust <u>lies</u> with Steve Shelley and since his trust <u>lies</u> with you, I can tell as many <u>lies</u> as the next one.

So, bring 'em on!

Best regards,

Lee Hazlewood

The advantages of an unusual name had, even by the age of twenty-seven, rarely revealed themselves to me. Suddenly, something which had always seemed a bad joke at my expense—courtesy of parents who'd plausibly named me during a high scoring game of Scrabble—had now endeared me to my hero. I was no longer 'Indie Wyndy', nor even 'Windybottom'. I was Wyndham Wallace, and Lee Hazlewood had endorsed me. At least for the time being.

Lee's firm but flippant message, found dangling from my fax machine on Valentine's Day 1999, set the tone for much of what followed. To begin with, his correspondences were brief; some were light-hearted, others to be catalogued among what were known as his 'hate faxes'. But our dialogue became increasingly relaxed, peppered with casual asides, and early on he conceded, if unenthusiastically, that he'd talk to the press some more. I speedily lined up chats with the *Sunday Times* and the *Observer* before he changed his mind again. If he'd known how the latter's headline would read—'The Return Of Nancy's Boy'—perhaps none of this would ever have happened.

Flush with success, I took another step, this time beyond the boundaries of my publicist's role. My proposal caught Steve off guard: Lee, I'd decided, should perform live. It was a naïvely ridiculous idea, and even if he acceded

I knew that setting up a show would involve a tremendous amount of work. But its greater significance to both Lee and his fans was initially lost upon me: I'd failed to realise that, up to that point, he'd never played solo in the UK.

Steve understandably believed the concept to be a lost cause, and—irrespective of whether it was Lee's debut or his thousandth British concert—in private moments it struck me as futile as well. If picking up the phone to speak to a journalist was an effort for this sixty-nine-year-old man, then the idea that he'd put down his whisky to fly over to London and rehearse musicians was surely out of the question. Nonetheless, I persevered, if only to know I'd tried.

My vision of this grizzled cowboy prowling the boards of a darkened venue—singing his songs to a devoted audience who never thought they'd see the day—preoccupied me. I daydreamed about who might constitute his backing band, and in my mind lined up opening acts willing to pay tribute to his talent. Money was surely no object; fans, I was certain, would part with sizeable amounts of cash for tickets, perhaps even more than the prices their rare vinyl commanded. Furthermore, the list of coverage in the UK media that I'd by now managed to confirm should entice potential concert promoters.

I knew, however, that it wasn't just a promoter I needed to win over. That, in fact, might prove the easiest part of the job. First I'd have to convince Lee himself.

I called a promoter I knew socially, and with whom I'd worked a number of times. I explained the theoretical show, and he swiftly provided me with a budget that was far from unattractive. But then I had another idea: a better, more distinguished possibility. News had reached me that Nick Cave was about to be announced as the curator of that year's Meltdown Festival, so I tracked down David Sefton, the head of artistic development at the South Bank, where the festival took place. As the man responsible for overseeing the event, he could talk to Nick, and it took them little time to make an offer. The money was an improvement, yet I still wondered if it would be enough to drag Lee away from his pool, his alligator, and his Chivas.

Surprisingly, Lee wasted no time in responding. Maybe he wanted to prevent me wasting any more of his time. Perhaps he simply had nothing better to do. Either way, he blasted UK income tax rules. He refused to pay for English musicians. He wouldn't play fewer than two shows. Opening a concert was out of the question, he added mystifyingly, but he wasn't important enough to close one, either.

After consultation with the venue, I explained how his taxes could be minimised. I added that only a single show would be necessary—a performance at the Royal Festival Hall, which he would headline—and emphasised that he was free to use his fee to choose any musicians he wanted. Slowly, to my cautious delight, he began softening to the idea.

All the same, he argued, the money wasn't enough. I returned to Sefton, whose next offer was again deemed unacceptable. Timidly, I informed the promoter he was going to have to up the figure once more. Again, Lee rejected the proposition, but refused to clarify why. I began to feel way out of my depth; I had no experience of booking shows of this size, let alone working with artists of such eminence, and what kind of money would be reasonable—or, better still, respectful—remained a mystery to me. These, though, were facts I had to hide, and not only from Lee and Sefton: I'd been forbidden to discuss the negotiations with anyone else at all.

My determination to overcome the shortfall led me to seek a sponsor. Most targets were laughable, and—in one of my less imaginative decisions—included Lee Jeans, who never so much as replied. The most promising candidate was Seagrams, makers of Lee's beloved Chivas. Their whisky had been crucial to Lee's work, and he'd frequently recognised this by name-checking their product. It was, I felt, time they put their money where Lee's mouth was. I sent the head of marketing a copy of the new album, hoping that the liner notes—containing references to a 'Scotch bus', with 'a huge Chivas sign on the side', driven by famed guitarist Al Casey to the recording studio—might be enough to persuade them this was a smart way to spend their cash.

'The opportunity outlined is definitely not appropriate for us,' the suits at Seagrams replied. They didn't explain why, but it probably hadn't helped, I later realised, that my first fax was sent on April Fool's Day. They instead offered to send over 'some of our full, fruity, rich Scotch whisky.' Pitching their product to a man of Lee's standing—a voluntary spokesman who'd already been advertising on their behalf for half a century—seemed impertinent. To my surprise, however, the promise of a free bottle seemed to provide Lee with added incentive to visit London so he could collect it. He apparently loved a drink even more than I imagined.

As the deadline for the announcement of the Meltdown line-up approached, I was forced to take a step that—to my mind, at least—required considerable courage. Calling journalists I'd never met was often intimidating enough, so disturbing someone I revered petrified me, especially someone I pictured relaxing in the grounds of the extravagant estate that I imagined his accomplishments had earned him. Faxes, at least, could be polished, whereas it often amazed me how many feet I could fit in my mouth. I had no choice, though: I needed to pin Lee down.

Late one evening in my Brixton flat, I dialled the thirteen digits for Lee's home. There, it was still afternoon, a presumably reasonable hour at which to call a reclusive legend for the very first time, but I was nervous as a farmhand asking an aristocrat for his daughter's hand in marriage.

A female voice answered my call.

'Jeane?' I guessed, though for all I knew it could be a housemaid busy clearing up empty bottles after another wild night round the pool.

'Yes … ?' she replied, in a comically puzzled tone. I guessed she didn't receive many calls from unfamiliar British voices. Their number must be a closely guarded secret.

'It's Wyndham,' I said cautiously. 'Lee's UK publicist.'

'Wyndham!' she replied, seemingly delighted. 'How are you?'

I responded politely but briefly, eager to get on with business, concerned that her warmth might burn out fast if I outstayed my welcome. She and Lee were no doubt cut from the same tough leather.

'I wondered whether Lee is home?' I enquired.

She paused a moment. I heard a distant click and for a moment wondered if she'd hung up.

'I'm afraid he's out. Can I help?'

I hoped so very much, but doubted it. Jeane might have been responsible for typing the faxes that I'd been receiving—perhaps occasionally interjecting a line of her own—but Lee was in charge. She—like Steve, like me—presumably did as she was told. Still, I might as well sound her out.

'It's about the concert,' I dived in, my enthusiasm outweighing my professionalism. 'I just really want it to happen.'

'I know,' Jeane agreed, surprisingly excited. 'It would be amazing.'

'So … do you think there's any way at all he can be persuaded? What do I have to do?'

'Wyndham,' she sighed, 'I know how much you want this to happen—so do I—but all I can say is I know he won't do it unless he gets paid what he wants.'

'But what does he want?' I begged. 'How much does he need? He just tells me to get him more. I get him more, then he tells me it's not enough, and we're almost out of time. They need to announce the show. If he doesn't confirm, he won't be on the posters, and if he's not on the posters, there won't be any show. I reckon I've got one more chance before they run out of patience, and if I don't get it right then we're stuffed.'

There was another pause. These, I would later discover, were rare for Jeane.

'I shouldn't talk to you about this,' she confided at last. 'He doesn't like me interfering with his business. If you ever tell Lee we had this conversation, I'm a dead woman.'

She sounded oddly serious, then exhaled, perhaps a little theatrically.

'I think that if you get the fee up by another £2,000 he'll do it. But I never told you that, OK?'

'Really?' I said, excited at a figure I could grasp, though in indie-rock terms—the ones I was used to—this was a pretty substantial sum. I knew bands that were lucky to get a tenth of that to play.

'I'll call them tomorrow,' I replied. 'I can't promise anything, but I'll do my best.'

'I can't make any promises either,' Jeane said, 'but from what I've heard him say, I think that's where he'll settle. Just remember: I never told you.'

I phoned David Sefton the next morning. A short time afterwards, feeling distinctly pleased with myself, I despatched a message to Kissimmee. Before the end of the day, Lee Hazlewood had, in principle, confirmed his first London show. By the end of the night, I was very, very drunk.

* * *

The first time I meet Lee Hazlewood I'm so tense I start smoking again after two years. Despite the giant Margarita fulfilling its duty, I can't take the anxiety scalding my nerve-endings. Lee pulls cigarette after cigarette from his packet, sucking up smoke and nicotine as the Chivas softens his edges. But this doesn't help me: it's all I can do to sit still, trying my hardest to remain composed. Finally, unable to resist any longer, I point at his Marlboro and ask if I can take one.

'Sure,' he smiles. 'Go right ahead. But I've got some I haven't punched yet.'

The word 'punch' makes me hesitate. I look up at him, perturbed, as he reaches into his jacket and pulls out another pack.

'Here you go,' he says, slinging them to me. 'They're yours. Unpunched. I've got this device that stamps holes in the filter. It's supposed to make smoking healthier.'

He pushes his open packet across the table.

'See?'

I pick them up and notice the top is perforated with holes no bigger than pinpricks. He shows me his 'puncher', which he says he got from the Cedars-Sinai Medical Center in Los Angeles. It looks like a cartridge stamp—the kind that marks documents 'Top Secret'. He places it over the end of his current packet and demonstrates how it stabs the filters with needles designed to ensure that more air is breathed in with the fumes.

'May I try one?' I ask, passing the untouched packet back. 'I don't really smoke anymore, so perhaps I should stick with the healthy ones.'

'Fine with me.' He smiles again. 'Go ahead.'

Putting one to my mouth, I pick up his lighter. The first drag is so thin it's barely there. I check it's lit and try again. Lee takes his Zippo back and places another cigarette between his teeth, though his last is still burning in the ashtray. I soon understand why he's chain-smoking: healthy also means pointless. I might as well be sucking on the straw that came with my drink. I try covering the holes with my lips when I take a drag. Only this way does the cigarette give up any poison.

'So, you're not coming tonight? To the dinner?' Lee asks.

'I won't be there, no,' I tell him hesitantly, momentarily disappointed by news of a meal at which I'm apparently not welcome.

'Ah, OK. Well, don't worry,' he replies, reassuring me. 'It's just us and the band and one or two other people.' He tosses the information out casually to soften the blow of my not having received an invitation. 'It's not really a business thing.'

'I figured as much,' I assure him in return. 'It's all right. I've made plans with a friend anyway. I'll be at the party tomorrow.'

'Good,' he grunts.

The party is why I'm here, in fact. Steve's throwing a bash to celebrate the first batch of reissues, and when he offered to contribute towards my flight costs, I found it impossible to resist his invitation. Back then, I'd not even spoken to Lee, and the slim chance that I might get to shake his hand was worth coughing up the rest of the money. It's funny how things turn out, though: in the end, it had been Lee who—after agreeing to the Festival Hall show a few days earlier—had demanded our private meeting.

'So, your father's a military man,' he says, changing the subject again after a second or two's silence. 'You know what a wildcatter is?'

I shake my head. I'm guessing it's nothing to do with wild cats.

'My father was a wildcatter,' Lee explains. 'He worked the oil fields until World War II started. We lived in Port Arthur, Texas, 'cos that's where all the refineries were. Then he went to work helping to make refineries for the government. That's where I bought my first record, when I was twelve. Roy Acuff's "Wreck On The Highway". You know it?'

He doesn't wait for an answer.

'I bought it at the Kress store, and it cost thirty-nine cents.'

More ash is tapped with a stout finger into the ashtray.

'I've got friends that will tell you that the reason I wasn't more successful was I had one really happy childhood. I liked my mom and dad, loved them, got along with them fine, and if you would just do the things you were supposed to do I was probably the freest kid in my whole life, from the time I was in the first grade to the time I was in the last grade, up 'til I went to university. Because that's the way they were: if you did what you were supposed to do, then they gave you lots of freedom. In fact, most of the children that I knew wanted my mom and dad for their mom and dad, because it seemed like I could do about anything I wanted. I've been teased about it, because, you know, to be in the business that you're in, that I'm in, you're supposed to have an unhappy childhood, because that will make you write better.'

It soon becomes obvious that he enjoys discussing his family, and he wants to know more about mine. There's something comforting in the way he addresses me, a hint that he's beginning to trust me already, and I appreciate his interest in my life. I'm wary, of course, just in case this is a test, in case he's probing for information that he might later hold against me, but if there's a tyrant within, as had once seemed, he's retired to the shadows for now. His jokes, admittedly, are sometimes off-colour, groaning under the weight of vulgar puns, but for Jeane, who works her way through a green packet of Marlboro Menthol next to him, they're a boon. He calls her his 'keeper'; their mutual fondness is evident, and whenever she stands up he kisses her extravagantly on the lips, before welcoming her back afterwards with a hug or an affectionate snuggle.

'More drinks?' he says.

We watch her head to the bar to fetch another round.

'That's my girl,' he adds proudly.

When he turns to me again, his face is suddenly solemn.

'So,' he pronounces gravely, 'looks like you're gonna give me some trouble.'

'Excuse me?'

I swivel back to him, startled.

'All these goddamned interviews you're giving me.' He picks up his cigarettes and stuffs them into his breast pocket decisively. 'I can't take a shit without getting another request. What are you telling these idiots?'

'I don't have to tell them anything,' I say, still a little taken aback, but relieved that this is the only kind of trouble he means. It is, after all, the kind I'm being paid to give him. 'All I'm doing is sending out your records and they're doing the work. People are excited, you know?'

'I sure as hell don't. And, by the way, most of those records aren't worth the plastic they're pressed on.'

'I don't know about that,' I reply firmly. 'I mean, I've been a fan of yours for years!'

'Yeah, yeah, of course you have. A youngster like you. Did your grandmother introduce us?'

His sarcasm is scathing.

It may only have been six years, but ever since I first heard Lee sing I've thrown myself into an obsessive search for his records and anything vaguely associated with him. Unfortunately, I was a latecomer: his records have long been out of print, and most of whatever vinyl was once available has been snapped up by collectors and is now changing hands for absurd amounts of money. It's one of the music industry's more intriguing contradictions that success is usually indicated by the widespread availability of an act's releases, yet obscurity can sometimes confirm authentic artistic value. Nonetheless, I've become pretty well versed in Lee's work, and the struggle it has taken emphasises what an honour it is to be granted this rare audience.

'Well,' I eventually concede, 'I don't have all of your records, but friends have made compilations for me, and ever since I first heard *Cowboy In*

Sweden I've been trying to track down whatever I can. I've been picking stuff up in charity shops and places like that.'

'Charity shops, eh? I could do with a little charity myself, you know. Perhaps I should give them a bunch of records and they'll give me some charity for free. Ha!'

His lips curl upwards, but he shakes his head gloomily, as though he thinks he's joking but can't locate the punch line.

'I found some CDs, too,' I add.

'Goddamn bootleggers. I never see a penny from those motherfuckers.'

'Well,' I offer, increasingly concerned that I'm alienating him and therefore keen to emphasise that I've also bought music legitimately, meaning he got paid, 'I've also got the *Fairy Tales & Fantasies* compilation—the one with Nancy Sinatra that Rhino Records put out. I picked that up last time I was here. Do you mind if I have another cigarette?'

'Sure,' Lee says, retrieving the sealed packet from his breast pocket. 'Like I said, it's yours.'

He flicks it across the table.

'I hope I'm not making you nervous,' he adds.

'No, not at all,' I deny as Jeane flops back down beside him. 'Well, maybe a little.'

'Well, don't be. I don't bite.'

'Oh, sometimes you do,' Jeane giggles, leaning in to plant a wet kiss on his cheek.

'And you love it,' Lee replies, and a dirty grin spreads across his face.

Jeane squeals and kisses him again, this time on the mouth. Squirming slightly at their public display of affection—though admittedly I find it touching, too—I move things back to the topic of interviews. At some point I'll need to raise the subject of his show, but finding a way is proving difficult. Up until now it's not even been mentioned.

'So anyway,' I smile bravely, 'there's all these journalists who've heard a little of your stuff, and now, all of a sudden, they're getting sent copies and realise it's as good as they hoped. And there's a great story they can tell, too.'

'Well, their stories are normally a mound of horse crap,' Lee grumbles. 'What they write about me is unbelievable. These critics don't know shit, but they're more than happy to spread it.'

'That's why it's important to do interviews,' I counter. 'It's your chance to put them straight.'

'They don't listen,' he says firmly. 'And, by the way, it doesn't make any difference what I tell them: they just write what they want to believe. Nancy and me, we used to see these things written in magazines. They'd say they saw us in a club in Atlanta. I'd have been locked in the studio for a month producing something, and Nancy would be off doing something somewhere else in the world, and she'd say, "Did you read it, Barton?" She always called me Barton, by the way. It's my first name, as you ought to know by now. "Did you read it, Barton? I've never been to Atlanta!" And I'd say, "Yeah, I read it. Boy, we must have had a good time. I don't even remember."'

'You know,' I tell them both, bracing myself in case this should cause him to explode, 'the first person I ever talked to about you told me you'd had an affair with Nancy. He said you got chased out of America by Frank.'

I regret the comment immediately. This is way too personal too soon. I'd thought it might be smart to address the rumours, but instead I sound clumsily prurient. Fortunately, Lee takes this gossip in his stride, as though it's the most tedious story I could tell.

'Oh, they say that,' he groans. 'I've heard that before. But honestly: look at Nancy. Why would a girl like that get caught up with a guy like me? If there was anything going on, I didn't know about it, and nor did Nancy!'

'I know, I know,' I say, 'but that's journalists for you. What can you do?'

I figure that my regular betrayals of the media—the very people whose existence provides much of the reason for my own—might display a welcome empathy with Lee's predicament. But his eyes narrow and he leans towards me combatively, so close I can see tufts of grey hair in his ears. I sit back, out of reach—just in case—then realise he wants to make a confession.

'I'll tell you what, though: there was something going on.'

I stare at him, motionless. He surely doesn't know me well enough to be sharing secrets this soon.

'I loved her.'

The entire hotel falls silent. Every car outside slams on its brakes. He must be drunk already.

'I still love her very much,' he proceeds. 'And I know she loves me.'

He leans back in his seat, satisfied with the visible effect his revelation has had upon me. I glance at Jeane, worried about her reaction to this bombshell, but her face gives nothing away. The waiter arrives and places more drinks in front of us. Lee waits patiently for him to leave.

'But not that kind of love!' he qualifies at last, mugging triumphantly.

I breathe out again quietly.

'You know,' he continues more sincerely, 'I couldn't handle that. And she couldn't have either. God! Who wants to sleep with the record producer? I know a lot of artists have, but … no. We had a lot of fun. That's all.'

'I knew that,' I assure him. I'm his publicist, after all. 'The funny thing is,' I add, feeling more confident, 'the same guy who told me you were chased out of America also said he'd heard you became a monk.'

'A monk?' Lee splutters.

'Can you imagine this man as a monk?' Jeane shrieks. 'That's the funniest thing you've said so far, Wyndham! Lee, a monk?'

'Where the fuck do they get this stuff from?' he sighs. 'I'll remember that one. A monk. I'd sooner be a monkey than a monk!'

Jeane wipes her eyes. I now feel rather proud of myself for causing so much merriment with my idiocy. Leonard Cohen may have pursued such a path for a while, but any signals that Lee is spiritually inclined have been as hard to discern as copies of his earliest singles are to buy. Looking at him now—just short of his seventieth birthday, cigarette in hand, whisky melting ice in his glass, leather jacket scrunched up towards his neck—it's patently crazy to imagine him in a robe and tonsure, however scared of Frank he might have been.

In fairness, these are the days before Google. Anyone who cares enough will have struggled to uncover any more about Lee's life since he left Sweden in the mid 70s than that he reunited with Nancy Sinatra onstage in 1995 during a short series of American shows. Tales emerged of brief appearances by her side—Lee playing the laconic, wisecracking drinker to Nancy's demure go-go girl—but afterwards he vanished as mysteriously as he materialised, his image as a shit-kicking rebel-rouser in leather boots and rock star shades intact. In the absence of hard facts, hearsay has since filled the void. Perhaps the only thing more perplexing than allegations of Lee's monastic exploits is that I've not heard much more inventive inanity.

Devotees often speak of Lee as a legend, but that classification suggests some form of narrative, and information about him is so scarce that he hasn't even made it into the latest *Rough Guide To Rock*. Even his name is frequently misspelt on the rare occasions that one sees it. Beyond the press biography that Steve has provided, and the information his most ardent fans have collated, Lee exists beneath a shroud of contradictory myths, fantasist explanations for his absence from the musical landscape. The more I've listened to his records, the more I understand why that is, and the more complicated the shadowy image he presents becomes.

His signature tune, of course—the one everyone knows, 'These Boots Are Made For Walkin''—is ostensibly an unassuming song with throwaway lyrics and a relatively straightforward structure. Like much great pop, it's hard to know what separated it from the mass of music released every week to make it the success it became. It's the kind of composition that often ends up slipping through the cracks—as had most of Nancy's work until Lee started working with her—but something about it captured the world's imagination. Perhaps it was Nancy's coquettish delivery and her easy-going, feline charm. Possibly it was the lyrics, which hinted wittily at female emancipation in a manner blithe enough to disguise the song's intent. Most likely it was the novelty of its bassline—performed on both upright and electric bass—which slid down a quartertone at a time. Most writers work only in semi or full tones.

'I'll tell you a story,' Lee announces, as our afternoon meeting threatens to stretch into the evening. It's a phrase I'll soon hear repeatedly, and if I'm not already sitting down I'll always find myself a chair. 'There's a guy called Chuck Berghofer, a bass player. I used Chuck all the time, because Chuck worked at the jazz club that wasn't too far from my house out at Toluca Lake in LA. He's a great jazz player, so I absolutely wanted him when it got to "Boots". And it was no problem: Chuck wasn't overworked. So it was November when we cut "Boots", and in January we're working on the album. I hadn't seen Chuck since, but the single had already sold five million, or something like that, anyway.'

He says this like it's nothing, a drop in the bank vault of his sales.

'So Chuck came in and popped himself down. He's a big, tall, lanky guy. Parked himself down and said, "You son of a bitch!" And I said, "What are you doing? How was your Christmas and everything else?" And he said, "Just unbelievably wonderful, and I'm supposed to give you a hug and a kiss from my wife and my two kids," and I said, "You touch me and I'll …"'

Jeane slaps him softly, disapprovingly, on the arm.

'Anyway, I said, "What have I done now? I'm always doing great things for worthless old musicians." He said, "I've been playing jazz for twenty years and I bet I haven't signed a hundred autographs. After playing on 'Boots' I must have signed two hundred in the last week. The kids even come over to my house!"'

Whatever the reasons for its mass appeal, 'Boots' barely hints at the strange realms that further listening to Lee's songs reveals: 'Sugar Town', another of the summertime tunes he penned for Nancy, is a veiled reference to drug-taking; 'Arkansas Coal Suite' is the tragic tale of a woman's search for the father she lost in a mining disaster; 'Sand' is engorged with desire.

Independent of Nancy, Lee goes further. He writes odes to drinking—'*I'll give you my shoes for a glass of booze / If you won't tell / They don't smell / No better than I do after six*'—and odes to ill-starred romance—'*Where there's sky there must be rain / Where there's you there's me*'—and odes to what might have been: '*The loneliness and the emptiness / And the hopelessness are fine / Because sometimes my cloudy brain remembers / For one moment you were mine.*'

He pens songs by convicts for whom he never struggles to build sympathy: '*They say I shot a man but I never shot, I ran / That was my first mistake, I'm telling you.*' He sings too about life's losers, in a way that suggests he's seen it all: with 'Houston', he has Dean Martin, a man not known for his poverty, sing convincingly of how '*I saw a dollar yesterday / But the wind blew it away*' and '*I haven't eaten in about a week / And I'm so hungry when I walk I squeak.*'

Subversion is Lee's speciality, and his imagination seems inexhaustible. The soon-to-be-reissued *Trouble Is A Lonesome Town*—his 1963 solo debut, which features offbeat but fascinating spoken word introductions to each song—focusses exclusively on fictional versions of characters he met in the places where he grew up. '*You won't find it on any map,*' he warns us, '*but you can take three steps in any direction and you're there.*' There's an intimacy to his sketches, too, whether of himself or others, and on 'My Autumn's Done Come', written when he was only in his mid-thirties, he even poignantly imagines his dotage: '*Kiss all the pretty ones goodbye / Give everyone a penny that cries / You can throw all my tranquil pills away / Let my blood pressure go on its way / 'cos my autumn's done come.*'

Then there's his voice. When Lee sings, it can rumble like distant thunder, ominous and disconcerting, yet sometimes it's butter melting on toast. He's unafraid of sentiment, and able, in his own way, to croon like his Rat Pack friends. But he also knows how to inject songs with menace, tragedy, and humour, whoever delivers the lines. 'Sing like a fourteen-year-old girl who fucks truck drivers,' he'd instructed Nancy at the session for 'Boots'—or so the stories go, and Lee has never chosen to deny them. His own recording of the song even deconstructs the original as he interjects, '*And this is the part of the record where everybody said, Why, that can't be number one!*'

Lee and Nancy's pinnacle achievement is arguably 'Some Velvet Morning'. It leaves me speechless each and every time I hear it, the flower-power romance at its heart transformed into an unnerving psychedelic trip, its eroticism twinned with doom. His solo work enlarges further upon the dichotomy between the love that he longs for and his apparent, cynical conviction that all pleasure is fleeting. The spoken-word prelude to 'Come On Home To Me'—from his second album, *Requiem For An Almost Lady*—begins, '*And you wake up one morning, and you say: I feel good. I don't miss her, I can live without her.*' Still optimistic, but with reality starting to seep in, he continues, '*and you soon learn that time will come. But,*' he concludes, his voice now clearly resigned to the facts, '*it wasn't that day …*'

The raconteur now opposite me has learned things that few of us can articulate. His work speaks to us all, even if much of it remains largely unheard. His songs, equal parts humour, compassion, and bitterness, address subjects as diverse as romance and its price, imprisonment and capital punishment, violence, poverty, injustice, racism, and a life that is, at best, '*two drops of happy, one pinch of pain*'. Each one seems to have lived a lifetime. It could seduce the most beautiful and enlightened of all humankind, but has also had its heart broken a multitude of times, had the crap kicked out of it, or even kicked the living crap out of someone else, deserving or undeserving. Then it's drowned its sorrows in moonshine before bedding down on a lonely, sandy blanket beneath the stars. '*I've been down so long, it looks like up to me.*'

Lee inhabits his songs so completely that I can't separate them from the man sitting in front of me. Each time he refers to someone as a 'goddamn little fucker' I remind myself to stay on the right side of him. Every time his hand comes to rest on the table I flinch instinctively, imagining it balled into a fist aimed at my nose. But this is more to do with his reputation than his songs, which suggest he's caressed many more faces than he's ever struck. He's the quintessential American hero: tough as rawhide, soft as old boots. So while the ice in his glass continues to thaw, and my Margaritas drop salt to the table, he charms me even more than my imagination of him had earlier terrified me. When the time finally comes for him to leave, long after his proposed departure time, an urge to hug him threatens to overcome me. Yet Lee isn't quite finished: there's one more story he wants to share.

'From the time I was about five years old—when children generally stutter because they talk too fast—I started to stammer,' he begins, 'and I stuttered 'til the third grade. That's just long enough for everybody, wherever you live, to make fun of your stutter, and I really hated it. We're in Oklahoma one summer, staying in this little house by the train tracks, and my dad's drilling oil wells. The hobos used to come by our house to get something to eat, and this one old hobo, just a guy like you or me, he got to the door and asked my mom for a little something. My mom always gave them bread and beans, which they loved, and I sat down with them because they told good stories. They were even better than radio programmes.'

He drains the last dregs from his whisky and adjusts the bracelet on his wrist.

'Neither my mom, my dad, or my uncles had ever mentioned my stutter, although to say good morning sometimes took me thirty minutes. And so I'm sitting there talking to this guy, and he says, "You stutter, don't you, boy?" My dad had never said that to me. My mom had never said that to me. Either they were ashamed or they didn't want me to know. Of course, everybody said, "He'll get over it," but I didn't get over it. I was in the third grade, and that's rough. Anyway, he said, "You stutter, don't you, boy?" and I said "Ye-ye-ye-yes, sir." He said, "Do you like to stutter?" and I said, "N-n-n-n-no, sir." And he said, "Do you want to stop?" and I said, "Ye-ye-ye-yes, sir!"'

He breaks off a moment to sweep salt from the table in front of me.

'And I'm really watching this guy because he interested me suddenly. He was magical. He said, "If you don't like to stutter, I know how you can stop." And I said, "Ye-ye-ye-yes?" And he said, "OK, here's what you do. Can you whistle?" and I said, "Ye-ye-yeah." He said, "OK, when you start to stutter, whistle, and then say what you've got to say." In my child's mind, by the next day I didn't stutter. And even in my mom and dad's mind, within that month I'd stopped stuttering.'

He sighs quietly.

'I never saw him again. God, I wish I could find him. I'd set this man up as good as any man has ever been set up ...'

He stares off into the Manhattan distance through the windows beyond us.

'That's beautiful,' I tell him, when I'm certain he's finished. 'It's like a fairy tale.'

In the years that follow, I'll ask him regularly to share this memory, like a child requests a bedtime story. Unusually, its details will remain consistent.

'How come you never wrote a song about that?' I add.

'Maybe I did.' A smile crinkles his eyes as he turns back to me. '*Shu-shu-shu-shu Sugar Town …*'

He tilts his head to one side slowly. He may have even winked.

'Anyway …'

He stands up from the table without further warning and reaches out to me.

'It's time to go,' he declares. 'We'll see you at the party tomorrow.'

'You will,' I reply, getting up hurriedly to shake his hand. Jeane rises beside him. 'Most definitely.'

The London show remains an unspoken secret, as though its possibility barely exists. As business meetings go, this has been a poor one. But I'm surprisingly unconcerned; any sense that we've failed in some way to use the time wisely is lacking. We've established a connection, and it's different to any I have previously initiated with a client. I hesitate to think of it as a step towards friendship—a concept far too rash at this stage—and yet within me I recognise the unlikely possibility of building an attachment to this old man.

'I think we'll call you Bubba,' Lee suddenly announces, much to Jeane's amusement. 'Nice to meet you, Bubba. Yes. I like that. Bubba: that's what we're going to call you.'

I'll never understand why, but I'll never really care. The name feels like a medal.

CHAPTER TWO

GOT IT
TOGETHER

With only four days notice, Lee arrives at Gatwick Airport on a fresh Saturday morning. I'd checked in advance whether he'd prefer to be picked up by a cab, confident that my antique Volkswagen would be far too dilapidated for him. But he replied in a fashion that I'm beginning to recognise as characteristic: 'I would far rather ride in a Polo than play the damn game.'

He's never seen the car, though. Grubby and battered, it boasts a loud rattle from under its back axle, pages of an atlas are scattered in the boot, and there's mud all over the floor. The glove compartment, too, has a habit of falling onto the legs of those in the passenger seat. I once tried to win over a woman by driving her to a festival where I'd arranged for us to have VIP passes, only for her to emerge ungratefully from the vehicle when we reached the site with both her knees bruised purple blue. Even 'Some Velvet Morning' couldn't save the day that time.

Lee's decision to visit London, however unexpectedly, is perhaps shrewd. There's so much to discuss, so much to organise, that I've been burying him under lengthy faxes almost every day since I returned from New York two weeks ago. Work permits, payment methods, rehearsal spaces, equipment rental, hotel bookings, catering, lighting, taxes: all manner of things about which I have little knowledge have to be arranged, and I don't feel qualified to make decisions without his approval. No, scratch that: I simply don't feel brave enough.

In New York, business was sidelined. I was too cautious, too in awe of him, too flattered by his attention. He in turn was enjoying his Scotch too much to care. After our meeting we barely spoke for the rest of the weekend: I attended the launch party Steve had organised, but there were so many people there who wanted to talk to him—people of serious import, indie rock stars and other associates of Steve's, some of whom had also flown in especially—that we only exchanged a few words.

Four days notice, though, is troublingly short. What, moreover, am I going to do with him? Lee's uncompromising advance warning that he's heading my way for a long weekend insisted only that he see the Royal Festival Hall and the hotel they intend to book for him. Otherwise, he told me only that 'I'm coming over to discuss all matters concerning this concert with you before I sign my name to anything. No press, no interviews (unless the promoters plan to pay my airfare and hotel).'

Of course I can take him to see the venue, but that's going to take all of one hour, if I'm lucky. Am I supposed to show him the Tower of London as well? Buckingham Palace? Madame Tussauds? Or is he going to submit the Charing Cross Hotel—the place recommended by the team at the Royal Festival Hall—to an inch-by-inch examination to confirm that it's worthy of his custom? And what if he doesn't like what I show him?

His message is especially intimidating because I've already started telling people that he'll be performing. I can't imagine the fallout if he decides things aren't to his liking. I'm worried that he's come to the conclusion, after my barrage of enquiries, that I don't know what I'm doing, and that perhaps this venture is doomed to be an administrative nightmare. I've yet to experience anything worse than one of his 'hate faxes', but even a hint of his notorious temper is more than enough to unnerve me. And with good reason, I'll occasionally find out.

He's dressed the same as he was the last time we met: leather jacket, black T-shirt, black jeans, and black baseball cap. This time, however, his hair is jet-black, too. I load his bags onto a luggage cart and we stroll through the crowds to the car park. He extracts a cigarette from his packet long before we reach the open air and lights it the moment the sliding doors let us out onto the walkway to the garage. It seems a moot point that this is legally premature.

I point to my vehicle. It needs a good clean, but he says nothing and heads straight for the driver's door.

'Did you want to drive?' I ask, wondering whether my insurance will cover this. Accommodating his inclinations seems easier than contradicting them.

'No, no, you drive,' he replies, moving around the car before crushing his cigarette underfoot as I unlock the passenger side. 'I'm just used to getting in on the right. Jeane always drives me.'

I dump his suitcase into the cluttered boot and climb in beside him. The car starts first time, which is a relief. We manoeuvre our way out of the car park and, as soon as we reach the airport exit, Lee rolls down the window and lights another cigarette.

'You don't mind,' he says, 'do you?'

'No, go right ahead,' I advise him. 'I smoke in here too.'

'I thought you didn't smoke,' he says.

'I didn't 'til I met you.'

He looks round at me. I might be imagining it, but I swear there's a hint of affection in his smile. Could my faxes have actually worked in my favour?

I leave him to rest at his hotel around midday. When I return some time towards 6pm, he invites me up to his suite, where his open case—a green canvas bag with stitched initials—stands at the end of his bed, his clothes still carefully folded inside. I can see an immaculately packed wash kit on a counter in the bathroom.

'Jeane does that for me every time I travel,' he says, catching me inspecting his belongings, though he doesn't seem concerned. 'When I leave, I won't be able to fit half these things in. She has this talent for organising. It's her German roots. You want one?'

He waves his Marlboro at me.

'Sure,' I say.

'Sit down.'

He gestures towards his unmade bed. I take a seat at the dressing table instead.

'Scotch?'

There's a bottle of Chivas on the table—the one that Seagrams offered. It's already open. I'd hastily arranged for them to send it because, as my mother taught me, you should never look a gift horse in the mouth. And, of course, because Lee had reminded me.

'I asked room service for ice, but it never came,' he points out. 'Luckily I was tired enough to sleep without a drink. Help yourself.'

'I'll hold off on the whisky. Perhaps a beer.'

'I don't think there's any in the minibar,' he apologises, 'but we could have something sent up. If they remember to bring it.'

'No, that's fine,' I tell him, uncomfortable at such extravagance. 'I'll wait 'til we go out.'

'Then we'd better go out soon!'

Shortly afterwards, we make our way down the richly carpeted stairs of the hotel and walk out onto the Strand. Trafalgar Square lies to our left, with Nelson's Column towering above. The hustle of Charing Cross Station emphasises our central location.

'Boy, you got me right in the heart of town, didn't you?' he observes as we stroll towards Covent Garden. 'I wouldn't be any closer if you'd put me at the Queen's.'

'Well, this is the place the Festival Hall recommended. The places I normally put bands probably aren't what you're used to!'

'You may be right,' he chuckles.

'The Festival Hall is just the other side of the river, so you can actually walk there. We'll go on Monday. There'll be someone to show us around if we need. I don't think you'll have any problems.'

We turn into Bedford Street. Lee spots a TGI Friday's sign jutting out of the brickwork a hundred yards or so ahead.

'That'll do,' he announces. 'They know how to cook a burger.'

'Really?' I ask, surprised. 'You want to eat there?'

'Sure,' he says. 'Good American food. Better than anything you Brits can manage. We'll be safe there.'

I'm perfectly happy with the decision. Since he's never discussed his dietary preferences, and I don't know Covent Garden's restaurants well—in fact, given my income, I don't know many restaurants well—this takes quite a weight of responsibility off me. We duck inside, where a youthful waitress, resplendent in a red-and-white-striped shirt like a football player, guides us to a table at the back.

'So, what can I get you guys?' she asks, before we've even settled into our seats.

'How about a few moments of silence, so we can sit down and think?' Lee says, a sudden, bitter edge to his voice.

'Well, of course,' she replies, oblivious to his tone. 'Anything else?'

'No, thank you,' Lee mutters drily. 'That'll be all.'

'I'll be right back,' she tells us.

'Damned bozo waitresses,' he says. 'You could shoot them in the head and they wouldn't be any less dumb.'

'Or any less happy,' I reply, trying to keep up with him.

'Right,' he agrees, opening the menu.

The waitress is back mere moments later with a jug of iced water.

'So what can I get you?' she asks again. Her informality seems as artificial as the décor.

'How about the same as last time?' Lee raises his head and looks the waitress squarely in the eye. 'We'd like a few moments of silence so we can think.'

'Sure thing,' comes the breezy reply.

'Don't shoot her,' Lee laughs as she departs, perhaps a little too loudly. 'Shoot me.'

He orders a burger, insisting half the salad be removed, and milk with a separate glass of ice.

'If I wanted to pay for ice,' he explains, 'I wouldn't order the milk.'

I watch him select cubes once the drink has arrived, adding them to his milk until he's satisfied with the temperature. When his meal appears—suspiciously fast—he nods again approvingly.

'Well, that's exactly how I'd expect it, Bubba, which is exactly how I like it.'

He updates me on the alligator at the bottom of his land. He's given it a name now—The Critic—and relishes its regular presence, but hints that he and Jeane might be relocating soon. Among the possible destinations is Ireland. It seems he's moved around for years, settling temporarily in Sweden some quarter of a century ago, living in Hamburg in the 80s and southern Spain twice in the 90s, where most of his time was spent in bars.

'That just came up because I went down with some Finnish people,' he elaborates, 'and I liked it. So I got me a flat and lived there on that terrible, old, ugly Spanish Riviera. Not conducive to much work. You just don't feel like that in Spain for some reason. Oh, you feel happy and you have good times. You have long talks with people. But not much work.'

This Irish idea, therefore, isn't entirely without precedent.

'Who knows, Bubba?' he says. 'If this little project you've cooked up here works, I might want to do more shows, and then I'll need to be closer.'

He toys with his food while I eat, seemingly more interested in chat than chow. It occurs to me that this is as good a chance as any I may get to find out more about his career, and it takes him little to get started. When I ask how he first began working with Nancy Sinatra, he doesn't hesitate to explain, though the roots of the story are eccentric: overwhelmed in the mid 60s by the British invasion of bands like The Beatles and The Rolling Stones, he'd originally chosen to step away from the business altogether.

'I thought, *why should I make records that compete against all these English groups?* I might as well retire. I'm very comfortable anyway. And I did. I was very happy to just sit in my backyard and watch the boats, swim in the pool. But then Jimmy Bowen from Warner Bros stepped in. He was looking for a house and I didn't like the guy who lived back of me. He said, "Boy, I love the area you live in. It's so close to Warner Bros." And I said, "You know, there may be a house for you. Now go over and talk to this guy." So Jimmy became my next-door neighbour.'

He lets slip a coy grin as he leans back.

'He was the one that asked me to do Nancy. I said, "I'm retired." He said, "Well, just meet with her and see."'

'Surely you were tempted right away?' I suggest. 'I mean, if only for the money?'

'I'd just finished a year of Dino Desi & Billy,' he replies, shaking his head as he recalls the Hollywood child trio formed by Dean Martin's son, Lucille Ball's son with Desi Arnaz (her co-star in *I Love Lucy*), and their school friend, Billy Hinsche. 'That's enough to kill you! I made money but—oh, boy!—twelve- and thirteen-year-old kids should not be in a recording studio with me. So I said, "I don't wanna do any second-generation records any more." That's really what I said, you know?

'And then he talked me into going over there, and she was something: smart, bright. So I signed the thing to work with her. Then my retirement went to hell, 'cos I lucked out too fast. We got her first chart record, "So Long, Babe". And then the second little song that I wrote for her blew the top of the charts off and was number one for a while, and that of course was "Boots". And we had several good records from then on for about three years.'

Sometimes, in years to come, Lee will tell the story differently, claiming that he was invited to a dinner where the idea of him working with Nancy—whom he called variously 'The Pope's Daughter' and 'The Sinatra Girl'—hadn't even been raised before her father appeared in the kitchen, congratulating him on his decision to produce his daughter's next record before they'd even sat down for spaghetti. Either way, Nancy's work to date had been pretty much ignored in her homeland: even if she'd enjoyed some success in Europe, she was apparently on the verge of being dropped by Frank's label, Reprise. Lee changed all that, rescuing her career from potential oblivion.

His reward was unusual, if fruitful. It was also something no one had expected: he and Nancy started singing together. As I dip fries into a portion of congealed mayonnaise, I ask him how that came about.

'It's so technically superior,' he sighs cheekily. 'I hate to mention this kind of stuff. I'd written some what I call "Boy / Girl songs".' He checks I realise he's being sarcastic before continuing. 'I had a couple or three of them lying around. I just used to sing the songs for her. "I like that one. No, not that one." "OK, forget it." "No, I want to do that one, too." That's the way she was. So we hunted around for people to sing with her and she just said, "Stop it. If anybody sings with me, it's got to be you, because they won't sound right. 'Cos if I'm gonna do these songs, I do them with you, 'cos I'll be unhappy if I don't hear that old whisky voice."'

His attachment to Nancy is obvious, though I remain convinced that he told me the truth about their relationship when we first met. It might even be argued that anything more intimate would have destroyed their magical—sometimes even tense—chemistry.

'My agreement with her,' he goes on, 'was, "If you are a good girl …"'— and she was, she was very professional, and giggly, and fun, and all that— "… then I'll put one of these on each of your albums." She bought it. And I bought it, too. I thought it was really great. Then one day Mo Ostin, who was the head of Reprise, called me up and said four cities wanted to take "Summer Wine" and put it out as a single. I said, "It was never put together as a single, and it won't be put out as a single." Mo talked to me and talked to me, and his wife, who I was madly in love with. I called her the Nurse, because she always took aspirin when we had meetings with distributors. I wouldn't go unless I had aspirins, 'cos I didn't want to blow up at them.

'Anyway, the Nurse said it, Mo said it, so after they bugged me a lot about it, I said I'd talk to Nancy. She said, "Well, it doesn't surprise me," and I said, "Well, it surprises the hell out of me!" I said, "I'll put this on the B-side, so that'll satisfy those four cities that wanted it." And she said, "What's wrong with that?" And I said, "I can't find a thing." I said, "Mo. It's the B-side on 'Sugar Town'." Then, you know, you want to slit your wrists, because they played "Sugar Town" for three months—it sold about a million and a half—then they turned it over and it sold another half a million with "Summer Wine". So what I did is give them a two-dollar record for a dollar. That hurts your producer's mind, and it hurts your publishing mind, and it hurts your writer's mind. You gave a two-sided hit. And I don't believe in two-sided hits. So that's how my wonderful singing career began.'

'But you'd done your own records before, right?' I enquire. 'Like, *Trouble Is A Lonesome Town*, your first album … that came out a few years earlier, didn't it?'

'I didn't make that record for myself,' he declares, pushing his half-empty plate to one side. 'I wanted somebody that was a really good singer to do it. But I took it to a friend of mine, Jack Tracey, who was the Head of West Coast for Mercury Records. In fact I was doing some other business with him. He said, "What's that?" So I said, "That's a demo of an idea I have. It's kind of folksy. See if you got an artist for it."

'So he took it home, and I'm just about ready to crawl in bed that night, and the phone rings, and it's Jack. And he said, "I heard that thing, and all I can do is laugh and have a good time with it, and I grew up in a little town like that and I know a lot of people who did. I love it." And I said, "Who've you got for it?" He says, "I want to put it out like it is." So I became a singer of my own demos. It sold enough for Jack to make the money back. He had so much fun with it. It was Jack's favourite thing.'

If I was struggling earlier to work out how best to keep him entertained, I needn't have worried: my role is to listen until he's done, and when we're finished with dinner it's apparent that such a time hasn't arrived. Picking up the bill and scornfully dismissing my attempts to pay my way, he suggests we return to the hotel bar rather than fight for space with tourists in nearby pubs.

He shuffles off down Bedford Street, his hand-stitched leather boots occasionally sidestepping debris and giving him a couple of useful extra inches. I continue my interrogation and ask how he met Duane Eddy, another of the stars whose career he helped launch.

'Duane used to come into the radio station down at Coolidge,' he says, recalling the time he spent in the mid 50s, working as a DJ in Arizona. 'He introduced himself: "If you ever have any extra country records …" So I'd have him a stack of eight or ten of them that we couldn't play every week. That's how we became friends. He'd play a little guitar for me, and we decided one day to make a record on him. But we wanted to make a record in a certain way. I loved Eddy Duchin, the piano player who played the melody way down low on the piano, and I wanted to know why they didn't do that on guitar more. So I asked Duane to do that, and he was the best at playing that. I don't know how many great guitarists today say, if it wasn't for Duane, they never would have played guitar.'

'Was that the station where you used to do characters on your show?' I ask, recalling something I'd read in the official press biography that Steve Shelley had provided. 'In fact, didn't you name the record label you released Duane's first recordings on after one of them? What was it? Something like Abe Lincoln?'

'Yeah, Eb X. Preston,' Lee laughs, adding that Duane had at first believed these people were real. 'Sometimes the characters used to get more mail than I did! There was teasing going on between the characters, and then these people would write in and say, "You shouldn't tease him." By the way, I thought, since I was doing myself and two other people, I should get three times as much money, but the owner of the station didn't buy that. He wanted me and the two guys that came with me.'

We continue strolling side by side, my feet swinging in slow motion to accommodate his slower pace and keeping time with his heels, which click hypnotically like a metronome on the concrete.

'And what about that huge sound you and Duane got? The twang? You must have been using some kind of effects on that, surely …'

'Yeah, I used a grain tank for an echo! I went out and yelled in grain tanks all day and finally got one. I asked the man how much he wanted for it, and he said, "Two hundred dollars." I said, "I'll pay two hundred dollars for it, but I want it delivered." He said, "Well, I have to charge for delivery." And I said, "Then I don't want your damned tank." So he delivered it, and we put it outside. Put a little cheap microphone at one end, and a little cheap speaker at the other end, and that's how we got our echo. That same chamber still has a place of honour in a nice two-million-dollar building in Phoenix.

'It was a wonderful little tank,' he adds nostalgically. 'The greatest problem I had with it was on a nice spring or summer day the birds liked it too. If Duane was singing very soft, we'd hear, *tweet, tweet, tweet, tweet*. So we sent somebody out to shoot the birds off.'

Cars drip past us along the Strand, air bubbles in a plastic vein, and clouds, golden mauve with the oncoming sunset, float above the horizon. London seems colourful and inexplicably peaceful in Lee's company, the normal battle for space postponed, the figures flitting past insubstantial, silent and blurred. The double decker buses, the black taxis, the discoloured stone faces of the buildings that line the street are all imbued anew with a romance that familiarity has in recent times rendered dreary. I fear disturbing its peculiar composure by turning off onto the cobbles in front of the hotel, tempted instead to prolong the occasion by extending our promenade.

'Are you listening, Bubba?' Lee suddenly demands.

I snap out of my trance.

'I said, I need to get some cigarettes.'

'Sorry, Lee. I got distracted.'

'Well, pay attention, Bubba. From time to time, you'll learn, I have something important to say. And, by the way, you'd better be a quick learner.'

I guide him to a newsagent on the station concourse next door—he requests two packs, tucking one into his shirt pocket and the other into his jacket—then back to the hotel. The lounge bar at the top of the staircase is unfortunately packed with loud, wealthy sightseers, the men's premature summer polo shirts garish, the women's make-up overwrought. I'd been looking forward to our relaxing together in its comfortable, faux antique armchairs, and returning downstairs to the lino-floored environment of the hotel's far less opulent café feels like an affront.

'Will this do?' I ask, rather hoping he'll instead suggest we find a pub.

Saturday early evening, however, is hardly the time to locate a seat for an elderly man, and I can tell he's in danger of becoming irritated.

'Do they serve Scotch?' he replies.

I look over at the bar.

'Looks like it,' I tell him.

'Then it'll do.'

He drags a cheap white chair out from under a table while I take care of the drinks at the bar, ordering myself a pint, and, predictably, a Chivas on the rocks for Lee.

'Tell them to put it on my room,' he shouts.

I cheerfully do as I'm told.

'You know, it's surprisingly nice to see you again,' I say, raising my glass to him once I'm back at the table, unable to restrain a burst of sentiment but spicing it up with a little mischief. He seems to like that, I've detected.

'It's tolerable to see you too, Bubba,' he smiles. 'But don't get any ideas.'

He lifts his glass and nudges mine.

'To good health. Now, about your little plan. I've been having a few thoughts.'

My heart sinks. I suspect these thoughts are going to be unwelcome. Instead, he begins to tell me about the musicians he's booking to play the show. His long-time friend and colleague, Al Casey, will be performing, and Lasse Samuelson, the arranger involved with many of the recordings Lee made in Sweden, will oversee the band. He sounds genuinely enthused but makes it clear that he still needs to see the venue before he makes his final commitment. I can't bring myself to tell him I've already done that on his behalf. My fear that he might pull out is tempered only by the fact that, should he feel that the plush surroundings of the Festival Hall are inadequate, it's unlikely he'll ever perform anywhere.

In our own far-from-plush surroundings, I settle in for a long night, though he's soon done with business. Each new whisky provokes further monologues, and those whiskies just keep coming. There's little need for me to ask anything: stories pour forth as fast as the lager slips down my throat. When I run out of cigarettes, he maintains the same 'I buy, you fly' regime that he established with the drinks: he sends me to the machine in the corner with enough money for two packs, insisting that he pay for both, ignoring the fact he's already weighed down with tobacco.

'I've had some fun times in London,' he tells me when I return, a twist of nostalgia in his voice. 'You know, I met Richard Harris here once on a TV show. You know who he is, right?'

'The actor, yeah? He made some records too. The guy from *The Wild Geese*?'

'Well, that's not his finest work, but yes. That's him. Anyway, I'm sitting there with five people from the record company, and of course he's sitting there with his people from the record company, 'cos it was round the time of "MacArthur Park", that hit he had, the one Jimmy Webb wrote.'

He waves his cigarette like a conductor's baton as he mumbles the famous melody: '*And someone left the cake out in the rain ...*'

'And by the way, I thought he did a tremendous job on it,' he states firmly, 'for a singer. For an actor, he did a hell of a job!'

He takes a nip of whisky, a drag on his Marlboro. He seems out of place among the white walls and furniture of the room, the pastel shades of the cheap, framed prints that hang pointlessly as decoration even more effeminate in his presence.

'Actually,' he continues, 'I met Jimmy Webb once. At the time he had a hit with "Galveston" and I had "Houston". I said to him, "I wish you'd be a little more careful with your songs." "Why's that?" he said, and I said, "Because Houston's pretty close to Galveston." So he said, "They don't sound anything alike," and I said'—here Lee checks to see if I can anticipate his punch line—'"I was talking miles, dummy!"'

His face creases, wrinkles shifting like ripples in honey, but he's told better jokes.

'Anyway,' he says, returning to his earlier topic as though aware he might lose momentum, 'I could see back in those days, not like today.' He lifts his glasses from the bridge of his nose and wipes the corner of an eye.

'I saw Harris at the other end of the room, kinda looking at me. So then he goes like this.' Lee curls his finger as though trying to lure me towards him. 'And I go'—he curls his finger again—'and then about five minutes after that'—curling his finger a third time—'and I go ...'

He bends his finger one last time, overacting now, lost in the story. It's hard to tell if he's talking to me or just reciting it to himself. I perceive a slight tremor in the movements of his hand. His copper bracelet is perhaps less effective than he hoped.

'So he sends this person over who says, "Mr Harris is kind of tired today and wants to know if you'd meet him halfway." My kind of guy!' Lee laughs, a rough splutter this time. 'So the guy goes back, and about five minutes later somebody whistles, one of those real loud ones.'

He demonstrates unnecessarily, and the bar's only other customers, a couple enjoying a peaceful sandwich in the corner, turn round, startled. The barman scurries our way. I lift my hand to signal everything is fine. Lee remains oblivious.

'So I stand up, and he stands up, and we walk towards the middle and meet. He says he's got something special where he is, and would I like to come over for a drink? I say, "Well, we have Chivas over here," and he says, "Show me the way!" So we sit and talk for a while and finally it's time to go. He says, "What are you doing this evening?" and I say, "I'm going to bed early to save this fantastic voice."'

Belittling his own singing is one of Lee's well-established habits.

'Then he says, "I'm going to go to a little party this evening, and I'd love to have you go with me. I'll send a car."'

The party was to take place at the home of a wealthy aristocratic lady. Lee struggles for a moment to remember the host's name. It's unimportant.

'So we get there about 8:30, and of course we sit around and talk, but about 11:30 it's packed, and I haven't seen Harris for thirty minutes. I don't know where the hell he is. So I say to the lady, "If you run into Mr Harris, would you tell him I'd like to see him?" For thirty, forty minutes, I didn't see him at all. So I just got up, said, "Good night, thank you very much"'—he tenderly mimics an upper crust English accent—'and I walked out the front door and found his driver. I said, "You haven't seen Mr Harris round here, have you?" And the driver says, "No, sir, I haven't. He usually stays pretty late." And I said "Well, I'm not staying, so could you get me back to the hotel?"'

He lifts his baseball cap, smoothing down his hair. Images swirl in my mind: a Chelsea drawing room, chandeliers overhead, young Lee Hazlewood—like a bohemian, moustachioed cowpoke—lounging exotically on a velvet chaise longue, much like he did on the cover of 1969's *Forty*.

'So I go home,' he continues, interrupting my reverie, 'take a shower, and crawl into bed. I've got really, really comfortable, just got to sleep, when the telephone rings.' He adopts a posh accent again, this time pitched higher, most likely based on parodies of the Queen he's seen on television. '"Is that Mr Hazlewood? This is Mr Harris's personal assistant. You haven't seen him, have you? We've lost him." And I say, "Well, I'll get out of my bed and check around if you want me to, but I really don't think he's here."'

He sits back and laughs. I smile broadly, although he's tailed off rather suddenly, like a clock that's run down. This sometimes happens with Lee; without the structure of a song, he can sometimes take a ponderous route to his finale. It seems to be something he knows, though: he begins self-consciously moving cigarette butts around the ashtray with a lit Marlboro.

'To be fair, she didn't know you,' I laugh, trying to lift him a little with flattery. 'I mean, you were always more of a ladies' man …'

'Oh, God!' he snorts. 'Five-eight, with a ski-chute nose, solid grey since I'm thirty years old—just like my dad—and I'm a ladies' man? Oh yeah, sure. I tell you what: I have been very fortunate in some respects that I don't think had to do with PR or publicity or anything. I've gone with, and lived with, several beautiful ladies. Sometimes I'm amazed at myself when I think back about it, 'cos I'm an old man, and of course I have a pretty nice looking lady now, too. But I did spend a lot of time with ladies about half my age. All legal, but half my age, a lot of them! There was something about each one of them that I liked, and I knew when it had worn itself out. And one or two of them that I broke up with hurt me, and one or two of them that broke up with me hurt me. You think if you did all the breaking up … well, I didn't do all the breaking up. I probably caused all the breaking up, put it that way.'

He scratches his ear with a stubby finger, poking it into the fold of his earlobes as he considers his next words.

'I have a friend who said, "The reason he only goes with young women is that he doesn't like wrinkles." That is not true! But usually the ladies I went with were adult enough to fit in with these other people, and they usually walked away saying, "You got the weirdest group of friends in the world." And I said, "Well, they think I'm weird 'cos an old man like me is hanging out with you … "'

With Lee's spirits restored by this remembrance, I excuse myself to visit the loo. When I come back, there are two full drinks on the table.

'You don't have to go yet, do you, Bubba?'

'Not yet,' I say. 'I'm good for another.'

'Great,' he says. 'I'm enjoying myself.'

'I'll be paying many more visits to the bathroom, though,' I add.

'Then hang on a second.' He reaches into his pocket. 'You should try one of these.'

He hands me a little red pill. I examine it, unable to mask my shock.

'It's just an old man's pill,' he explains. 'It'll help you piss less. It certainly helps me.'

Many years later, it was still in my wallet. The strangest things end up as souvenirs.

* * *

With two more hangovers under our belt, I fetch Lee late on Monday morning. He complains that he didn't sleep well the previous night—'goddamned jetlag means I still watch the news 'til dawn'—but the only sign that the preceding evening might have had any effect on him is the fact he's wearing shades.

We cross Waterloo Bridge slowly, heading for the Royal Festival Hall.

Inside, in preparation for the night's show, technicians are zipping across the stage, leaping into the auditorium, grabbing cables and shouting tetchily at one another. Lee stares silently at the space, the rows of seats stretching back far further than I remember. He turns, deliberately, to face the front, as though the room might alter its shape with each new perspective. Ahead of him, a grand piano stands draped with a heavy black blanket, and a vast organ nestles in the wooden backdrop at the rear of the stage, its pipes a bucktoothed, metallic smile that taunts us. I'd understand if the scene intimidated him, but I hope he's also impressed.

'So?' I say at last. 'What do you think?'

Lee looks mutely around.

'The sound's pretty good,' I add, trying to cajole some kind of response from him. His face gives nothing away.

'It's big,' he says, finally. 'How big exactly?'

'It's about two thousand capacity,' I reply, struggling through the fog of my headache to remember the numbers David Sefton gave me. 'Two thousand, two hundred, I think.'

'Two thousand, two hundred,' he repeats slowly. 'And they think they can sell enough tickets?'

'I reckon so,' I reassure him. His tone is sceptical, even if he's trying to hide it. 'They're paying a lot of money, so they must be confident.'

'Doesn't matter anyway,' he shrugs, 'as long as they pay upfront. Some of it, anyway.'

'That's in the contract,' I say. 'You get a good third of it as soon as you want.'

'Well, I want it now, but I don't think they'll like that.'

'Probably not,' I concede. 'Not 'til you sign, anyway.'

'That's the mistake people make, you know,' he says, striding slowly along the front row. 'You've got to get paid upfront. Then you're not worrying about money, and you can do the job properly.'

He climbs up a staircase hidden to the left of the stage and looks back through the venue.

'If I get paid before I go onstage I'm not going to be thinking about whether they're gonna argue with me afterwards. "Sorry, Mr Hazlewood …" and right there you know there's trouble. "Sorry, Mr Hazlewood, but we only sold this many tickets," or "Sorry, Mr Hazlewood, but our budget's not as big as we thought." If I've got the cash there in front of me then I stop worrying about that. 'Cos by the way, that's always my biggest worry: the money. That's what I'm doing this for. It's just another job. And it'll keep you and Steve happy.'

I'm not sure who he's trying to convince.

'And they want me to go on last?' he checks.

'Yes.'

'And you really think people will come?'

'I'm sure.'

'You're an optimistic young chap, aren't you, Bubba?' he smiles. 'I hope you're right, or the guys here may not be so fond of the name Hazlewood.'

'Well, that's their risk, I guess.'

'You're learning …'

He glances around another time, shakes his head and steps back down off the stage.

'Can you show me the back? That's where I'll be spending most of my time. I wanna make sure the boys will be comfortable. And, by the way, they need to be. Al's not a well man, and these guys aren't much younger than me …'

* * *

By the time I leave him I'm once again drunk. The rush of anecdotes has remained unabated—Jeane, I guess, must have heard all his stories already—while my attempts to focus his mind on what lies ahead have proved almost entirely futile. Most of the questions I've faxed to Lee's home remain unanswered. He's travelled from Florida to London simply to chat. He has, however, found time to sign the deal. I stuffed the papers back into my bag in seconds. They are now my most valuable possession.

When I return the next morning, he immediately picks up the conversation in the same spirit.

'Did I tell you,' he says, even before we've buckled up, 'that Cynthia Plastercaster got a hold of me back when I worked with Nancy?'

'No,' I say, surprised to hear him mention the name of this notorious artist. 'Tell me more.'

'Well,' he laughs, 'she didn't get actually get a hold of me. I wouldn't do it!'

Given her chosen profession, I'm not entirely surprised. Plastercaster has spent portions of her career taking moulds of rock stars' penises, and since the late 60s it's been considered quite an honour to be invited to have one's member immortalised for posterity. This has been more in theory than practice, however: her subjects may have included Jimi Hendrix and Anthony Newley, but the quality of the list soon drops off. I once worked with her when she talked at a club night I publicised, and she'd brought along a suitcase with a selection for display, afterwards signing a Polaroid of the two us together with the words 'Pardon my sweaty disgusting brow'. She'd made no mention of the plaster-of-Paris private parts behind us.

Wondering if this has been Lee's shortest anecdote ever, I ask him why he turned her down.

'Well,' he laughs, as though he's been waiting all along for me to tee this one up, 'it certainly wasn't my morals. I'd just be afraid I'd be walking down a Los Angeles street one day and there'd be a sign: *Ten Lee Hazlewoods, One Mick Jagger*. I just couldn't handle that …'

By the time we arrive at Gatwick, my cheek muscles ache from smiling. It's something I recognise as the same dull pain I get when I spend hours with older relatives to whom I wish to show respect as much as amusement. I accompany him to the check-in desk, his bag slung over my shoulder, and he presents his passport and ticket. Boarding card in hand, we stroll on towards security.

'It's been fun,' he says, and he really seems to mean it.

'Thank you,' I reply, flattered. 'I thought so too.'

'So I'll be back in a few weeks' time,' he adds.

'That'll be fun too,' I answer, 'but I'll be talking to you before then, I'm certain.'

'I bet you will,' he grouses cheerfully. 'See you soon, Bubba.'

I shake his hand solidly. A strange sensation, much like when I waved goodbye to my parents at the top of the school drive, comes over me like a shiver.

'Thanks, Lee. Have a safe journey.'

He lets my hand go, picks up the bag I've put down on the ground beside us, and shambles off. I watch him leave, his baseball cap pulled low over his head, his green satchel matching the case over his shoulder. He blends into the crowd immediately, another American tourist on his way home. I continue to monitor him as he steps through the X-Ray and collects his bags, and then, without looking round, he's gone.

I walk slowly back to the car and climb in. As I close the door, the glove compartment drops to the floor.

CHAPTER THREE

NOT THE
LOVING KIND

May 13, 1999

Dear W.W. (Bubba),

Jeane and I are sending you a little gift to show our thanks for all your help.
A thousand thanks.

Jeane and Lee

* * *

May 13, 1999

Dear Steve,

In the future—starting now!—I'll do interviews with journalists who
interview <u>me</u> and <u>not</u> a group of old <u>losers</u> I've known for the last 40 years.
The interviews will be <u>with</u> me and <u>about</u> me and not a bunch of quotes from
people from my past.

That's it! When someone hurts someone in my family—trust me—I'll find a
way to hurt him.

Please inform Wyndham, no one from MOJO is to receive free tickets to the
concert. Let the bastards pay $45 just like everybody else.

Regards,

Lee Hazlewood

* * *

June 1, 1999

Dear Jeane,

Here's a weird and possibly tactless question that I wondered whether you could help me with. The journalist from the Observer wanted to check how many times Lee has been married, and to whom. I think this is to avoid any Mojo-style errors. Can you help me with that?

Best,

Wyndham

* * *

June 1, 1999

Dear Wyndham,

This message is from Lee.

It is tasteless. However, Been married twice, divorced twice, will not give out names, but both kept my name. My keeper and love for several years is Jeane Kelley—we ain't married—and don't plan to be—just too happy how we are.

Be sure and type this for the nosey son-of-a-bitch, so he'll get it right.

Regards,

Lee Hazlewood

* * *

June 15, 1999

Dear Bubba,

I got—14 inches of dick and a pisspot full of balls!!!

And that idiot from the Observer calls me a BOY???

Regards,

Lee Hazlewood

June 16, 1999

Dear Steve,

As of June 21, 1999, no more interviews—no exceptions. This is forever and concerns all media. I've wasted time with 30 or 40 of these illiterate assholes and with the exception of the NY Times and maybe one other, it's all garbage—and doesn't help you, your label and most especially me.

So, please, pull Wyndham off anything to do with me. I like him, however, these unimportant 2nd year journalism students I've given many, many hours to are not only brain dead, untalented, scum-sucking, uninformed cretins of the first order—they are assassins!

My God! I've let myself be surrounded by assassins!!

NO MORE! Include me out!

Best,

Lee Hazlewood

* * *

June 25, 1999

Dear Bubba,

See if you can arrange a reservation at the little Mexican restaurant we went to when I was last in London.

It's close to the hotel—we can walk over and walk back saving about 5,000 pounds in cab fare.

Regards,

Lee Hazlewood

CHAPTER FOUR

THE
PERFORMER

Monday, June 28 1999, and as a bell rings out in the foyer of the Royal Festival Hall to signal the imminent start of Lee Hazlewood's first British solo concert, queues form at the doors, young, middle-aged, and even old alike waiting for amiable, ageing ladies to check their tickets. Indie kids balance beers carefully and ease their way down the aisles past their more punctual, formally dressed elders and betters.

The room swells with chatter as an unfamiliar version of Bob Marley's 'No Woman, No Cry' seeps from the PA, while Lee, with only minutes to go, watches from a gloomy corner, just out of sight of the front row of the audience. His cigarette glows as he takes frequent, surreptitious drags, but otherwise he betrays little sign of whatever thoughts he must have about the huge space he's about to fill. Beside him, his musicians mill around in the shadows, joking half-heartedly with one another, their shuffling feet and random glances a sign that their composure has not been established so successfully.

Less than three months after we first met, it's show time. A bearded stage manager taps me on the shoulder, a signal I pass on to Lee and Lasse, his bandleader, as the lights begin to dim. Applause and sporadic whistles pierce the solemnity of the setting before raucous cheers—screams, even—greet the band as they step out of the dark to take their places, their music stands lit beneath muted red and blue spotlights.

As Lasse raises his baton, a hush descends. Lee takes a pace forward, as though impatient to begin, and then halts just as impulsively beside me.

I recognise faces in the front rows of the audience, and their suspense is unmistakable. My own expectations surge uncomfortably.

'Here we go, Bubba,' Lee says, just loud enough for me to register, deeper than ever. If he says anything else it's buried beneath a vigorous opening drum roll and fanfare. Lee drops his cigarette and grinds it carelessly into the floor. There's no time to wish him luck before he's gone, striding up the steps to face his fans, embers still smouldering at my feet. He's not even reached the stage by the time we've heard our first bum note, but, as the crowd spots Lee, and the riotous introduction slips into the more sedate opening of 'Rider On A White Horse'—hardly one of the most prominent songs in his catalogue, but still a firm favourite of the devout—the mistake is submerged beneath their roar.

Only then do I notice what he's wearing.

In front of over two thousand fans, celebrities, and the 'horse's asses' due to review his concert, the genius we have all come to eulogise has reappeared in ill-fitting jeans and a novelty sweatshirt almost certainly purchased in a souvenir gift shop. 'Movie Facts' is emblazoned over his heart. A list of notable film trivia decorates its back. My mother dresses better for gardening.

Twenty-five years after he all but vanished from sight, the spotlight has finally found Lee Hazlewood. There he is, one hand tucked stiffly in his pocket, sauntering onstage like a man returning from the toilet.

* * *

Again insisting on the personal touch, Lee had asked me to collect Jeane and him upon their arrival in London little more than forty-eight hours earlier. I couldn't help but get a kick out of the fact that he was engaging in this adventure in what I thought of as an 'indie rock' fashion. Even when he solicited me to add a second journey to Gatwick in order to collect the other two musicians he'd brought from the US, I had few qualms about confirming my commitment to his cause.

Admittedly, I'm not sure he gave me any choice: these were instructions rather than requests. But to find myself invited to shuttle Al Casey—a member of Hal Blaine's fabled Wrecking Crew, no less a man than the guitarist who played the opening riff to The Beach Boys' 'Wouldn't It Be Nice'—in a decrepit vehicle that surely reminded him of his own, worryingly impending mortality, was a request few music fans would turn down. Al and his colleague Brad Bauder, however, might have preferred a little more luxury: every time I braked, the backs of their heads were struck by Al's guitar case, which had been stacked on top of their luggage behind them.

Although I'd barely have time to sleep for the next few days— my kitchen the evidence, the sink piled high with plates covered with leftover food in varying stages of decomposition—I approved of this DIY ethic. I was uncomfortable with the end-of-the century music industry's wastefulness: the reliance on couriers instead of the post to compensate for poor organisation; the use of taxis instead of public transport purely for convenience; the decadent partying for which there was no reason other than proving there was money to burn. I was especially self-righteous when I couldn't capitalise on, or participate in, such activities. If Lee's decision to employ my car may have been miserly, it suited my principles to a *T*.

The Glastonbury Festival was taking place that weekend, and as I waited for Lee to emerge from baggage claim, another imposing figure strode out through the sliding doors surrounded by a prodigious entourage. A suited chauffeur hustled up alongside him, grabbing his bags before directing him towards the exit. I was impressed: The Reverend Al Green looked immaculate, every inch the soul-man turned preacher-man, and everything about him screamed 'Star!'

Some ten minutes later, Lee quietly materialised, sporting grey stubble and shades. I resisted an urge to run towards him, as I'd often done when my parents arrived to collect me from school. His diminutive height helped hide him from curious onlookers, though if there were any I couldn't spot them. Jeane walked alongside him, pushing their luggage trolley. Lee paused briefly to locate me, his baseball cap still atop his head, just as it had been a little short of two months ago when I'd waved him off not thirty metres from where I now stood. Beneath it, his hair looked like it had again been dyed black, but this was the only concession he seemed to have made to the days that lay ahead. This time it was the modesty of his manner that impressed me: Lee rarely, if ever, screamed 'Star!'

While this unassuming style was one of many things I was beginning to like about him, it wasn't long before I wished that he'd scream 'Star!' just a little more often. Perhaps this spoke more of his confidence in his musicians than of a failure to recognise his fans' high expectations, but he'd decided that one solitary rehearsal, and a lengthy soundcheck the next afternoon, were all the band would require. In fairness, Lasse Samuelson had been instructed to spend the previous days in Stockholm drilling his men through the set that Lee had drawn up, but it quietly troubled me that they'd underestimated what might be necessary, especially given the additional musicians arriving from America with only hours to prepare. The words to one of Lee's songs gently taunted me:

> *Can't you tell by my clothes I never made it?*
> *Can't you hear that my songs just won't sing?*
> *Can you see in my eyes that I hate it?*
> *Wasting twenty long years on a dream ...?*

It was almost as though he couldn't be bothered to try.

* * *

I pick Lee up punctually at noon the following day. The rest of the band has already travelled separately to the Putney rehearsal rooms but Lee, as always, has requested special care. Whether he feels he's above sharing a minibus, or simply wants to spend time with me, I haven't yet figured out.

Jeane appears first, skipping out of the hotel full of energy, her mood as sparkling as the white polo shirt she's wearing under her Superbowl jacket. Lee slouches behind, giving me a sly smile as I open the boot of the car so he can put his stuff away. There's a light in his eyes that I've learned to identify as a sign that his mood is affable. After Lee's struggled, childlike, with his seat belt, we head through Trafalgar Square, on to the Mall towards Buckingham Palace, and then down Horse Guards Parade. I point out the tourist attractions to Jeane, who squeals repeatedly, both at the sights and at my driving on the 'wrong' side of the road.

'What are the chances of going to rehearsal today?' Lee interrupts, playfully bored.

'I thought we'd slip that in at some point,' I assure him, checking in the rear-view mirror that I've understood his tone.

'Oh, thanks a lot,' he smiles.

'I thought the sightseeing was probably more important,' I add.

'Not to me,' Lee chuckles. 'I'm not a tourist. I've seen castles. They're dark and damp and full of dungeons.'

We head on down Birdcage Walk, a milky sky turning slowly grey overhead, the windscreen spotting with drizzle.

'I stayed in the Connaught Hotel once,' Lee announces, just loud enough for me to hear over the roar from the window he's opened to allow his cigarette smoke to escape. 'This was back in the 60s. My business managers put me in there. They're laying out my clothes, they ask where you're going and what you're doing, and every floor has its own kitchen. I'd have people up there at one or two o'clock in the morning. I'd say, "Is anybody hungry?" and I'd punch a button, and here comes the guy and cooks anything you want! It was an experience for a cowboy like me! An expensive experience! But they just said, "Relax, Lee, and let it happen, 'cos you're not going to have to do anything in that hotel." I guess it was the first time they pressed more jeans than suits …'

It strikes me that his response to the high life isn't so dissimilar from mine to his company: a sense of amused incredulity that such things can happen to folk like us. There is, however, a genuine humility to his tone as he shares these stories of the beau monde, whereas I know perfectly well I've been showing off about our growing acquaintance. He's put a swagger in my stride: that he's trusted me enough to come this far means a whole lot, and I worry sometimes that my pride might be going to my head. I recognise an urge—usually unfulfilled, since I fear Lee won't appreciate it—to bolster my status by revealing his identity to anyone we meet. 'This is Lee Hazlewood, don't you see? *The* Lee Hazlewood. Yeah, that's right. With me, Wyndham Wallace. He calls me Bubba, you know?' But then I feel a bit sad that this might be necessary. I shouldn't crave validation. Nor should Lee require an introduction.

In Putney, half an hour or so later, we fall out of the tiny car, relieved. In keeping with a traditional English summer, the day is becoming increasingly cold and miserable. We hurry through a tall garden gate to the studio door, past inappropriate antique farm machinery and rusting, rotting cartwheels, before entering a warren of corridors lined with amplifiers, drum kits, and cables. Tracking the sounds from various rooms, we find Lee's musicians, who've set up in a semicircle facing a battered, brown leather sofa on which Lee is soon lounging. The studio's chilly and damp, a musty smell in the air. It's embarrassing to see them in such surroundings, but I take comfort in knowing the Festival Hall team has selected the location: I'll blame them if I have to.

It's Lasse Samuelson, examining the score with his glasses tipped far down his nose, who's ensured that the band is ready the moment Lee arrives. On first sight, it can't be said that they're the hippest group a cult singer songwriter could have chosen after years in the wilderness. Al sits nearest the door, amply filling a red New York T-shirt, his head crowned by a white golf cap. Brad, a diminutive grey-haired man who played on Lee's latest record (as well as some of Lee's former protégé Duane Eddy's 70s recordings), is blowing on a saxophone, smiling shyly as though worried the noise might bother us. With them are another four Swedish musicians, dressed in what might best be described as 'casual wear'. After years of indie-rock uniforms, this isn't what I'm accustomed to seeing.

Soon, however, I'm equally concerned by what I'm hearing. They begin with 'The Fool', Lee's first hit, scored with Sanford Clark in 1956.

'I wrote a cowboy song once, three or four chords,' he'd tell me, a year or two later, 'and I thought it might really do good in the cowboy market. I was very young and dumb. Al put a blues lick on it that the world still knows, and my dumb cowboy song—which, by the way, is a little Shakespearean, gather-round-me-buddies, hold-your-glasses-high, not your typical cowboy song—well, it didn't sell anything cowboy, but damn did it sell pop! Suddenly I was a pop writer!'

Even Elvis Presley cut a version in 1970, in Nashville's famous RCA Studio B. Lee and the King had crossed paths before: Lee would sometimes boast that, back in the 50s, when he'd worked as a DJ, he'd been the first to play Presley's records.

'A guy brought it back,' he explained, another time, of his first Presley disc. 'A local country artist named Chuck Mayfield. Chuck'd gone down to Louisiana Hayride, and he said, "Lee, I want you to listen to this record. He does country, but he does it like a black guy, and it might be something you can play." I'd never heard of Elvis Presley, but I played it and got some calls from people saying, "Get that black person off the air!" I got a lot, though, from the younger people going, "Play more by him." Elvis found that out. When Nancy and I were playing at the Stardust, he was playing at the Hilton, and the first time I met him he said, "Thank you, 'cos I understand you were the first one to do it in Phoenix." And I said, "I'm guilty. Should I not have done?" And he said, "No, I'm glad you did. Wasn't for about ten of you that did it, or I'd still be out driving a truck."'

'The Fool' is undeniably—almost gratifyingly—simple, but this afternoon, someone somewhere in the room is playing it wrong. The musicians fiddle with their manuscripts, scribbling notes furiously, but when they try again they're only marginally more successful. As I take a seat beside Lee, I remind myself this is just a warm up, but attempts to continue with a medley of his most familiar compositions—something he's planned for the show's climax—fare little better.

'Where were you, Lee?' he mumbles after coming in late, impatience flashing across his face. It's a good question. He's been gone a while, and it's often not enough for a star to 'come back': they must match the vision their admirers have for the occasion or else risk squandering their reputation. Lee may not have recognised it, but there's a lot at stake here, even if his fans feel this more keenly than he does. He needs to justify their patience and passion. If he's really thinking of doing something like this again, he cannot afford to let them down.

Initially, I'd hoped to hook Lee up with a contemporary band, knowing full well that there were many who'd leap at the chance. An aborted attempt at a tribute album in the early 90s had revealed plenty of high profile fans—from Beck and Nirvana to The Jesus & Mary Chain and Sonic Youth—and I wanted to capitalise on Lee's legendary name by employing one of the acts I'd come to know in recent years. They'd lend the night a cutting edge, suggesting Lee was in tune with his followers just as much as they were with him. But Lee had had other ideas, as he always did, and my concept barely registered. His trust in Lasse was beyond dispute, and they'd worked together in Sweden on so many projects that it made sense. I just never expected everyone to be quite so old. I never expected them to be quite so *square*, for want of a better word. And though it pains me to say it, I never expected them to sound as rusty as the agricultural machinery outside.

The band presses on regardless, Lee bizarrely delivering the chorus to 'Sugar Town' in a voice borrowed from Sylvester The Cat. Despite his outward nonchalance, there are still errors enough to concern me, and indications of Lee's unease slowly begin to increase. He stands up, pacing the dirty carpet with one hand in his jeans pocket, and Jeane, noticing his declining mood, slips quietly outside. The problem isn't that this line-up has never performed together. It's almost as if, in the years since Lee last played live, they've been separated from their instruments altogether.

My enthusiasm can't hide the fact that they need far more time than has been booked for them in this pokey room. As the afternoon drags on, Lee struggles to maintain his composure, interrupting songs irritably, groaning from time to time as another stray note prods harshly at his pride. He collapses onto the sofa as though participating is too much and, making things tenser still, his gentle criticisms are often imprecise, leaving Lasse to turn vague observations into concrete solutions.

Eventually, things start to come together. It isn't slick, but I hope— we all hope—things will improve further after the next day's prolonged soundcheck. All the same, I'm thankful when a studio employee sticks his head around the door and asks for a quick word in private. A chance to step away is surprisingly welcome.

'Are you going to be here much longer?' he asks.

'Well,' I frown, wondering if he's heard the massacre taking place and is eager to get the amateurs out, 'we're booked in for a little while yet, and they need all the time they can get.'

'Ah, OK,' he says. 'It's just Nick Cave was asking to meet Lee. He's rehearsing here, too.'

I'm tickled that a man like Nick, the gentleman behind the very festival at which Lee will be appearing, needs my permission to visit.

'Of course,' I say authoritatively. 'Send him in. I'm sure Lee wants to meet him.'

Back in the dungeon, I warn Lee that Nick might pop by in a short while. He seems as bothered as he is pleased. I keep an eye open for Nick's arrival, but we remain uninterrupted. Finally, still dissatisfied, Lee calls things to a halt. I sidle up to him as the band start packing up.

'How'd that go?' I ask. It is, I realise, a thoughtless question.

'I think you heard everything as well as I did,' he grunts. 'How'd you think it went?'

'Well,' I tell him diplomatically, haltingly, 'it sounded like the guys had a few mistakes to get out of their systems. I'm sure tomorrow will be note perfect.'

Lee nods thoughtfully.

'Listen,' I add, trying to change the subject, 'I assume Nick still wants to meet you. Shall I try to find him while you guys are getting ready?'

'Sure,' he smiles, visibly cheered by the idea. 'Tell him to stop by soon as he can.'

I step out into the foyer. Apart from the muffled sounds echoing from behind a few heavy doors, the place is as silent as a run-out groove. I'm pointed down a gloomy corridor to a room at the furthest end and knock tentatively. The tones of a piano can be heard, so I rap gently again. The music persists. After a minute, I screw up the courage to push the door slowly open.

Nick Cave sits preoccupied at a grand piano. He makes a perfect black silhouette against a window so bright that, despite the grim weather outside, it seems as though all the light missing from the nearby studios has been sucked into this space. The only thing that's lacking to complete his Mephistophelian appearance is a cloak.

Approaching him across the room's polished wood tiles, I introduce myself humbly, a lowly serf. Perhaps he mistakes me for a court jester: he certainly looks bemused by the sight of a blue polyester-shirted clown in purple corduroys. The man I've left behind at the other end of the corridor makes me feel much more welcome.

'I'm with Lee,' I stammer, spooked by Nick's presence. 'I heard you wanted to meet him. They've just finished their rehearsal.'

'Right,' he says, barely looking up. 'I'll be out in a moment.'

'I guess we'll be in the studio or out the front once they've packed.'

Nick says nothing further, and simply turns to his instrument. Sensing I'm less than welcome, I head back the way I came so I can help carry gear outside, where a minibus has arrived to take the musicians to central London. Mist hangs in the air, and while we wait we shelter under a nearby bridge, the corrosive smell of pigeon shit rankling our nostrils as I discuss the rest of the day's schedule: interviews for Al, downtime for Lee, dinner in a couple of hours. After ten minutes of aimlessly biding our time, Lee, not surprisingly, starts to get tetchy.

'Where is this guy, then?' he demands. 'It's too cold to be hanging around. Go and fetch him, will you, Bubba?'

I slope back into the building, though I'm not sure I have the powers required to 'fetch' Nick Cave for anyone.

'We need to head off to the hotel, Nick,' I say nervously to the figure at the piano after first waiting for him to notice me. He keeps playing.

'Shall we wait for you outside? Or do you want to meet him tomorrow?'

'I'll be there in a moment,' he repeats, again barely acknowledging my existence. Aggravated and embarrassed to have to tell Lee to wait a little longer, I re-join the gang outside.

'Nick says he's just coming,' I try to reassure Lee.

But he doesn't. We kick our heels on damp pavements. The drizzle continues. I send the band on their way. In all honesty, if it was up to me, I too would climb into my car, taking Lee and Jeane with me: as much as fame and success impress me, they don't excuse the discourtesy it takes to leave a sixty-nine-year-old man out in the rain. I anticipated more from our Meltdown host, and clearly so did Lee.

'Where is he, goddamn it?' Lee finally snarls. 'Doesn't he know I'm an old man? I'll die of cold out here.'

I shake my head, aggrieved on Lee's behalf.

'To be honest,' I tell him, tired of defending Nick's behaviour, 'he's just sitting there playing the piano. I don't know what's holding him up. His songs go on a while, but not forever, surely.'

'Well, if he doesn't get here in the next minute we ain't waiting any longer. I've got better things to do than stand around in the cold.'

Seconds later, Cave at last meanders towards us. I play my role by formally introducing them.

'Thanks for flying over,' Nick says, shaking hands with Lee.

'My pleasure,' Lee replies, his earlier frustration carefully hidden behind a mask of good will. 'I appreciate you inviting me.'

'How did it go?' Nick asks.

'Not bad,' Lee lies. 'We'll have another run through tomorrow, and that should iron out any kinks.'

'Good,' says Nick concisely.

There's a long silence, a burst of small talk, and then more silence again. It seems painfully apparent that there's little chemistry between the two. Given his reputed love of Lee's music, and the fact that much of the public credit for Lee's imminent resurrection has gone his way, I expected Nick to exhibit a little more interest.

'Well,' Lee says, discreetly picking up the slack, 'I reckon we'll see you tomorrow?'

'Yeah,' Nick replies hesitantly, and I begin to wonder if he's simply shy. 'Looking forward to it.'

With that, he heads back to his studio. Lee looks at me and shrugs. It's the first time I've seen him nonplussed. He may even be hurt, though if he is he does his best to hide it.

'Hell,' he mumbles, fiddling with his bracelet. 'That was pretty strange.'

* * *

If a taciturn Nick Cave is strange, it's nothing compared to the sight of prominent indie-rockers like Primal Scream's Bobby Gillespie, The Charlatans' Tim Burgess, and Placebo's Brian Molko standing casually at the bar in their finest threads when I wander into the Royal Festival Hall's lobby some twenty-four hours later. Backstage, even they are overshadowed by the presence of actor Harry Dean Stanton, who with his occasional country band represents one of the night's two opening acts. The star of my favourite film, *Paris, Texas*—in which he sometimes looks like a younger Lee, had Lee been a broken man by forty—is pounding the corridor in a white linen suit similar to the one he wore in some of its best scenes. I keep my distance: dealing with one hero at a time is enough.

The day has been spent repeatedly travelling between the bowels of the building and its foyer. The musicians loaded in early, setting up from 10am, and rehearsals have gone on almost all afternoon while I deal with a barrage of phone calls: last-minute attempts to get on the guest list, questions about tax deductions, discussions about photographers, negotiations with the taxi firm scheduled to get everyone to the airport the next morning. Fortunately, once the official working day is over, there's lull enough to grab food, but peace renders me fidgety. Backstage, where there's no mobile phone signal, I worry someone might be trying to call. Out front, where I feel obliged to mingle, I'm concerned I'm neglecting my duties, or that I've overlooked some vital detail. With only minutes to go before doors open and the first of the three acts, Conway Savage, takes the stage, there isn't exactly a great deal I can do, but I still go on the hunt for problems.

'Everything OK, Lee?' I ask, having found him in his dressing room, where he sits quietly with Jeane, his arm slung over the back of a leather sofa, an unusually full ashtray the only sign of strain. The simple white T-shirt and baseball jacket he's been wearing throughout the afternoon have been replaced by a baggy top.

'Everything's fine, Bubba,' Lee replies. 'Nothing to worry about here. Go and check on the band.'

'Everything OK, Lasse?' I ask next door.

'Everything is good, Wyndham,' Lasse replies, his Swedish accent pleasantly melodic. 'Did you check in with Al? He's in the next room along.'

'Everything OK, Al?' I ask, poking my head round the door of his dressing room to find him resting in an armchair, strumming his guitar.

'Everything's under control, Bubba. How's Lee doing?'

I begin to feel redundant. Killing the interminable hours between soundcheck and Lee's arrival onstage is proving tough. I head out to the front of the venue again to meet my parents. It's the first time they've attended a concert with which I've been involved, so this has the potential to be a gratifying occasion for me on both a personal and professional level, something they plainly recognise. My father, as for all formal occasions, has put on a sports jacket and tie, while my mother is in her best summer dress, the previous day's overcast skies having been replaced by an afternoon of sunshine, or so I have to assume, having barely seen daylight since I arrived. My sister's here, too, and I take them all to their seats during the first interval. But much as I want to sit beside them and watch Harry Dean Stanton, I find it hard to concentrate. I'm forced to offer excuses about how busy I am—hoping perhaps my commitment to work will make an impression—and circle back to Lee's dressing room.

'Everything's still fine, Bubba,' Lee says, entertained by my behaviour. At least his mood is upbeat. 'Did you find your folks?'

'Yeah, they're inside already,' I tell him with a pang of guilt.

'You should go hang out with them. Distract them from the disaster ahead.'

'Fair point,' I tease, 'but I think I'm happier making sure everything's running smoothly. I can keep the disasters at bay.'

'Not this one, Bubba. Some things can't be helped. Let's hope they've got insurance for acts of God. Look, everything's running smoothly. Sit down, for Christ's sake. Grab a drink.'

'Are you sure?' I ask, wondering whether this is actually what I want to do. 'I don't want to risk getting in the way.'

'You're not in the way, Bubba. I'd tell you if you were in the way.'

I give in and help myself to a beer. It's the first I've dared have.

'You want anything?' I ask. Fetching him a whisky will give me something to do.

'No, I'm fine,' he replies. 'I don't drink before shows.'

Abstinence hasn't previously seemed one of his strengths. The open bottle in my hand makes me feel self-conscious.

'Sit down, goddamn it,' he says, waving towards the chair again, this time a little irritably.

I do as I'm bidden.

'That's better. By the way, am I going to meet your folks?'

'I hope so, yes. They'd love to meet you.'

This seems to gratify him. He gives me a lopsided, sentimental smile. Actually, they're apprehensive at the prospect, but I'm as keen to introduce them as Lee appears to meet them. A real-life legend gives my work substance. Even my grandmother has heard of 'These Boots Are Made For Walkin''.

'How's Al?' Lee asks next.

'Fine,' I assure him. 'He says he's fine.'

'Good. Good. I worry about him. He's not well.' He stares into the distance a moment. 'You know he started playing guitar for me when he was sixteen and a half? He married a woman named Vivienne. He called her Corky, so we all called her Corky. Don't know why. You know he taught her to play banjo on their wedding night?'

'Really?' I laugh, though he's hardly waiting for an answer. 'Wow.'

'Yeah, ain't that a grand thing to do on your wedding night? I thought that was wonderful. She said so, too.'

'Well, it's hardly traditional, but I guess it's memorable. Unless it was a metaphor?'

Lee glances at me, puzzled, then smiles knowingly. In the silence we can hear music from the hall piped in over a speaker above the dressing room mirror. I stand up to turn it down.

'Sit down, Bubba!' Lee snaps bluntly. 'For God's sake! You're making me nervous. Shut up and I'll finish what I was saying.'

Chastened, I once again do as I'm ordered, though he tries to pretend he was just having fun.

'You know, we started making Duane Eddy records in 1957, in Phoenix, Arizona. That's over forty years ago. Corky Casey'—he relishes the sound of her name as it rolls off his tongue—'played rhythm on a lot of them. She didn't play in the band in person, but Corky was always on the records. You know, what Corky Casey may have been is the first American rock lady guitarist in America. I haven't found anybody who can say otherwise, and I've talked to several people about it. They say, "1957? That's waaaay back there, isn't it?" So if you know of anyone, Bubba—and I don't mean your grandmother who played in a band—then I think you ought to tell me.'

'I don't think my grandmother ever played in a band,' I laugh, surprised by the notion, since I'm not sure I've ever mentioned her before. 'She was more of a wannabe poet.'

'Aha! I like the sound of her.'

'Did your family listen to a lot of music?' I ask.

'Well, my mom liked pop music. You know: Bing Crosby and Perry Como and Frank Sinatra, those kind of people. My dad liked good old-fashioned bluegrass. And he liked all the hill music. He didn't care about anything else. I mean, he'd listen to anything, but he didn't care about it. He just liked Lester Flatt and Earl Scruggs, or somebody like that. And when we were down in Texas, he let me go to a blues club, because he knew the guy that was the bouncer there. And you had this little white face in the middle of all those people who didn't have white faces—in the back of course, 'cos I was too young to be in there—and I'd see all the blues, you know: Little Willie John and people like that, and B.B. King. Anyway, there was a clash—not violent, nor very verbal—between my mom and my dad's musical tastes. And as time went on, I bought them better and better equipment. So my dad could blast my mom out of the back bedroom or kitchen, or she could blast him out of the back bedroom or kitchen.'

He reaches into his packet for another cigarette. For a moment I wonder if I saw his hand tremble. He's smoking Camels today. Perhaps they make him nervous.

'When I was growing up,' he continues, 'we had this beautiful piece of land, all green with cotton trees on it. You'd drive in this big, long driveway, and expect to see this southern mansion with all these giant pillars and everything on it. But there was just a little Tobago house at the back. My dad bought it with the land. It was a nice place, but hidden from everything by twelve or fourteen beautiful cotton trees. And I remember: my pop and I had to chop them down.'

He shakes his head sadly.

'One time, I came buzzing up the driveway and my dad was sitting out on the front porch, reading a paper. Right behind me came a police car. So I stopped my car and the cop came over and opened the door and said, "Step out here," just like they always do, you know? "What's your name?" he said, and I gave him my name. And my dad just sat there. Now, he's far away from us, but he could hear, and the policeman said, "You really might be in some trouble, so let's take a look in the trunk of your car." And I said, "Well, that would be nice, except for one thing: it's locked." I think my Dad must've heard that part, so he stood up and walked to the car.'

I picture a scene from *The Dukes Of Hazzard*: dungarees, dusty tracks, a small-town sheriff chewing straw. I can't help it if that's patronising: it's the way Lee tells them.

'My dad introduced himself like the gentleman he was,' he goes on, 'and the policeman did too. "What's the problem?" my dad said, and the policeman said, "Well, we just want to take a look here in your son's car." So my Dad said, "I tell you what: I want a reason before you do that." The cop told him, "Last night, about eleven o'clock, there were two new tyres stolen from a gas station up here. They broke the window."'

Lee taps ash onto a paper plate balanced on the sofa arm. The sandwich hadn't looked terribly appetising to begin with.

'My dad said, almost as a joke—well, to me it was; it probably wasn't to the cop—"Did you steal two tyres from the gas station up there last night?" And I said, "No, sir, I was home at 10:30." The guy said, "Well, you could've got them before that. Go on, ask him again: has he got them?" So dad asked again: "Did you steal two tyres?" I said I didn't. So my dad said, "That will be all. If he said he didn't, he didn't."

'So the cop said, "I'd still like to take a look in the trunk." But my dad said, "No. You can go and get a search warrant if you want to, but if he told me he didn't take the tyres, then he didn't take the tyres." So the policeman mumbled and grumbled, but my dad just walked away from the whole mess and went back to reading his paper.'

He smiles at me.

'So what did you do?' I ask.

'Well, let's see … I got out of my car and went back to the house! The policeman sat out there for a while, and eventually drove away. You see, the one thing you didn't dare do is, you didn't lie to my dad. And the policeman knew that. That would get you more than a couple of straps. That would get you grounded, and I could stand anything but grounding, you know?'

Lee's fondness for his father gleams in his eyes, perhaps heightened by memories of mischief. I wonder whether he actually stole the tyres, but I don't have time to enquire. Without even pausing for a cigarette, he launches into another tale.

'In the 1930s—we happened to be living in Oklahoma at the time—my dad was friends with Bob Wills. So he said, anyway: as I got older I believed my dad less and less about that. Bob Wills & His Texas Playboys were probably the biggest band in the South, and that's from San Diego to

Miami. They were a country swing band, meaning it had trombones and trumpets and everything else in it. He used to go to a place in Tulsa called Cain's Ballroom, where Bob Wills was playing. And of course it was a good time for oil field workers like my dad—the wildcatters—and outlaw fiddle players like Bob Wills to get together and have a drink. It was prohibition time, and my dad always seemed to have something in his boot, and so did Bob Wills. And they always told me that when I was small, half the time I sat on his neck while he played fiddle in front of the bands. He'd just walk me around the room, me just hanging onto his hat. We were great buddies. This was when I was three, four, five years old, and of course I don't remember any of it.'

He reaches down to a bottle of Coke at his feet and twists the top off, taking a swig before he continues.

'So when I was in the army at the start of the Korean War, I saw that Bob Wills & His Texas Playboys would be playing at the NCO Club. I knew this old Sergeant, and said, "I don't belong to this or anything else, but could I just get in for a few minutes?" And he said, "Sure, come on down." So I sit at the back and watch and it's packed! Oh God, all the redneck soldiers were there to see him. And he's good. Oh, he's goooood!'

That last word is delivered in such a low rumble that I'm pretty sure Lee enjoys the sound of it as much as I do.

'If that's your kind of music,' he adds hurriedly, almost apologetically. 'But if it isn't, it should be! So, anyway, I walked backstage and there he is, sitting with that foot-long cigar on his little stool with his big cowboy boots crossed. He told me to come in, and I introduced myself and told him all this stuff about Cain's and my dad, Gabe Hazlewood, and how they always carried a drink in their boot. He just looked at me, and I didn't know if he was looking at me like I was crazy, or if he was looking at me like I was all right. As soon as I got through my story, he put his arm around me and said, "How's old Gabe Hazlewood doing these days?" So he did know my dad! The stories were true! And that made me very proud.'

I smile, checking my watch discreetly to see how much time we still have.

'I remember,' Lee's ongoing nostalgia nudges him further, 'the summer before I was sixteen, me and a couple of friends wanted to go to the Mardi Gras. It was going to be a big adventure. Well, my mom said, "absolutely no", but my dad, he said, "Those boys are big enough to take care of themselves." And we were. We were big old boys. Mom said, "What if they don't have anything to eat?" Well, that's mothers for you. My dad said, "You can pack them a little lunch and they'll get rides."

'So,' he continues, 'my mom asks, "Where are you gonna stay?" And I said, "We'll find somebody. We know a couple of people down there and we'll sleep out in the park if we have to." They had some warm places in those days where you could kinda lay. People would come down, because they didn't have any money, and they had some fires there where you could just, you know …'

Lee's interrupted by applause coming through the speakers. It sounds like Harry Dean Stanton is warming up the crowd successfully.

'Well,' he says, once the noise has subsided, cleaning his glasses with his sweater, 'we walked about three miles out of town to get on the main highway. The first guy that picked us up was a friend of my dad, and he was going in the right direction, so we went with him. Then the next guy who picked us up was going right to New Orleans, and he worked for my dad for two to three years. So we got out there, and it was dark, and it was getting kind of cold. We got a sandwich and were sitting out by those fires to stay warm, just watching everybody.

'Anyway, this guy who was a foreman on my dad's last job down there, he came up and said, "Why in the world are you boys here?" And he had his wife with him, so we sat and talked. He bought us a Coke or something, and he said, "Where in the hell are you guys staying tonight?" "Well, we were going to stay here." "No," he said. "We've got a room up there with a couple of beds in it. Just go up there, I know the guy." It was a hotel, a little French hotel. "Just get a pillow and a blanket for each of you and you can sleep on the floor."

'We got up in the morning, cleaned up as best we could, and went out and spent a day there. The other two guys—they were bigger than me, one may have been a couple of years older—they sat and drank beers. It was New Orleans: nobody cared. But I didn't drink, so they were having a better time than me. I didn't like beer and there was no drugs. Well, of course there was drugs, but we didn't know about drugs, so …

'That night we ran into him again, and he said, "The room is still up there. I want to find you boys in that room. You're not sleeping out." So we slept in that room again.'

Stories of Lee as an innocent teenager always guarantee my attention. Though the wisdom of his character nowadays suggests he's as ancient as the plains, he hasn't always been a gruff, unpredictable man. There was a time before the hits when he was a teenager, just like I was. In fact, I travelled to New Orleans as a nineteen-year-old, and can picture his youthful figure strolling the same night-time streets that I explored some half-century later.

He reaches for yet another cigarette. There's a scratch of flint. He takes a deep drag and smoke flows from his nostrils. Drinking may be off the agenda tonight—possibly for the first time since he visited New Orleans—but he's making up for it in other ways.

'So the next day we got up, and he said, "We're going back today, and I expect you boys better come back with us as there may be a lot of people trying to get a ride out of here." They took us all the way back to the house. My dad was all ready to hear about our great whoring adventures, but there wasn't any. We were just kids having fun.'

'So you were taken care of by your dad's friends the entire way?' I ask.

'All the way,' he replies.

There's something romantic in the way Lee speaks of what has always seemed to me a mythical America—a place where everybody knew your name and helped you out. I live in London, a city where everyone does their best to avoid sharing a bus seat, let alone a hotel room, and where I don't even know my neighbour's name. The world Lee conjures up seems friendlier, if tougher, and I understand the affection with which he recalls it.

'I think I only had ten dollars,' he concludes. 'My mother slipped it in my pocket just before I left. You know how moms are: "You just hang onto that in case …" And as I'm going out the door, my dad slipped some money in my pocket too. He said, "Be sure to call your mom," so we called a couple of times. And, by the way, I think I had a ten left in my pocket. I remember giving that back to my dad and he said, "Oh, you just keep that. I've never seen nobody coming home from Mardi Gras with money!"'

'My grandmother was like that,' I tell him, his sentimentality reminding me of her. 'She always used to give me cash, sneak it into my hand when she hugged me goodbye. She'd call it jingle jangle.'

'Jingle jangle,' Lee repeats dreamily. 'I like that.'

He tips his head back and looks up at the ceiling, revealing his neck's wiry sinews.

'I could tell these tales forever,' he sighs.

I could listen to them forever, too. Following him requires concentration—something I sometimes struggle to maintain—but with the reality of his fast approaching comeback threatening to bite us both in the arse, I want him to keep talking and talking and talking. It takes my mind—and most likely his—off the real reason we're here. He'll never admit it, but I think he's as nervous as I am, and right now neither of us knows how this story will end.

* * *

I feel like I've got to know Lee over the preceding weeks, but how little I understand him becomes clear moments after he's walked out onto that stage in his jeans and scruffy sweatshirt. After my initial panic, I realise Lee hasn't made a sartorial misjudgement at all: these are exactly the clothes he intended to wear. Dressing up isn't his style. Years later, Jeane will offer me the blazer he wore to his daughter's wedding: it had never come out of the wardrobe again.

Clothes, I should have learned by now, are of little concern to Lee. As a young man he looked casually dashing, but these days he seems almost to disdain fashion. If that's what people care about, then he doesn't care for them. Perhaps, when you've been in and out of style as often as he has, you're forced to disregard it.

Fortunately, his outfit doesn't seem to trouble his fans: whatever they might have first thought, the moment he opens his mouth to sing—and for an opening line, '*I have walked, walked on your water*' is a pretty smart gambit—the crowd falls silent. His extraordinary voice resonates through the hall, the shouts that welcomed him breaking out again as he finally reaches the first verse's payoff line: '*Some of your women love me*'.

The response remains uniformly passionate throughout the performance. Part of the reason is Lee's banter: admittedly he works from a script—it's laid out on a music stand in front of him—but if he's judged one thing perfectly, it's how to gratify an audience that, until not so long ago, he scarcely believed existed.

'You paid £20 to get in?' he wisecracks early on. 'You wouldn't pay £20 for an old horse, would you? Well, you just did.'

Such self-deprecation always seems to work for him. His humility provokes people to protest their loyalty louder, to respect and defend their idol. It also serves to reinforce an idea that perhaps lies behind some of their allegiance: that Lee has been cheated of the rewards he deserves and, in the process, been ground down so far that he no longer believes he was worthy of them anyway. Some of these people, I suspect, identify with the imaginary figure they've created over the years of his absence, and to champion him is in some way a substitute for the appreciation they themselves crave. Lee stands for the little guy, whose vital work remains underappreciated. But perhaps that's just how I see it.

Whether Lee believes he's been hard done by is hard to say. At times I interpret his disdain for his own work as a way of shyly pleading for approval— proof that beneath his tough public exterior lies a singularly insecure man. It might also be a way of avoiding disappointment: if he's the first to dismiss his work, no one else can hurt him by doing the same. There are moments, however, when he really does seem to hold his career in low regard, and this always dismays me, because there's little I can do: trying to console him with compliments never works. Still, this evening he won't need them.

'Tonight' he announces, 'what we're going to do is some obscure songs, the kind that the Hazlewood addicts like.'

I smile, noticing how he deliberately pronounces the word as 'addicks'.

'Now, I love you guys. I named you guys that because I don't have fans. I know I don't have fans because everybody has fans, whereas I have *addicks*. Say there's a song of mine that you want a copy of, but you can't find it. Well, if you're a fan, you'll take your little tape machine over to make a copy, and that's it. But not the Hazlewood addicks. No way! They've got to go out, pay sixty, seventy, eighty, ninety pounds in some dark alley for a bad-sounding Singapore bootleg!'

He sounds almost angry for a moment, much as he did when I recounted my own attempts to track down his recordings. But then he hastily adds, 'And I love you for that! You're really great!'

He chuckles audibly as the addicks applaud him. This may be the very moment he realises just how great these addicks are.

'So we're going to do a bunch of obscure songs, as I said, and in fact we just started off with a couple. This first one, "Rider On A White Horse": that comes from a German film in the middle 70s. Except that it wasn't in the film. Now, the director loved it, and the producer loved it, and of course I liked writing the song to the film and everything else. But they must have thought—being German—that I was from Poland or Czechoslovakia and they wanted to get me for nothing! And they don't know this old redneck Indian: you've got to pay some money for him! So it wasn't in the film, but it could have been. That's close.'

I lean against the doorframe at the side of the stage, at last beginning to relax.

'And "Your Thunder And Your Lightning": I've taken this song to at least twenty or thirty artists, and what they usually say is, "You know, Lee, when you write a song it's got two, three, four hidden meanings in it. But, boy! With this one you just put it out! It's too personal. It's …"'—he lowers his voice—'"… it's dirty …" And I said, "Oh, my God! A dirty Hazlewood song? That's a wonder, isn't it?"'

It's true: the lyrics leave little to the imagination. Lee and Al even exchanged boyish grins during rehearsal yesterday as Lee sang the second verse:

Take these rough hands gently while I lay
My head down upon your swollen breasts.
Then I'll kiss each secret place
So wet and warm and waiting to be free.

But while he specialises in double-entendres—albeit usually more poetic double-entendres—Lee insists to me that only his famous duet with Nancy Sinatra, 'Some Velvet Morning', ever presented him with problems from the censors. They'd misheard the line about how Phaedra *'made it end'*, finding something troubling instead in the idea that she might have *'made it in'*. 'What's it about, Lee?' they'd asked, before it could win approval for the national TV special in which it was to be unveiled. 'Oh,' he'd replied, 'it's about three and a half minutes,' before correcting the lyrics and leaving them to question their own filthy minds.

Up onstage, Lee perseveres with his audience chatter, explaining the premise of his latest album, made up of songs his dad sang after a few drinks back when Lee was a child. Privately, he calls them 'two-beer numbers', but it's clear they mean a lot to him. It's no coincidence that later that night he chooses to dedicate 'She's Funny That Way'—rather than one of his own compositions—to Jeane, still 'my keeper and my love'.

These songs are not really what the audience has come to see: this new record has received uneven reviews, and most people long to hear him sing the older material they've spent their money and time hunting down. But a handful of jazzy standards—as well as a two-song interlude given over to Al Casey while Lee takes a cigarette break at the side—are a small price to pay for the chance to see their hero perform. The indulgence has been earned, as long as Lee also gives them what they want, and this is something he's understood. The majority of the set calls upon unacknowledged classics like the painfully resigned 'If It's Monday Morning', the crudely comic but still touching 'Dolly Parton's Guitar'—'that's got to be the happiest goddamn guitar in the world,' he points out salaciously—and a song whose unlikely subject he describes with relish as 'a dead hooker named "Feathers"'.

'I know the addicks are here tonight,' he says as he peers into the audience, flushed with pleasure, 'because they know these freaky songs that nobody ever heard of before! I have an eighteen-year-old grandson, Dion, and he says, "Granddad, I know what obscure means, but an obscure song? Is that one that didn't make any money?" And I say, "Yes, get the hell out of the house and don't came back here anymore!"'

His most famous songs—the likes of 'Sugar Town', 'Houston', and of course 'These Boots Are Made For Walkin''—appear towards the set's end, slipped into the medley the band worked so hard to perfect during rehearsal. Some in the audience are mystified by the decision to dismiss these in as little as a single verse and chorus, but they fail to understand that while these hits may have delivered Lee's Chivas Regal, he's playing for the fans whose faith in his music reaches way beyond the mainstream, the ones who have helped keep his solo work alive. He may have misjudged their desire to hear his 'freaky songs' almost entirely at the expense of his commercial successes, but reading the reviews that condemn this decision over the following days, his response will be succinct and unsubtle: 'I guess they expected me to sing the girl's parts, too? Well, screw 'em!'

While Lee is banging out these final hits, trouble is brewing at the side of the stage. The curfew, organiser David Sefton warns me, is rapidly approaching, and playing on beyond the allocated hour could result in significant fines due to the overtime that staff can accrue. Inflexibility like this exasperates me: Lee only has his encore left, and it's one that, personally at least, I'm determined to hear at any cost, although I'll probably want to check prices with the venue first. Of greater concern, however, is the fact that Lee wields his temper like a sock filled with pool balls, and the news could turn things ugly. Sefton wisely retreats as Lee cuts the applause short at the medley's conclusion.

'Let me tell you something,' he says, gesturing to his musicians to remain seated, almost as though he's sensed the discussion going on in the shadows to his right. 'That is the stupidest thing that anybody who sits on this stage does. You know damned well I'm coming back. People go out, come back. I just like to sit here on my butt and keep on going.'

David Sefton nods approvingly. I pray Lee won't choose this moment to elaborate upon his thoughts about stage etiquette. Instead, he begins to pick out people in the audience, directing a spotlight towards them so he can thank them: Nick Cave, Steve Shelley, his publishers, his daughter Debbie, and naturally the ever-loyal Jeane. With the seconds ticking away, I urge him silently to wind things up so he can get that final song done, but then he thanks 'the PR man who's worked his *cojones* off, Wyndham "Bubba" Wallace'. It's like my headmaster has singled me out for praise in front of the whole school—except that this time my peers admire the source of the acclaim and it's for something they actually respect. I really could hug the old man.

With the formalities over, Lee readies himself for the grand finale.

'Now,' he states calmly, 'in the 50s, somebody recorded … it's a rock record, naturally, and it sold two or three million, and I really liked this record. I've never been fond of a record more than this. But I think they did it wrong.'

He's toying with the crowd. I know what's coming, and I anticipate the imminent bathos. Ridicule is nothing to be scared of.

'You hate to tell an artist who's sold two or three million records that he did it wrong. But to me it's a love poem, and it should have been done as a love poem. So, tonight, I'm going to do this song the way it should have been done.'

With Lasse clicking his fingers, the band slips into a subdued swing tempo. Lee leans into his microphone, and—his voice now shuddering with reverb, deeper even than it has been all night—intones the opening lines:

Come on over, baby…
There's a whole lot of shaking going on.

A wave of recognition ripples through the audience as Lee continues to deliver the lyrics in a gravelly spoken voice. Fans nudge friends, checking to see if they realise what he's playing. The song is done the way only Lee Hazlewood can do it—as a sexy, lewd, dustbowl crooner who could give Barry White a run for his money. It's perfectly calibrated, playing both to the strengths of his voice and the peculiar image he's cultivated of cowboy and lover. It's also one last number for the devotees, a rare gem recorded for 1976's *20th Century Lee*. The addicks are overjoyed, and none more so than I.

This bizarre interpretation of a beloved rock'n'roll standard provides a victorious climax, but as Lee trots offstage—the band still playing, the crowd's approval deafeningly loud in our ears—it falls to me to inform him that the curfew has arrived. The grin he sported as he moved out of the spotlight disappears before I've even finished the sentence. It's obvious that he's in no way ready to retire: it's been a third of his life since he faced such a crowd, and to deny him a few extra minutes can't help but feel cruelly draconian. Sefton sensibly retires to the shadows as a terrible end to an amazing evening looms ahead.

But Lee buries his fury. He accepts the verdict and lights up a cigarette, smothering his grumbles with smoke. Soaking up the applause from the shadows—the way he so frequently has—he also accepts the long-awaited, calming Chivas on the rocks that Jeane has prepared. He takes a grateful sip and his grin returns. Nothing can spoil this now, not even England's bureaucracy.

Back in the auditorium, with the house lights up, most of the audience are refusing to leave their seats. I step over to Sefton and whisper in his ear. He nods grudgingly but benevolently. I relay the exchange to Lee, whose smile widens a little further. He bounds back onto the stage to bask in the attention one final time.

'I'm sorry, gang,' he explains. 'That's it. That's the curfew and they're closing our butts down. But thanks so much. You're one hell of an audience!'

The response is as dismayed as Lee's own, moments earlier, but the mood passes just as fast and the cheers simply multiply. He leaves them with a final Hazlewoodism.

'And you're all invited up to Al Casey's room for a drink!'

* * *

I lie awake that night trying to piece together the events that followed, my thoughts like balls in a bingo machine. Though the behaviour backstage was restrained by the age of the show's participants, the atmosphere was exuberant all the same. Lee welcomed both my sister and my parents—with whom he spoke at the expense of everyone else for the short time they could stay before their last train left nearby Waterloo—and the close friends I smuggled backstage. The fridge was emptied, and more crates of beer obligingly delivered, while Lee liberally shared his Chivas.

'The best thing,' he announced at one point, his smile threatening to split his cheeks, 'was I was talking about doing obscure songs, and appreciating all these people coming and everything else, but, you know: "Really, guys! I'm seventy years old! Where were you back when I needed you?" And someone with a Cockney accent says, "We weren't born yet, Lee!" I go, "Yeah, you got that right. You're all twenty-eight years old. You weren't born yet!" Nothing gives me chills, but that did.'

Even when we finally left the building, long after the Tube had shut down, he graciously accommodated the queue of fans who'd waited loyally outside the stage door for autographs. Had he been allowed, one sensed, he'd have loitered in his dressing room 'til dawn, so long as the whisky kept coming.

Towards the end, as Jeane and I were congratulating ourselves quietly on a job well done, she'd reminded me of our first phone call, and how eager we'd both been to make the concert happen. Without her help, I knew, it probably never would have.

'You know how I told you never to tell Lee about our little chat?' she recalled. 'You never did, did you?'

'I didn't,' I stated happily. 'Now you know you can trust me.'

'Oh, I do,' she giggled. 'And so does Lee. He was listening on the other phone the whole time we were talking …'

Back in my bedroom, as the boom of bass from passing cars on nearby Coldharbour Lane rattles the garage door that passes for a wall, this recollection of Lee's puckish side fuels my insomnia. I'm still elated by what has taken place, but peculiarly sad too: I'll miss Lee's company, and now we have no further plans together. His growl has become a fixture of recent days, and I've come to rely on the confidences he's shared to give me the confidence I normally lack. As with a school holiday, the end was always inevitable, but now it seems unbearably premature.

My mobile phone lies by my bed, its alarm set early enough for me to be conscious when everyone leaves for the airport in the taxis I've arranged. If they fail to catch their flights due to some last-minute administrational bungle and I'm not available to sort it out, that will be the last thing they'll remember of the trip. There's no way I'm going to risk that.

In the end, an alarm proves unnecessary. My phone rings shortly before dawn, the number withheld.

'Bubba?' a shrill voice shrieks. 'It's Jeane. You have to help me. Lee's frantic. You've got to call the venue.'

I sit up in bed and rub my eyes, trying to catch up with her words. She sounds hysterical.

'OK, Jeane, slow down,' I say, trying to take command of the situation. This is hard: a hangover is in full effect, and each syllable pierces my eardrum, just as each word I utter seems to stick to my tongue. I lay my head back down on the pillow, the phone pressing painfully into my temple.

'Tell me what's going on …'

'Lee's lost his sweatshirt,' Jeane gasps. She couldn't have sounded more distraught if he'd lost his eyesight. 'He loves that sweatshirt more than me! You've got to help. Lee's relying on you, Bubba …'

SIDE B

I love Wyndham, but he's never been
associated with any hit in his life. He only
deals with underground groups. That's
really the truth. I've told him before.
    'Tell me one hit you've had anything
to do with.'
    'Well, this album sold 30,000.'
    'Hell, I sold 30,000 on a bad album!'
LEE HAZLEWOOD

CHAPTER FIVE

MY AUTUMN'S DONE COME

Lightning claws the sky like bony fingers, throwing the mountains that surround Las Vegas into sharp relief. The phrase 'shock and awe' keeps coming to mind, the way the sky is lit an immaculate vision of an otherwise now heartless euphemism. There's no sound, just a wild beauty to the storm, and as we prepare to descend into the desert, its proximity is unsettling, although I still can't stop myself watching. There's nothing else to look at anyway: beneath us lies mere emptiness, a barren wasteland that stretches as far as the eye can see.

That's until the plane banks around and there, laid out before us, are lights twinkling like golden coins, a hint of the treasure trove that pilgrims to Vegas seek. The aircraft bounces and shakes as we head down over the plain in which this shrill, surreal city is settled, the famed strip of casinos looming larger and larger in our view, while around us the mountains are bathed erratically in violent bursts of phosphorescence. It's a suitably theatrical arrival for the weekend that lies ahead.

Lee Hazlewood is dying of cancer. He knows he may not have long to live, and he's not making any secret of it. It's been that way right from the start.

'I'm off to the hospital for a while Monday,' he'd written to me, a year or so earlier, breaking the news of his illness to me in a typically frivolous fashion.

> I spent 12 hours with these folks on Friday while they took gallons of blood and stuck me with spears. They then spake 'it seems you have a mass'. I inquired was this a Christ-mass, a Catholic-mass, or just a mess-mass.

Anyway, I refused to stay in hospital Sat & Sun, told them I had more important things to do—with fear-lined faces and over active tear ducts they let me go. So I spent the weekend working on arrangements with Lars Samuelson in Paris. I'll go back tomorrow for a biopsy to see if I have the big 'C'. If so, I'll take none of their treatments until I return—middle of April.'

The trip to Paris had been set up to enable him to begin work on a new album. Even before he began, he warned it would be his last, although its morbid title, *Cake Or Death*, was in fact borrowed from a sketch by one of his comedic heroes, Eddie Izzard. The confirmation of his renal cancer following these initial tests had done little to soften his resolve, and even his more pessimistic observations on the subject continued to be delivered with that distinctive wit.

'Every month is a year at my age. My green fruit buying days are over.'

The invitation to celebrate with him a year later was similarly succinct. 'My last (?) birthday party is July 8th in Vegas. Try to make it.' When he put it like that, it was hard to refuse. With Lee, most things are.

After the first time I visited Las Vegas I swore I'd never return. I spent less than twenty-four hours in its heart—if a soulless city can be said to have a heart—and experienced the same sense of shame that hopelessly drunken, outspoken nights sometimes inspire the next morning. Walking through its streets, dwarfed by a fake Eiffel Tower, a mock Egyptian pyramid, and the garish colours of the Excalibur Hotel's castle, the place seemed little more than a film set—a series of facades hiding a grim desperation to be anywhere else but there. Nothing was as it claimed to be, either: the free drinks available to gamblers were watered down and warm, the all-you-can-eat buffets far from a steal, given the dubious nutritional content they offered. I felt soiled by the experience, by this gaudy display of wealth designed to appeal to dreamers who believe that anyone can win at the craps tables or the fruit machines that ring out ceaselessly in every corner, even now, in the airport, as I make my way to baggage claim. I can't believe I'm back. Again.

I guess it's some small measure of how far my life has progressed that my mind dwells on my unwelcome need to return to Las Vegas instead of the once inconceivable idea that I'm here to attend Lee Hazlewood's most likely final birthday. So blasé have I become about our relationship that I even considered skipping the festivities. In my defence, however, the last few years of my life have been tumultuous. Late in 2000—little more than a year after Lee's first performance at the Royal Festival Hall, and following four years of working in London for City Slang Records—I'd partnered up with a freelance marketing consultant to run the label's business and simultaneously start our own. Almost exactly twelve months later, five days after planes had flown into the World Trade Centre, he'd hanged himself. The two events were unconnected.

Lee sent condolences, and his words were unusually comforting.

> I seriously doubt there is anything I can say or write to ease your pain. I can only tell you about myself and what I've had to do in a similar situation. Seven of us grew up together as close friends. There are only three of us left. When we get together and speak of the missing four, we tell stories about them as if they were still with us. We laugh at their frailties and screw-ups as they relate to us, and it seems they are just missing that day, and not gone.

> When next we meet I hope you'll tell me stories and we'll touch glasses and drink a toast or two to someone who will be missing that day and not gone.

But my business partner *was* gone, and it was a devastating blow. To add to my misery, only days after he'd died, our accountant revealed that the company stood on the brink of bankruptcy. There were, I would discover, troubling reasons for this that didn't speak well of my former colleague's 'frailties and screw-ups', and the subsequent nightmare of trying to save the business led, eventually, to its dissolution: City Slang's British affairs, and my job, for a while at least, became the concern of EMI Records, and the label I'd founded was shuttered. The strain eventually made me ill.

Fortunately, salvation appeared soon after my partner's suicide in the shape of a relationship with another City Slang employee. This led me to travel to Berlin every month or so to spend long weekends in the city, where I slowly fell in love with its Bohemian lifestyle and elegant, affordable apartments. Each time I returned there it felt like an escape and, after two and a half years of commuting between Germany and England, I realised I needed a fresh start. Although my girlfriend and I had by that time broken up, I remained certain Berlin would offer a chance to take stock of my life. Resigning from my job in early summer 2004, I worked out my three months' notice, took a short holiday, and then, in October, set off in my car—by now I'd upgraded to a Vauxhall Astra whose glove compartment remained firmly in place—to drive the fifteen hours east with only what I could fit inside.

I wasn't sure what I'd do. I had money enough to survive for a few months, and knew only that the music business had never seemed so unattractive. I swiftly landed work as a staff journalist on a quarterly magazine for the outrageously, unattractively wealthy, but after nine months, in a bittersweet stroke of irony, the company announced significant financial cutbacks and the closure of the magazine. Luckily, I had another option: a Berlin-based record company was eager to see me start a new imprint on their behalf. I was reticent to return to a profession that had brought me to my knees once already, but a contract was agreed, carefully negotiated to allow me to work on other projects alongside. I called the label Ever Records, its motto insisting that 'Music Is For Ever'. I would quit two and a half years down the line.

Lee and I had enjoyed a host of adventures in the five years since he'd left the stage in London in '99, but after I'd quit the UK we initially kept only sporadic contact, and I visited his home just once. There was little for me to do: although he'd decided to return to the studio, my involvement was largely unnecessary. I was instead called upon to administer one solitary assignment: a duet with a former Eurovision song contest winner based in Norway. Lee's list of demands was short: flights and accommodation for us both, a studio that 'must be less than 180km from Oslo', and an impressive, one-off fee. He'd justified the upfront payment with another simple fruit reference: 'Lee wants no royalties. He doesn't buy green bananas.'

We'd spent five days lounging around the foyer of the city's Bristol Hotel, listening to the piano player, dining in expensive restaurants, charming his temporary duet partner, and purchasing a Rolex watch for Jeane. Oddly, the latter task was handed over to me after the price forced the store to call Lee's credit card company, inevitably provoking a flourish of his unpredictable temper.

'Can you confirm the name on the card?' I was asked, after the phone was passed my way.

'Yes,' I replied. 'Barton Lee Hazlewood.'

'Barton Lee Hazlewood?' The name was mulled over for a moment. 'You mean like the singer guy, Lee Hazlewood?'

'Yes, exactly like the singer guy, Lee Hazlewood.'

'Is that who I'm talking to?'

'No, his representative.'

'No way! I'm such a big fan!'

'Well, he's pretty mad that you won't let him spend his own money. Can you fix this before he takes it out on me?'

They did, and afterwards Lee patted me on the back like a small child. Our trip confirmed we were friends—a clumsy if nonetheless accurate word—but when he invited me to his birthday party during my first summer in Berlin, I decided I was too busy with the early stages of setting up Ever Records. Although the party was only in Paris, which was hardly a long way to go, I couldn't afford the travel anyway. Later on, I'd realise the true gravity of Lee's illness had failed to sink in, and I'd regret not having made the effort, but at the time it was hard to believe I'd be missed. Away from the work I did on his behalf, I doubted my presence carried any significant weight, and such insecurities outweighed his benign petitioning for me to change my plans. Imagining he was sincere simply seemed presumptuous. We got on well, but we normally only hung out when there was a job to be done.

A year on, however, I can't say no. This time I really don't want to. I may be in the midst of endless travel in pursuit of new bands, but recently, to my amusement—and as I spend increasing time helping him find a home for his final album—he's made our business relationship official. It ensures I can't decline his invitation while preventing me from feeling like a sycophant when enjoying time in his company.

'I've got you a gift,' he'd told me on the phone. 'I don't know whether this means anything to you, but perhaps one day it will.'

He'd paused. It could have been for dramatic effect, or maybe a brief exchange with Jeane. It was hard to tell if the voices in the background were simply from his television.

'You can start putting my name on your letterheads or emails,' he'd finally announced, 'or whatever it is you do. You can call yourself my manager.'

'I'll be proud to do so,' I'd told him, without hesitation. 'Thank you!'

My response was heartfelt and humble. It was the first time he'd ever sanctioned such a post, and the appointment meant a lot. People had been attributing the role to me for some time, but usually I qualified the title by correcting it to 'quasi-manager', so his recognition was welcome affirmation.

This time, though, I had no need to diminish my own contribution. Lee did it on my behalf.

'I want you to put "Europe" in brackets after it,' he added with a cautionary tone. 'No fucker interferes with my business in America.'

'Right,' I conceded immediately, though I was actually close to finalising a deal that included the US. '"Manager (Europe)" it is. I'm honoured.'

Whatever he chooses to call me, it's a notional title: no fucker tells Lee Hazlewood what to do, wherever they are. All I've really done is make things happen when he wants them to, although occasionally they're my suggestions. To some, including myself, I'm less a manager, more a gopher, but however anyone sees me, it's a position I enjoy, and I value the added authority my new office affords me. Besides, I always like it when Lee rewards me. I've rarely earned much money from our work—a low percentage on the few deals I've handled directly, a bit of pocket money if the mood takes him—but I'm not doing it for the income. His and Jeane's smaller gestures often prove far more endearing, if eccentric, and answer a greater symbolic need within me: a Sound Soother Alarm Clock & Radio from Sharper Image; a giant Margarita glass; a bag of Taco Bell Hot Sauce sachets that Lee swears turn scrambled eggs into a culinary tour de force.

As Lee's new, official Manager (Europe), I know I should be by his side on his birthday. Moreover, with his health declining, I find myself appreciating our bond more than ever, and the feeling seems to be mutual: though this remains unspoken, I sense he needs me, too. There's another factor at play as well: Lee rarely suffers snubs gladly, and our association is as fragile as he chooses to make it. God knows I hate it when he gets angry.

So it's way more than loyalty that insists I attend, and far more than mere business. He's taken my last two girlfriends under his wing, sending them Christmas cards and friendly faxes. He continues to enquire fondly of my parents, voicing respect for my father, whom he calls simply The General, and extolling the beauty of my mother, known only as The Lady. I in turn have met some of his closest relatives and friends, stayed at his home, eaten from his TV table, and shared a thousand drunken anecdotes, confessions, and problems.

So, yes, of course I have to be here. Even back in the early days, Lee had signed a picture for me with the words 'You're family now.' This has become ever truer since. If this really is to be his last birthday, and possibly my last chance to see him—as his doctors suggest is the case—then I can't miss the opportunity. If it means anything to Lee to have me here in Las Vegas—and it seems to me that it does—then it means even more to me.

* * *

Jeane meets me at Las Vegas's McCarran International Airport. She and Lee are so different that his closest friends never saw their relationship lasting more than a matter of days.

'They thought I was just dating her because she was a barmaid,' Lee likes to laugh. 'Why would I do that? I only drink Scotch. I don't need a barmaid to fix a Chivas on the rocks.'

While Lee is charming, kind, and witty, sullen, moody, and demanding, it's become clear to me that Jeane—most of the time, anyway—is there to provide fun. She worships Lee, lifting his mood—especially now he's sick—in a way that no one else seems able. Her mission is to keep him cheerful, and he in turn does the same for her.

When I first met them, I took their relationship at face value, but familiarity has underlined how unlikely a happy couple they are. Quite apart from the fact that she's around twenty-five years younger than him—and her politics skew to the right of his broadly liberal minded Democrat values—he's a brooding poet with a dark, if sometimes unsubtle, sense of humour: a blend of Tommy Lee Jones, Robert Duvall, and Lee Marvin. She, on the other hand, is a cartoon character, a whirlwind of one-liners, laughter, and indiscreet stories, as excitable as Shelley Winters playing Charlotte Haze in Stanley Kubrick's *Lolita*. Lee would no doubt abhor such casting, but since his favourite film is apparently *The Terror Of Tiny Town*, his own choices might not be any more appropriate.

They still have no plans to marry. Lee's been burned before. It's something about which he makes little secret. His bitterness at the nature of his split from his first wife still seems as fresh as when the judge issued his settlement.

'In 1949, when we got married,' he once sighed, explaining the title of 'Buying Back', 'I had ninety dollars. Twelve years later, the woman took much, much, and more: property and money and everything else. Californian divorce laws are really heavy. On one of my many trips back to where I come from in Texas, somebody said, "Boy, Lee, you're buying back what you used to give away," and I said, "Yeah …"'

I spot Jeane coming for me as I'm waiting at baggage claim. She's accompanied by Lee's only son, Mark, a conspiracy theorist *par excellence*. In a book he published in 2001—*Blindsided: Planet X Passes In 2003*, which Lee passed on to me with evident scepticism—he predicted the end of the world. Now that it's 2006 and we've avoided the cataclysmic coming of Planet X, I'm no more inclined to read it. I find him an eccentric character:

often full of a nervous, excessively enthusiastic energy, his eyes wide as though permanently stunned. Jeane will confide to me some day soon that he's recently been following a diet in which he chews food for its nutritional content, only to spit it out afterwards. He is, she advises me, not the best person to take to a restaurant.

After we've exchanged warm greetings, and my luggage has been rescued from the carousel, Jeane starts gushing about the new car Lee's just bought her. He calls it her 'prairie schooner'.

'I bet you can't find the CD player,' she squeaks excitedly, once we've navigated our way through several brightly lit levels of a parking garage and are inside the vehicle at last. Sure enough, I can't. It's buried behind the GPS.

'I expect you've got a DVD player here too,' I sigh.

'Oh, yes!' she giggles. 'The grandkids have one in the back!'

She cracks jokes at such a pace all the way home that I barely see her pause for breath. Having not slept the entire way from Europe, it's all a bit much, although I manage to throw in a few little quips of my own. But she, too, seems somewhat drained; Lee's been in pain recently, and his moods go up and down. She's also taken on arrangements for the party, and it's keeping her up at night. It's not going to be a big bash— approximately thirty close friends and family—and to keep things simple, it will be held in their home. But she's sorted out all the catering, the carpet-cleaning, the hotel-booking, the airport runs, the lot. Nothing has been left to chance, and this is where Jeane excels. Lee still loves to remind me of her German ancestry.

She delivers me to the Sunset Station Hotel & Casino, five minutes drive from their house in the Vegas suburb of Henderson. It's convenient, and Lee also loves to spend time here, but while it's extravagant, it's also serenely depressing. Making the fifty-metre walk from check-in to the elevators that rise up to the rooms, I eavesdrop on a middle-aged couple waddling behind me.

'I can't believe they haven't put a moving walkway here,' the wife complains. 'They can't expect us to carry our bags this far.'

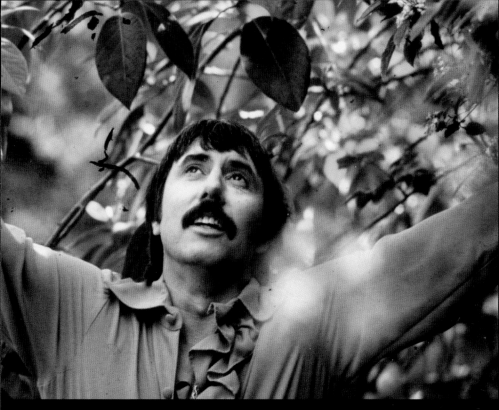

ABOVE A force of nature: Lee, long before his autumn done come, some time around 1970.
LEFT '... like a bohemian, moustachioed cowpoke': Lee during the photoshoot for the cover of *Forty*.
BELOW A billboard advertising Lee's debut solo album in 1963.

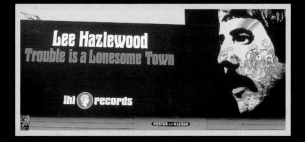

ABOVE The single that started my story: Tindersticks' 'A Marriage Made In Heaven', released in March 1993. **LEFT** New York, April 24 1999: Kalle Axelman, Torbjörn Axelman, Lee Hazlewood. **BELOW** Lee and future wife Jeane Kelley in Spain in the mid 90s. **OPPOSITE PAGE** The first fax I ever received from Lee, which now hangs proudly on my wall.

Lee Hazlewood

1970 East Oseola Parkway
Suite 320
Kissimmee, FL 34743
Fax (407) 825-9009

February 14, 1999

Dear Wyndham Wallace,

If I had a name like Wyndham Wallace I would not associate or correspond with anyone with a simple name like mine. However, since you have lowered yourself to such depths, how can my old Indian heart (west not east) not respond favorably.

Now that the B.S. is out of the way, I enjoyed your fax very much. So, as you wrote, I am not the biggest fan of interviews (in fact I may be the smallest fan of interviews). The English press has never been kind to Jerry Lee Lewis, Prince Philip, or me. But I've made more and done more than all of 'em with the exception of the Prince. So, you, Steve Shelley, and little ole me will forget our grudges and pretend this is virgin territory we are prepared to let attack us.

My trust lies with Steve Shelley and since his trust lies with you, I can tell as many lies as the next one.

So, bring 'em on!

Best regards,

Lee Hazlewood

Cc: Steve Shelley

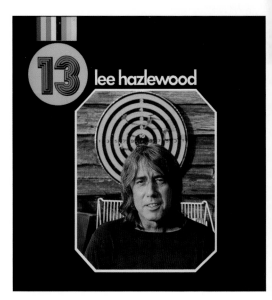

ABOVE The cover of Lee's 1972 album *13*, taken in the grounds of Torbjörn Axelman's home, Brucebo, on the Swedish island of Gotland. **LEFT** Over a quarter of a century later, on July 10 1999, Lee revisits the scene. **BELOW** Torbjörn Axelman and Lee enjoying 'a box of cat's piss' outside Torbjörn's studio on the island of Lidingö, Sweden, July 8 1999. **OPPOSITE PAGE** Lee backstage at London's Royal Festival Hall on June 29 1999.

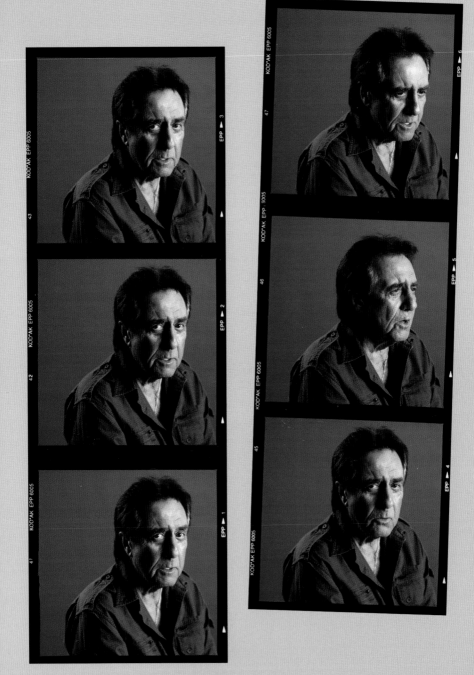

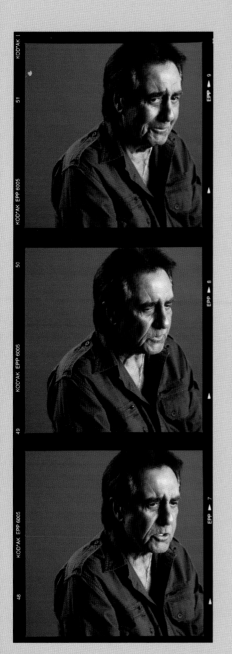

The many faces of Lee: a promotional photoshoot for the release of *For Every Solution There's A Problem*, London, May 2002.

ABOVE Bela B. and writer and TV presenter Charlotte Roche in Berlin with Lee, February 25 2006. LEFT Jeane, backstage after Lee's third and final show at London's Royal Festival Hall, August 4 2004—his last public performance. BELOW Lee meets members of the City Slang Records team in Berlin, April 26 2002.

ABOVE Lee signs copies of his records
backstage at the Royal Festival Hall,
September 22 2002.

LEFT Lee shares stories with Bela during sessions for 'The First Song Of The Day', Berlin, February 26 2006. **BELOW LEFT** Lee and Bela in the vocal booth that same day: 'Let's just hope this song will never be the first song of the day for anybody else.' **BELOW** Lee as I remember him best: lighting a cigarette.

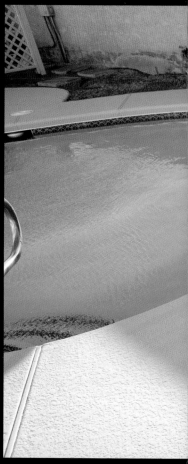

ABOVE Lee by the pool at the back of his home outside Las Vegas, October 6 2006. **LEFT** Lee poses in the Studio At The Palms Hotel, Las Vegas, for the *Cake Or Death* promotional campaign. **RIGHT** Lee at home during interviews in support of *Cake Or Death*.

ABOVE A short, short-tempered photoshoot
in Berlin's Gendarmenmarkt, April 20 2006.
Afterwards, photographer Kevin Cummins
and Lee chatted like old friends. Another
shot provided the cover to *Cake Or Death*.

LEFT Lee celebrates his 'Last (?) Birthday Party' at his home in Las Vegas, July 8 2006. **BELOW** Nancy and Lee at the Palms Casino Hotel, Las Vegas, February 2007; Lee, myself, and Nancy Sinatra.

LEFT Cake and death: Lee's last birthday party, July 12 2007. **ABOVE** 'You're supposed to film the cake!' Nina Fingskes (left) tries to placate Lee, as daughter Samantha delivers the cake to the accompaniment of Lee's best friend, Tommy Parsons, on guitar. **BELOW** Lee's Memorial Party, Phoenix, September 15 2007. Left to right: Erik Paparazzi (Cat Power), Joey Burns (Calexico), A.J. Lambert (Nancy Sinatra's daughter), Joe McGinty (musician and promoter), me, Kalle Axelman.

When I stroll to a nearby mall the next morning, people slow down their cars to stare. It begins to seem as though boots are made for driving here, and feet are for putting up. The streets don't even offer sidewalks, and they're certainly not paved with gold: the only other pedestrians are pushing shopping trolleys filled with empty bottles, desperately scraping deposits together for food.

I visited this hotel once before, losing $700 in a catastrophic, two-afternoon gambling spree when all I was trying to do was keep Lee company. The place is vast, a labyrinth emitting an endless, chiming noise that stops just short of cacophony, row upon row of bright, flashing lights repeating uniform patterns. In front of them sit largely emotionless faces hypnotised by the sounds and sights. It sometimes seems like there's more life in the machines than the players: balding old men with glazed eyes, paunches close to popping buttons on loud Hawaiian shirts; wizened old grannies with oxygen tanks by their sides; young couples sitting silently, sadly, next to one another; fading playboys optimistically eyeing up the fading peroxide hostesses.

There was a time, not so long ago, when I was in love with America: its open-mindedness, its friendliness, its generous prosperity; a land Lee sometimes lovingly describes. But those days look long gone. The America of George Bush has dined out too often on its own success and become a dreadful parody instead. It's a country that's sought only to please itself, and no city is more emblematic of this than Las Vegas. It makes little sense that Lee, a staunch Democrat who boasts on *Cake Or Death* that he's never voted Republican, should live here—until, of course, one learns about its tax breaks. The fact that these hadn't materialised in Ireland a few years earlier had been enough to lead him to cut short his relocation to the small town of Midleton in County Cork.

Around the playground of machines and poker tables lies a ring of restaurants and souvenir stores. The place is a monument to consumerism, and the cuisine on offer reflects this. Gamblers stagger to and from their filling stations, flashing American Dream currency, but Lee favours a place where he can cash in points he's earned as a casino regular. It's called, inevitably, the Feast Buffet, and it's an all-you-can-eat experience that offers food from every corner of the globe: Mexican, Italian, American, Asian, and the catchall 'International'. There is, of course, a separate section for desserts.

This is where Lee meets me for lunch the day after my arrival. I wait for him outside the entrance, marvelling at décor that allows the casino to host the illustrated, kitsch golden sunset that justifies its name whatever the season. I'm clutching a black briefcase, one Lee left behind after visiting Europe earlier in the year. Disappointingly, it contains only a friend's record sleeves awaiting Lee's signature, but to amuse myself I slip down my shades, hiding my eyes to look like a mobster guarding cash. No one gives me a second glance. I'm clearly unconvincing. That, or far from out of the ordinary.

I spot Lee limping inconspicuously towards me through the crowds, supporting himself on a silver-topped cane that he switches to his left hand so he can shake mine firmly.

'Hey, Bubba!' he says, his eyebrows briefly raised above the rim of his sunglasses.

'Hey, Lee,' I smile, as he releases his grip. Then he slaps me on the back and we embrace.

* * *

Thoughts of Lee's birthday always return me to Sweden, to a dark taxi ride that took us both out of Stockholm up into the overlooking hills one Friday morning in early July 1999, some two weeks after he'd left London. Our destination, a former industrial district, was the setting for the Fanclub Festival, an event that had been pursuing Lee to perform ever since it was announced he'd play Nick Cave's Meltdown. While our involvement had at first been strictly limited to British territory, after the success of his show Lee soon asked if I could take over the reins for this second concert. He was distrustful of the festival's methodology, and his confidence in their setup took a huge knock when they cancelled the event altogether the day after his triumphant comeback, only to announce a few days later that they'd reinstated it on a smaller scale.

Lee nominated me as his representative, making it thoroughly clear what he would and wouldn't accept. One demand was particularly flattering: my presence was to be a prerequisite, and they were to pay for both my flights and my accommodation in the stately SAS Radisson Hotel Lee always favoured when in the city. Since he'd headed on to Stockholm after the London show—looking to spend further time with friends—he argued he'd saved them money on his airfare by not demanding transatlantic flights. They could instead splash out on me.

Our schedule in Stockholm was, for the most part, hectic. It began dramatically with the delivery—in cash, as Lee regularly preferred—of the considerable fee I'd renegotiated. A nervous promoter brought it in person, apologising at length for the complications of recent weeks. He failed to reassure me; this new event had been hustled together within a matter of days and he appeared nervous, even desperate. Lee, however, didn't care. Once the money was in his possession, he sat me down in the vast atrium that doubled as a restaurant at the furthest end of the hotel lobby.

'You've earned your dinner,' he announced. 'Pick whatever you want.'

I did exactly that, peaking with a plate of fresh strawberries and basil with ice cream that tasted of a perfect mood. As the midnight sun drenched our table, even Lee's conservative tastes conceded it was wonderful.

It was as the 60s turned the corner into the 70s that Lee had first drifted towards Sweden. In the immediate wake of his success with Nancy, he'd gone on to work with other distinguished performers, including her father—for whom he produced 'Somethin' Stupid', Frank's duet with Nancy—and actress Ann-Margret, who teamed up with him for the absurdly overblown *The Cowboy And The Lady*. But something had drawn him to Northern Europe, and I couldn't help but wonder what it was.

'Oh, ho,' he laughs. 'Well, it might be that I enjoy living in Sweden. I stayed here in the summers, and then always went back to America too. And

I stayed a couple of winters here. Winter is a great time to write. But I just wrote what I felt like here, and it was easy to do it. I had plenty of company in my apartment—I wasn't lonely—but the only thing is I could work when I wanted to, just me and the tape machine. That was all.'

It wasn't, I realised, quite the prolonged exile that people had suggested. By renting an apartment in Stockholm, he'd been able to come and go as he pleased, keeping his whereabouts here and at home hidden from all but his closest friends, and sometimes even from them. Lee found it hard to settle down, but harder still to be accessible.

'You know, Björn Borg used to come by my place in Stockholm,' he informed me, as we nursed swollen bellies after our meals. 'I met Björn's father, too. I asked Mr Borg, "Why tennis?" And he said, "I was at one of those Rotary Club meetings, and they had a prize draw." And I said, "And you won a tennis racquet?" He said, "No, the tennis racquet was second prize. I won first prize, but traded it as a favour and took it home for Björn." And that's how he started playing tennis. Isn't that an interesting story?'

Lee winked and then looked around to check whether he could smoke.

'Let's take a walk,' he said. I hailed a waiter and ordered the bill on his behalf.

'I liked Björn,' he added, as we waited. 'We used to run into each other in clubs. Clubs all over the world!'

'You played tennis?' I laughed. It took him a moment to realise I was joking.

Outside, beneath a bright night-time sky determined to deceive us, we ambled along the quay upon which the hotel was situated. I manoeuvred our conversation towards the records that Lee had made while he lived here, some of which were being re-released by Steve Shelley. Albums like the brassy *13*—its arrangements provided by Larry Marks, a composer for Hanna-Barbera cartoons—had meant little to people outside of Scandinavia at the time, but to those who'd recently discovered them, they were conclusive, if overdue, proof of Lee's special talents.

'Sometimes I just did an album for the fun of it,' he observed unassumingly, 'but *Cowboy In Sweden* was one of the best-selling things they had.'

In fact, it had started out as part of another unexpected detour brought on by his move to Scandinavia, this time into film, courtesy of a man who would soon become a close friend, director Torbjörn Axelman.

'That was the biggest-budget TV show in Sweden to that date,' he beams proudly. 'We took six or seven weeks in the summer to do it. Really was pressed for time, with about maybe a ten-man crew. Everybody just did everything.'

One of their collaborations proved especially rewarding, 1973's *The N.S.V.I.P.'s—The Not So Very Important People*. A thirty-minute special featuring Lee and Swedish singer Lili Lindfors, it consisted of covers of Harry Chapin songs in theatrical, studio-bound performances, including especially moving versions of 'Taxi' and the eight-minute 'Better Place To Be'. In a display of typically Hazlewoodian contrariness, neither song had appeared on his album called *The N.S.V.I.P.'s*, which in fact had been released almost a decade earlier; never one to waste a good line, Lee had simply recycled the title.

The show won them the Golden Rose, the top prize at Switzerland's prestigious annual TV festival in Montreux, an event that honoured the best in 'Global Entertainment Television'. To Lee and Torbjörn's further delight and unconcealed amusement—especially given Lee's relationship with the media—the show also won the Press Prize. What gratified Lee most, however, was that an American effort, courtesy of Barbra Streisand, was pushed into second place.

Nonetheless, as boats creaked in the harbour alongside us, Lee confessed that his feelings about the prize were to become somewhat mixed.

'Two or three months goes by,' he explained, shaking his head, 'and the publicity's died down, and I said, "I've got an idea for a show that would really be great for next year's Montreux." They go, "What are you talking about?" I said, "Well, we won a Golden Rose. We'll try to win it, or at least a silver or a bronze next year for you." "Well, no, Lee," they said. "Let's give someone else a chance." You know, in America you've got one hit show on: get another hit show on! But in Sweden you take turns. That kind of hurt my heart a little bit.'

'I'll tell you what, though,' he added, kicking pebbles into the water as his mood lifted again. 'One time I was sitting on a yacht in Cannes. If that doesn't impress you, nothing will. Well, maybe this will: I was with Roger Moore. I was actually with Roger Moore when he was talking to somebody about getting the part of Zero-Zero-Seven.'

Muffled Swedish hip-hop leaked from a little cabin cruiser nearby. Lee rolled his eyes and continued.

'It seemed to me like it was one of the first calls he'd got. We'd only met a couple of days before, but he had a couple of my CDs—God knows why—and he invited Torbjörn and myself on the yacht. And we got to be friends those two or three days that we were there. I still consider him a friend. Every time he put out a new James Bond film, when it opened in Sweden he'd come to Stockholm, and he spent as much time up at my flat on Valhallawägen as he did at the Grand Hotel. And, by the way, good times were had by all! I liked Roger. He's still my favourite Bond.'

Valhallawägen—a street mentioned on a stupidly rare seven inch single, '(Let's Take A Walk) Down Valhallawägen', that Lee had released in 1972— was one of the places we'd visit during our trip. It was here—amid two lanes of traffic separated by a wide expanse of grass and trees, a place for promenades under parasols—that he'd led a group of kids, including his own, as they danced to the song for a TV show. '*Secretary Sue, I'm told,*' he'd sung mischievously, '*when she sniffs ain't got no cold,*' and then the kids had joined in with the joyful chorus. I reminded him of the tune excitably. He hadn't thought of it for years.

We stopped at the anonymous door of a low-level block of flats. He looked up from the pavement at its exterior, perhaps trying to reconcile it with his memories in much the same way as I would later at the Grand Hyatt in Manhattan. Then, coincidentally, he saw a man leaning over a balcony who'd lived there back when he did. Furthermore, they'd worked together.

Pleasure shone from Lee's face as they waved to one another. If Lee had ever had a home, it seemed, it was Sweden.

Before he'd get round to retracing his steps through the city, however, there was a day to be spent talking to the press. On our first full day in Stockholm, I led a procession of journalists and photographers into the grand two-room suite that had been allocated for his interviews. He'd agreed to co-operate as much as the promoters needed to help sell their festival, but it was clear he'd never expected such numbers. It seemed every publication in the country wanted a bit of him, as did a handful of other journalists who'd flown from overseas especially. From breakfast until dinner, with barely a pause, he answered their increasingly unimaginative questions, posed for their photographs, even signed their boots. In between, whenever he was asked which act he was most interested in seeing at the festival, he did his best to fulfil the promise he'd made as a belated present for my birthday, five days earlier.

Dear Bubba,

Choose one group you want promoted. Will only do one—Indians get too kind they'll start taking over our gambling palaces.

Built To Spill were the sole City Slang act on the bill. He'd never heard a note, but his outspoken dedication was conspicuous.

Even lunch was cut short—a rare sacrifice—in an effort to save time. But it was to no avail. As always, Lee's anecdotes were an unstoppable force, and long before his final appointments were completed, Torbjörn had arrived, accompanied by his son Kalle, as well as Nina Lizell, with whom Lee had sung on *Cowboy In Sweden*. She'd dressed up for the occasion, her smart suit pressed and pristine, her hair a classic Scandinavian platinum, perfectly brushed so it streamed down her back like a waterfall. They'd not seen each other for two decades, and she was obviously both nervous and excited.

The pressure to satisfy everyone became too much. Lee's temper began to fray, and he gave Nina short shrift. She was an intense and sentimental woman, a combination Lee frequently struggled to accommodate. He'd been warned, too, that she dearly wanted to join him onstage, and it was an idea he had no intention of entertaining. But it was the photographers who bore the brunt of his impatience and growing hunger: never a man comfortable with cameras, Lee growled at them, swore at them, and gave them a minute or two at most before telling them to get the hell out of his face. I elected to stand to one side, concerned that I'd make things worse if I intervened. Frankly, I was scared.

Fortunately, he had time to unwind the next day, once again in the company of Torbjörn and his son. Kalle and I had already met in London: I'd found him to be an earnest, kind man just a little younger than myself, and one obviously keen to follow in his father's footsteps. On an almost flawless summer's day, we drove together to Lidingö, an island lying in the northeastern reaches of Sweden's capital. Beneath a sky flecked with the palest of clouds, Lee and his friend of more than thirty years sat down around a table covered with ingredients for an exemplary Swedish lunch: fresh bread, cheese, cold meats, and salad.

Had these two tried any harder to represent the countries in which they were born, they'd have entered the realms of pastiche: Torbjörn, leaning back in his seat, sported blue jeans and a smart denim shirt, with a red kerchief tied neatly round his neck. His gold-rimmed spectacles nestled upon his nose, and a light breeze ruffled his remaining grey hair. Lee, meanwhile, sat slumped in his chair wearing an oversize navy-blue T-shirt that revealed his mild paunch, his still dark, dyed hair betrayed by hints of grey in eyebrows framed between sunglasses and the *X-Files* baseball cap perched upon his head. An additional pair of reading glasses pulled the seam of his shirt down to reveal what he always called his 'turkey neck'.

'In the US, you can sit next to an American for five minutes and know the person's whole life,' he'd told me on the way there. 'You can sit next to a Swede for five hours and no one says a thing. That's why I like the Swedes.'

That day, there was no shortage of chat. This was where Torbjörn kept his art studio, at the edge of woods in which they'd sometimes filmed, and it was the first occasion that Lee had visited in a long, long while. Kalle hovered on the sidelines, his camera recording the two men as they reminisced about the years they'd shared, while I sat nearby, a little back from the table, observing them with fascination brought on by the fact I still couldn't believe I was there.

Lee had talked repeatedly about the man opposite: of the movies they'd made, of the fun they'd enjoyed, and of the island, Gotland, where Torbjörn spent most of his time. If Torbjörn wasn't a legend outside of Sweden, he was in Lee's world, and if Sweden was a spiritual home for the singer, songwriter, and producer, Gotland was his paradise retreat.

The two were first introduced by Torbjörn's 'script girl', Gunilla Nilars, who was working with Lee on another Stockholm television production and felt certain that the two would connect. She wasn't wrong, which was probably why she went on to become one of Sweden's most successful TV producers. Over the following seven years, Torbjörn and Lee would collaborate on seven productions, united by a creative chemistry and sense of the absurd that belied their contrasting personalities: Torbjörn was serious, armed with a keen intellect and a dry wit, while Lee was both moody and sentimental, a man who loved a hearty punch line, though never at the expense of someone about whom he cared.

Observing them together, it was as though they'd been apart mere weeks, the only indication of their separation the fact that the central themes of their conversation were based around the past. While I struggled to open a box of Gato Blanco wine—'Gato' is Spanish for 'cat', Lee informed me, before joking that Torbjörn was serving us cat's piss—they cast their minds back to the friends they'd made and the characters they'd met, Lee pausing only to advise me to 'milk the box' before unravelling another well-worn yarn. On the rare occasions they broke off conversation altogether, birdsong echoed across the lake beside us.

'I love the silence,' Lee sighed, with genuine pleasure. I'd rarely seen him look so content.

Lee had retreated to Sweden partially, he told me, to prevent his son

Mark from being drafted for the Vietnam War. But though people back home had been under the impression that he was 'laying low', as he liked to put it, he'd continued working. Some of the solo albums that resulted, like *Cowboy In Sweden* and *Requiem For An Almost Lady*, were among his best. It was just that they barely travelled beyond Scandinavia.

'I think people meant more that my music was laying low,' he joked, before recounting a story about how his Stockholm apartment was once burgled while he was away in America. 'They only stole two things: my leather coat, and all of my records: the ones that I made. The policeman said, "Well, we know one thing: the thief is not a music critic …"'

Of those Swedish releases, few were as little-known and yet quietly beloved of Lee as the soundtrack to the last film that Torbjörn and he had made together in 1975, *A House Safe For Tigers*. So sought-after had it become that vinyl copies had later been known to sell for several hundred dollars. Inspired by and filmed amid Gotland's supposed Eden, *A House Safe For Tigers* was a baffling, half-Swedish, half-English 'semi-documentary' that Lee declared 'strange—very strange'. But, he added, 'We meant it to be strange.'

A home for Torbjörn much of his life, Gotland lies off the southeast coast of Sweden in the Baltic Sea. Now a popular tourist destination, back in the 70s the area was populated by a small community for whom outsiders were mainly restricted to artists and celebrities like Ingmar Bergman, who owned a place nearby on the province's small island of Fårö, where he died in 2007. Torbjörn was of such lineage—he also painted and wrote poetry—and his home was the setting for a significant portion of *A House Safe For Tigers*. Brucebo, he enjoyed telling us, was, 'a fantastic cultural building from the 1800s, whose roots were entangled with the Canadian artist William Blair Bruce and his Swedish wife, Caroline Benedicts-Bruce'. Torbjörn loved the house so much that he would later defend himself from eviction with a gun.

'Something happens up there every day,' Lee said fondly. 'But it's not important. All I do in Gotland is laugh. And not at: I'm laughing with. Because they think it's funny, too.'

'It would be nice if you came there,' Torbjörn added, turning to me. 'Because it's not Sweden. It's not anything.'

'It's beautiful,' Lee concluded.

* * *

Lee presents his 'boarding card' at The Feast Buffet's 'check-in'. They subtract points from his grand total, allowing us to pile our plates high with food. He's on good form, happy to be out of the house while Jeane continues her endless preparations, and in an impressively talkative mood right from the start.

'I remember I heard this DJ one day,' he says, in a voice so deep I expect lightning to illuminate the painted horizon. I'm still arranging the food on my plate that I scavenged from the various display cabinets: in front of me, the bones of various small animals glazed with sweet sauces lie among overcooked rice and a token vegetable or two.

'He was playing some funny little country song, but about halfway through he interrupts it and says he's playing the wrong side of the 45, takes it off, and doesn't say what the song is. So I pull the car over onto the side of the road and I call the guy. "What was that song?" I ask, and the DJ says, "Hey, Lee, nice to hear from you." "Yeah," I say, "but what was that song you just played?" "Oh, that? That was a mistake. I meant to play the other side." "Yeah, I heard you, but what was it?" And the DJ tells me, and I tell him to send me a copy of the single, and that was "Did You Ever". Soon as I heard it, I knew it was a winner. I knew it was a hit. Of course we changed it a bit for Nancy, added some flutes and stuff. But it was the same song.'

I love these grand fables, although Lee's perhaps more precise when talking about his family. Today's all about his daughter Samantha, and how proud he is of her recent promotion. Predictably, his recollections of an era when rock'n'roll was a truly subversive movement tend to appeal to me more. Fortunately, he can be easily directed.

'I remember going to a club,' he says, picking at a chicken leg, 'where there were all these kids eating sugar lumps. And I asked a friend what the hell they were doing. "Oh, they're taking acid," he said. And that's why I wrote "Sugar Town". And, by the way, none of the radio stations knew I was writing about kids taking acid, but that's 'cos the censors only see things literally. That's all they care about. It's like "Boots": "*You've been messing where you shouldn't have been a'messing?*" Messing? That's the F-word in Texas! When someone tells you they've been out messing around, you know they didn't spend the night alone!'

Sometimes Lee's eyes glisten with glee at the things he's done, just as they do when he recalls his family, the girlfriends he had, the parties he attended, the Hollywood house he once kept, and of course the money he's made. Lee loves his money, and he probably knows what he was paid for every job he's ever done—and, quite possibly, the price of every steak he's ordered. Nonetheless, despite his fondness for cash, rarely was a man less flash. I only discover he's paying for my hotel when I arrive at reception, and after this first lunch he leaves me with his boarding pass and its PIN number, telling me to visit the Feast Buffet at his expense as often as I want.

Lee also talks about his health. He's candid, aware of the fact that time's now against him, and impatient to complete the deal for *Cake Or Death*: he wants to see it 'escape' before he's 'in his urn'. To look at him, he still appears reasonably healthy, but he gets tired more easily and suffers from countless aches and pains. He explains how his blood is spreading the renal cancer through his body, and says his cat, Chewy, found the latest evidence: a lump on his skull.

'By the way,' he adds, 'the cancer's not in my brain yet, though some people might question that.'

He's due to attend the Mayo Clinic in less than two weeks for radiotherapy, and after that they'll put him on pills 'so experimental they've not even given them a name yet. They're called DX132 A Piece Of Shit or something. The doctors don't know if they'll work or not. But, if I'm going to die, I may as well help someone on my way'. He tells me how the doctors presented him with a leaflet that listed all the possible side effects. He says he read the first two symptoms and gave it back.

'I've spent my life trusting and depending upon the power of my subconscious,' he explains. 'I don't want to read what my body might do, because then it'll do that. If I don't know, then I might not notice.'

He speaks in a matter of fact way about the possibility of losing his hair, of the scars he already has from treatment, of the operation on his kidney that left the stomach muscles on one side of his belly limp.

'I know this lawyer who I don't have to pay to sue their asses. We just split the winnings. And I'm gonna get them for that fuck-up, those miserable sons-of-bitches.'

He means it, although it's something he's been telling me for quite a few months. Later on, he confides there are other people who, over the years, have screwed him, often financially, that he also wants to sue, but he'll have to leave it to his family once he's gone, assuming they're not already too busy squabbling among themselves. When he names names, I can see why he's waiting.

Conversations with Lee can last for hours. If he has an audience, he revels in it. His daughter Samantha will accuse me a day or two later of being a little 'goo-goo-ga-ga' when I talk to him, but I'm so grateful for his patriarchal presence in my life that I'll never apologise for humouring him.

Just how far he's taken me into his closest circle becomes yet more evident when we meet for dinner later on. Jeane pulls up outside the hotel and I spot an eight-year-old hanging out of the back window. I correctly assume it's Lee's granddaughter, Phaedra, her name inspired by 'Some Velvet Morning'. To this day, Phaedra thinks the song was written about her, and she loves to sing the line from the chorus, '*Phaedra is my name.*' Lee has rewarded her by re-recording the track for *Cake Or Death* with her vocals. It's a moment of well-deserved indulgence.

Phaedra sees me approach the car.

'Bubba!' she yells, big blue eyes gleaming. 'Grandma, it's Bubba!'

'You must be Phaedra,' I say, and, while I have no idea how she's recognised me, we soon become friends. We return to the house to pick up Lee and Mark, then travel to a nearby steakhouse, where we order more food than any of us can eat and Phaedra cheats at Tic-Tac-Toe on her tablemat.

'You know what the first thing she said this morning was?' Jeane asks me, looking at Phaedra, who's sipping on a glass of pink lemonade.

I shake my head politely. I know the answer, as it happens, because Lee already told me on the walk from the car, but I'm interested to see if he was telling the truth.

'She woke up and stretched,' Jeane laughs, 'and then she said, "Is Bubba here yet?"'

Lee confesses that he'd never realised they spoke about me so much.

On the drive to the restaurant, during a staring competition to which she'd challenged me, Phaedra had become a little overexcited, so Lee insists I sit in the front on the way home. He doesn't need the noise. Phaedra, never one to pay much attention to restrictions, leans forward between the seats, spotting the clock on the dashboard. It's just gone 8pm.

'I'm going to miss my favourite show,' she whines.

'And what's your favourite show?' I ask, twisting round to speak to her.

'I don't know,' she says innocently. 'I'll have to see what's on.'

* * *

Things at the Fanclub Festival didn't go well. That it was Lee's birthday added pressure to make memorable a situation about which he already had a less than positive outlook. Additionally, the rehearsal in a spacious Stockholm studio the night before hadn't run smoothly, and it was obvious as we drove to the festival site that the relaunch of the event had been ineffective: as our taxi climbed the hill, we passed only occasional, straggling lines of teenagers and twentysomethings, a paltry crowd to fill a sizeable space. Grey skies hung overhead like a bad mood.

I tried to keep things light, but it was hard, especially when the taxi returned us to a quiet crossroads, suggesting the driver had no idea where he was going.

Lee was impatient to get soundcheck out of the way, and these detours were another growing cause for concern about the likelihood of anyone coming. If a taxi driver didn't know how the hell to find the place, how would a crowd, sent off to a new festival location at only a few days' notice?

My chunky Nokia rang in my pocket. It was my mother. Hesitantly, she broke the news that my sister's pet dog, who now lived with our parents, had been put down. It was, my sister later told me, the only time she'd seen our father cry. Katinka was old, so her loss wasn't unexpected, but I was still surprised how hard I took the news. We'd all adored her, an athletic half-Doberman, half-Rottweiler mix whose nature, despite her appearance, couldn't have been more devoted.

Lee turned slowly in his seat as the call came to an end, positioning himself so he could eye me face to face.

'Everything OK?

The taxi driver pulled up at what seemed to be factory gates. Plastic tape flapped in the breeze, and underemployed security staff kicked their heels.

'Is everything OK?' Lee repeated.

'My sister's dog just died,' I sighed at last. It felt horrible hearing the words aloud. 'They had to put her down.'

'Oh, Bubba,' Lee answered sincerely, and his voice ached like my heart. 'I'm sad to hear that. Goddamn sad indeed. Tell your sister how sorry I am.' He shook his head. 'I've got a feeling it's going to be that kind of day.'

And so it was indeed. Lee played out on a stage that looked like the side of a giant ice-cream truck, his band's notes blown out of tune by a stiff breeze that failed to clear the clouds. He withered in front of a sparse audience who gradually shuffled away, their expectations disappointed by the return of the legendary adopted Swede that they'd read about over breakfast, their feet dragging across an empty parking lot. Reduced to the humiliating level of seaside pier entertainer performing at a supermarket opening—and all this on his birthday, too—Lee wilted and bristled at once, his temper twitching like a snake ready to pounce. There was no encore this time. Lee was undoubtedly crushed.

I knew I had to make myself available afterwards, but, cowed like a child summoned to his father's study, I gave him a few minutes before knocking on his dressing room door. As I pushed it open, he looked up from a chair at the end of the room, and for a moment, from the way he was slumped, I wondered if he was weeping. I took a step back, looking to close the door instinctively, but he told me to get the hell inside.

'How soon can we get the fuck out of here?' he spat. His mouth pinched tightly as he spoke. Sparks, not tears, flowed from his eyes.

Although I would later be well practised at talking down Lee's blackest moods, on this worthless afternoon I found myself inadequate. He was incensed and inconsolable at once: incensed that a festival could fail to bring an audience to its arenas; inconsolable that the show had been unmistakably a stinker. After London's victory, this was a shameful defeat. He wanted to lash out, but he recognised that was unhelpful. Instead, he held on to his wrath, at least until the festival saw fit to deliver an extravagant birthday cake to the catering room, where by now he'd re-joined his band. For the musicians, who knew only too well that they stood in Lee's line of fire, it was a welcome distraction. For Lee, it wasn't even worth the wax the candles were made from.

'Did I not fucking tell you, Bubba, that I don't want any fucking birthday cake?' he seethed.

It was true. He had. He'd made it seriously fucking clear.

'So didn't you tell them I didn't order a cake?'

I did. They obviously chose to make the gesture anyway. They were only trying to be nice.

'No! Fucking! Cake! Which bit don't you understand? Get me out of this shithole. Now!'

Then he sat down, dejected.

Luckily, Torbjörn had placed a call to a local airline after our country lunch in Lidingö, and the morning after the Fanclub Festival found us on a small plane heading gratefully away from Stockholm. It was another beautiful afternoon as we landed in Gotland, the sun streaming over the landscape, lifting Lee's mood as, swelling with pride, he explained how the colours on the island were so loud that they had to be muted on film: 'The blues are too blue, the greens are too green, and the sky is pink.' Climbing down the steps from the tiny twin-engine to the tarmac, I suspected this was the most exclusive, glamorous thing I had ever, ever done: even the air stewardesses looked like they'd stepped out of a vintage Pan Am commercial.

We drove to Brucebo, which turned out to be a magnificent house whose long, lush lawn led down to a stony beach where we drank champagne with Torbjörn's family as the sun dipped slowly towards the ocean. Apart from the mosquitoes that buzzed around our heads, it was as idyllic a setting as I'd seen. We sat beside the summerhouse where Torbjörn and Lee had conceived *A House Safe For Tigers*, a dartboard similar to the one under which Lee sat on the cover of 1972's *13* nailed to its weather-beaten boards. I asked embarrassed permission to take his picture underneath it, and he patiently obliged, entertained by my unaffected dedication to his history. Afterwards, we retired inside to dine around the long wooden table that made up the centrepiece for *A House Safe For Tigers'* front cover.

Two of the eccentric film's main stars had been Gotland inhabitants. The witch, Fedra—apparently not spelt 'Phaedra'—had been played by Inez Graf, an artist from whom Lee once tried to buy a painting, only to be refused and forced indignantly to buy another instead. Fisherman William Pettersson, meanwhile, was the film's occasional cross-dresser; his English was limited, but he and Lee managed to communicate in a weird form of sailor's Swedish.

'He had four dogs,' Torbjörn recalled, 'and they looked exactly the same. They were called Rasken I, II, III, and IV, and you knew III and IV. And Rasken III was toothless and ...'

'... mangy!' Lee interrupted.

'It ate cigarettes and it drank whisky,' Torbjörn continued cheerfully. 'But this dog, Rasken III, he didn't have a lead, he had a rope, and then William had this old double-barrelled rifle. And the dog was ten metres ahead of him as he rode his bike, and then he'd stop when he saw ducks and *Bang! Bang! Bang!* and the dog picked them up. And one day, when he was out shooting grouse, he missed, and the dog was so pissed it went home. And he was tied to the bike! He drove the bike home! He was so strong he drove it into the kitchen! That's true!'

Lee and Torbjörn fell about laughing once again, before Lee remembered the ducks that he used to feed during his summers on the island.

'They're not the same in winter,' Torbjörn reminded him. 'They don't want to come to you then. Because we eat them, you see? And when there was ice in the bay, and the swans were freezing—they froze their feet—then people made swan balls.'

'Swan meat in a ball!' Lee gasped at the memory.

'It's pretty good!' Torbjörn argued.

'You pick 'em like flowers,' Lee continued, turning to me. 'When they're frozen to the lake, you go out and pick 'em. I saw them, over in Lidingö one winter. There were women throwing salt, 'cos some ducks were stuck to the ice. They went to sleep and woke up frozen in the ice. So the ladies were trying to help them. They'd put salt on to melt the ice a little. And I'd go, "What are they doing?" I thought at first they were feeding salt to the ducks. Maybe they were going to have a Margarita or something. But they'd eat 'em sometimes, wouldn't they, Torbjörn! They'd eat 'em!'

He took off his glasses and wiped his eyes. When he laughed this hard he sometimes reminded me of a gnome, his kindness and appetite for life written deep into his furrowed features.

It was, all told, a beautiful evening, punctuated by long bursts of curious but lovable stories, threatened only by brief memories of the day before. They recalled Sand Hill Anna, the hundred-year-old woman who used to live on the island, and the chefs in *A House Safe For Tigers*, who'd honoured its creators by adding two dishes to their restaurant's menu, one in Lee's name and the other in Torbjörn's. They talked of friends, of films, of music, until all the bottles were empty and the midnight sun had begun once again to rise.

'There are a couple of songs on that record that I think are pretty interesting,' Torbjörn recalled sagely, as the time approached to head back to our hotel. He glanced across at his dear old comrade.

'I don't know if anybody would be interested,' Lee smiled. 'Maybe. Perhaps they are. Sometimes we have to wait thirty years to be discovered.'

* * *

Seven years on from that disastrous Swedish festival, the day of Lee's seventy-seventh birthday arrives. I share a taxi to his home with Fitz, the boss of Four Music, a German subsidiary of Sony with whom I am concluding a lucrative deal for Lee's album. Lee likes Fitz, and it's not just because he's so willingly agreed to the price I've demanded: the man has a reputation as something of a maverick and, despite being brash and often loud, he's deferential, something Lee appreciates.

With Fitz is Bela B., the drummer and arguably most recognisable and popular member of one of Germany's most recognisable and popular bands, veteran punks Die Ärzte. He's largely responsible for Fitz's offer, having initiated my most recent escapade with Lee when he invited his hero to duet on his debut solo album, which is coming out on Fitz's label. As always, I'd proposed Lee's considerable fee, and was startled when Bela approved it almost immediately.

Bela was even more amazed to have Lee on his record, and in a gratifying turn of events, the news had arrived on Bela's own birthday. They've swiftly established a rapport, and Lee now considers Bela one of the nicest musicians he's met in recent years; in the sleeve-notes to *Cake Or Death*, he will refer to him as a 'studio god'. All the same, Lee remains oblivious to, and uninterested in, the fact that Bela is so beloved in his homeland that to many of the country's citizens he's a god wherever he goes. This is perhaps because, around Lee, Bela seems endearingly awed and bashful. Fortunately, the lack of reverence with which Lee treats him—nothing atypical, but fuelled further by his ignorance of Bela's musical accomplishments and status—appears to be refreshing to the German, in the same way as the old man is sometimes amused by my own occasional impertinence. After all, even legends need time off from their day job.

Our taxi pulls up outside Lee's modest house, which stands in a quiet, wide street surrounded by other similarly respectable homes whose manicured lawns are immaculately maintained despite the endless, overpowering temperatures. Take one step out of the air-conditioned spaces in which most people spend their days—homes, offices, shops, cars—and the heat, shimmering off the pavements, slaps you like a spurned lover. Only the occasional gentle breeze provides relief, but it's shortlived, the desert dust gusting so it irritates the nostrils. It's no wonder the streets are empty.

Like all the places Lee's lived in since I met him, his home isn't ostentatious. But there's plenty of room, a two-storey hallway leading into a lounge area to the right that blends with a kitchen space left. There's a second living room that is rarely used, a dining table at its far end, upon which—until today—I have never seen a plate of food, and Jeane also has a little office off the hallway in which she likes to sit playing computer games into the small hours of the morning. Lee, meanwhile, has a spot of his own at the top of the stairs. This, too, is seldom occupied, with little in it apart from an old electric keyboard, some overflowing plastic boxes, and a handful of pictures that don't look likely to be hung any time soon.

There are two guest rooms up there as well, the shades down, just as they are in most of the other rooms throughout much of the day. I used to suspect it was because Lee prefers it this way, but it's just that the heat from the desert would otherwise be too powerful. Lee and Jeane's bedroom occupies most of this floor, and stands directly over the sitting room. I wonder sometimes how they sleep: one of them always seems to be downstairs watching TV, and Lee likes the volume loud. There is, at least, no need to creep around at night: the carpets are so thick that it's like walking on warm snow.

Bela, Fitz, and I arrive early, as arranged, in time to watch Germany take on Portugal for the third-place playoff in the FIFA World Cup. Lee gives us a warm welcome—with the record deal all but signed, the two Germans are guests of honour today—and immediately points to a cooler filled with ice and bottles of beer in the sun lounge behind the sitting room. He's taped pieces of A4 paper with our names to armchairs in front of the television, and gestures for us to settle in for the big match.

'You know, I paid for this damn game,' he bellows, wearing a bold red T-shirt Jeane has bought him especially for the occasion. It states, simply, 'I have nothing nice to say.' 'I had to pay to get this soccer channel just for you damned Germans.'

He's told me this on at least two occasions previously, and he always pauses, smiling, in the same place.

'It cost me eleven goddamn dollars.'

'Sorry,' Bela counters. 'But you're about to get a big pile of money from Fitz.'

Lee and Bela met soon after a bidding war had broken out in Germany for Bela's signature. He was also an actor, which added to his 'household name' status, and therefore quite the catch for a label. EMI was in the running at the start, and had initially tried to seduce him by asking what his ambitions for the record were. The label hoped it could help make these happen, thereby earning his gratitude, so when Bela expressed admiration for Lee, the A&R man's ears pricked up. I still had close connections to several people working in EMI's Berlin office, and the A&R man rapidly put Bela's associates in touch.

Cancerous or not, Lee was no readier to compromise these days, and his list of demands remained as idiosyncratic as ever. Among them were 'a room in a hotel with hot and cold running maids—I don't need a suite—maybe a "sweet"?' There was also a note of caution amid his instructions. 'I suppose Bela knows about my health problem. Sometimes I get a little tired. And sometimes I get a little bored, or at least pretend I am.' But, he'd added, 'I'd work with this man: I like his name. I've never known someone with the Christian name Bela, but as a child I loved the vampire Bela Lugosi.' At no stage did he ask a single question about Bela's music, talent, or status. One efficient negotiation later, he was on a flight to Berlin.

When he arrived at Berlin's Tegel Airport, Lee wasn't bored, or even pretending. He was simply in a foul mood: his fee had included business-class tickets, but this had been a chartered flight in which business class was barely different to economy. Adding insult to injury, not only had Lee suffered the indignity of being without the comfort that he'd earmarked as part of the agreement—something that was increasingly important to him as his health deteriorated—but as we shook hands and I asked him if there was anything I could carry, it also became clear he'd absentmindedly left his luggage in baggage collection. He added this to the list of things that were Bela's fault, and before we'd even left the airport he was threatening to pull the session.

After quiet, persuasive words with a security guard, I retrieved Lee's suitcase, working hard to calm his jetlagged mood as I drove carefully into town. That evening, after a rest I'd insisted he take, we met Bela for the first time in a renowned steakhouse that he and his personal manager, Claudia, had chosen. I'd called her as soon as Lee had headed for his room: she'd squealed like a child with excitement that he'd genuinely made the journey. She'd forgotten that he'd not yet been paid, and Lee always wanted what he was promised.

Bela might have been a drummer—'That's what worries me about him,' Lee joked—and a heavily tattooed one at that, but he was articulate, friendly, funny, and respectful, if transparently nervous. Claudia, too, won Lee over rapidly with her disarming sweetness. By the next day, after Lee had learnt that she was also a singer, he'd warmed to her so much that he invited her to duet with him on *Cake Or Death*. A French record company had been demanding absurd fees for Lee to include a song he'd originally recorded with one of its artists, so Lee decided there and then that Claudia—aka Lula—would replace her.

As we sat in the furthest corner of the restaurant, I overheard a couple on the next table discussing their plans for a new café. They were talking in English, too quietly for anyone at our table to hear properly, but something they said caught my attention.

'Excuse me,' I finally asked, leaning over towards them. 'Could you tell me the name of your business? I couldn't help overhearing, and I think it might be of interest.'

'It's called Hazlewood,' the woman, a Canadian, told me.

Lee looked slowly round at her.

'Would that have anything to do with Lee Hazlewood?' I asked casually.

'It would,' she replied cautiously.

'Then perhaps I should tell you, this is Lee right here,' I announced proudly.

'We were wondering, actually!' she laughed.

We talked excitedly for a few minutes, with Lee only half-jokingly threatening to sue them for the use of his name, before they offered to show us the café's logo. Lee took one look, turned away immediately, and started talking again to Bela. He didn't speak another word to them all night, even when they bade us goodbye. His name had been spelt wrong: 'Hazelwood'.

I'd arranged a second dinner for the following night, a bigger affair where a number of others would attend besides Bela and Claudia. Among them were collaborators on Bela's album; one of my former colleagues and his wife; my ex-girlfriend, of whom he'd been very fond; and a further selection of friends that were keen to meet him. I gave Lee a rundown as I accompanied him to the restaurant.

'Damn it, Bubba, have you brought a whole army for me to feed?' he barked, even though it had been his own idea to invite extra faces.

'It's OK,' I said, defending myself, worried that perhaps he might suddenly have gone off the idea. 'You'll know some of them, and you'll like them all. It's a great bunch.'

'Well, you make one thing clear, OK?' He turned to me in the dark of the taxi's back seat and gave me a look steely enough to be unmistakable in the shadows. 'I'm not going to stay out 'til dawn—I'm too old now—so, when I leave, you let 'em know: that's it. They're paying for themselves from then on.'

'No one's expecting you to pay for anything!' I protested. 'Everyone's taking care of their own bills.'

'Well, I'm not having that,' Lee grumbled, more amiably now, reaching into his jacket's breast pocket as he did so. A huge diamond ring twinkled ostentatiously on the middle finger of his right hand. 'Is this enough to cover it?'

He handed me a thick wad of rolled up Euros. I removed the rubber band—he apparently scorned billfolds for foreign cash—and saw they were all €50 notes. They must have totalled the best part of €1,000.

'That's more than enough,' I laughed. 'This is Berlin, not Beverly Hills! There's enough here to eat all month!'

I tried to hand the cash back.

'No,' he said firmly. 'You keep it for now. I'll tell you when I want to leave and you can pay. I don't want to make a big fuss.'

'Well,' I replied, embarrassed, 'why don't I take what I'll need, you take the rest, and I'll give you the change later on?'

'Keep it,' he insisted. 'But don't tell anyone I'm paying 'til the end, OK? I don't want the grasping motherfuckers thinking they can order the caviar.'

'There's no caviar where we're going,' I assured him. 'They'll have to settle for a schnitzel.'

We gathered in the Weltrestaurant Markthalle, a century-old Berlin beer hall, fourteen of us in total. Bela was already there with Charlotte Roche, a TV presenter and writer who'd also provided vocals for a track on Bela's album. Since both were significant celebrities in Germany, they drew inquisitive stares from nearby customers, but the two of them were touchingly more in awe of the old man, even if his own identity remained unacknowledged by the other diners. Together, they made sure he had everything he wanted, and I felt comfortable letting them relieve me temporarily of my responsibilities. Lee held court at the head of the table, teasing his audience with tales of fun times he'd enjoyed in Hamburg, and sharing jokes about the fierce volume at which he believed all Berliners spoke. Later—so as to be fair to everyone present—he made his way to the other end of the table to chat. Each person there, he believed, should have the chance to meet him, whether or not they'd asked.

Some time after eleven, he gave me the nod to pay. I had a discreet word with the waiter, who delivered the bill and ordered a taxi for Lee.

'Did you have enough money?' he asked as he put on his leather jacket.

'Without a doubt,' I laughed. 'I took the liberty of tipping the waiter lavishly.'

'So long as I don't have to be ashamed.'

'I don't think so,' I smiled, and handed over a receipt with the remaining money.

'Good boy,' he chuckled. 'Good work indeed, Bubba.'

The recording session was due to begin at 2pm the next day. After taking him for an American-friendly brunch of pancakes and eggs in a café near my apartment, I offered Lee a tour of the city, its streets decked with winter's dirty snow, its monuments—the Reichstag, the Brandenburg Gate—pointed out with as much pride as the plastic cows that climbed the side of an apartment building in the gentrified district of Prenzlauerberg.

Lee seemed in good spirits, maintaining a surreal commentary as we drove, announcing that he was happy to see portions of the Berlin Wall still standing because 'people can write pornography on it and all that good stuff'. Eventually, with our appointment looming, we headed back towards the studio via Karl-Marx-Allee, an extravagant avenue lined with imposing apartment blocks, a setting for military muscle-flexing during parades organised by East Germany's Communist government.

'Karl Marx tried to get a job on the *Times* in London,' Lee suddenly claimed. 'You knew that, didn't you? They turned him down, so he went home and wrote *Das Kapital*. And—just as good a story—did you know Fidel Castro tried out for one of the New York baseball teams? He didn't get the job, so went back and became a history professor, I think, and then a revolutionary. So … give these young people jobs, you know?'

'Keep 'em off the streets!' I agreed.

'By the way, in high school I got a copy—after a lot of problems—of *Das Kapital* in English. And my dad was a great reader, and I left it on the shelf in my room or something, so my dad read it. And I came home one day from my little job after school, and I saw my dad reading it. When he'd finished, he just closed the book—*Bam!*—and handed it to me. I said, "What do you think?" He says, "It won't work. They'll go bankrupt." And I said, "It's not about …" and he said, "I don't give a fuck what you say. It won't work, and they're gonna go bankrupt." And they did. But my dad said this—let me see—in '46, '47. It just didn't seem plausible to an old man who was a capitalist from head to toe.'

'But it's a real page turner …' I laughed.

'Yeah, it's a real page turner …'

I checked the rear-view mirror to see if he was finished. Not being an expert on Marx, I wondered whether this was a subject to which I could add anything. Lee, however, was already moving on in a typically arbitrary fashion.

'You know,' he said, 'Spanish tomatoes are fantastic. I took some seeds home and grew some the first time I lived in Vegas. And they're great tasting, but, you know, they're ugly. They put them on your plate for every meal, and of course when I first lived in Spain, they were just ugly little tomatoes and I didn't even eat 'em. Didn't pay any attention to them at all. Then one day I guess I had one Scotch too many, and I ate a tomato and I thought, *Oh my God! This tastes just like tomatoes did when I was a kid on my grandfather's ranch in Oklahoma.* And from then on …'—he put on his gentlest voice—'"… May I have extra tomatoes, please?" God, they were good! But God, they're so ugly. They're lopsided, they're not pretty to look at, but oh, the taste is magnificent.'

'Kind of like your songs,' I suggested.

'Kind of,' he permitted, as the compliment sunk in and a gentle smile crinkled his face.

Snow was falling as I parked the car in the back courtyard of the studio. Lee was already getting tired and appeared a little on edge as we waited for the goods lift that would take us upstairs. It failed to respond to repeated pushes of the button, so I called Claudia and told her we'd arrived, and that there was no way Lee would take the stairs up four storeys in his condition.

They sent the lift down, but when it arrived on the ground floor, the doors were locked. We were left out in the cold.

'Fuck this,' Lee muttered. 'Take me home, Bubba.'

'It'll only take another minute,' I assured him. 'Hang on just a moment.'

'I'm freezing, Bubba, and I'm a sick man.'

'I know, Lee, I know. Just hang in there and we'll get this sorted fast.'

'I'm just bitching so I don't kick this fucking door down,' he said, trying to keep a hold of his temper.

I called Claudia a second time. Lee strolled around the courtyard, trying to keep warm, hitting the toes of his boots from time to time with his walking stick to dislodge the snow. I'd seen him like this on too many occasions before, and I knew it signalled trouble.

'This is fucking unbelievable. I've come 8,000 miles to catch fucking pneumonia?'

We eventually made it into to the warmth. Lee needed time to thaw out, but before he'd even had time to remove his long black drifter coat, he was reclined on a leather sofa, revelling in new attention. People bustled around, offering drinks and ashtrays, while the producer and engineer introduced themselves, declaring it a great honour to work with him. Bela paced the room restlessly, sporting a designer rockabilly look—a smart black buttoned shirt with a screen-printed crown on the front—while his punk roots were still visible thanks to the keychain that curled from a belt loop into his jeans pocket. He tried to focus his attention on Lee, but his anxiety was evident—far more than Lee's— from the way his eyes kept darting impatiently towards his producer and engineers as they prepared.

Finally, Bela stepped out of the room quietly. When he returned, he was holding a black briefcase.

'Your money, Mr Hazlewood,' he announced.

'Aw,' Lee purred softly. 'You wrapped it for me.'

'But you have to guess the code for the lock, Lee,' Bela added.

'I have to guess the code?' Lee repeated, mystified.

'Yes,' Bela insisted. 'You're from Las Vegas. It shouldn't take long to figure out.'

He passed the case over to Lee, who rested it on his lap. Briefly bewildered, Lee turned the three rows of digits absent-mindedly.

'So Las Vegas is your clue, eh?' he said pensively, then looked a little more closely at the lock. Slowly, carefully, he lined up three sevens. 'That should do it, I reckon.'

He flipped the catch. The briefcase opened. People congratulated him as he peered in and examined the cash.

'I'll take that now, Lee,' Bela grinned.

Lee passed it over to me instead.

'You might want to work out how to change that code, Bubba, before these people take their money and run!'

With his self-respect restored, Lee suggested they start. He limped towards the vocal booth, Bela in his wake.

'If you hear something good,' he advised, 'for God's sake keep rolling. I never do something the same twice.'

The track Bela had written was called 'The First Song Of The Day'. It was an upbeat, surf-inspired piece of garage indie rock that expressed his belief that every day would start best if Lee's were the first voice one heard, as well as offering gratitude for Lee's music in general. But while Bela was obviously a fan, he hadn't considered Lee's style of delivery. Though the old man applied himself to the task with reasonable gusto, his vocal takes were many, often interspersed with asides about how these weren't the kind of phrases he'd normally sing. With Bela singing each line to him a few times in preparation, Lee tried and sometimes failed, his frustration and embarrassment increasingly detectable. When further assistance was suggested, his pride ensured that he less than gallantly refused.

'You don't have to count me in,' he snapped. 'I can feel it in my ass!'

It was agreed he should take one line at a time, the magic of studio trickery allowing the engineer and producer to paste them together seamlessly. With Bela looking on self-consciously, Lee squinted down at the lyrics I'd printed out on a recycled phone bill. '*Sometimes those songs are liable to drive your mind insane,*' he read aloud. He'd already told me that 'liable' wasn't a word he'd ever expected to sing, and, two lines below, it was harder still for him to deliver '*Music's too important, get yourself a good assortment, end this shame once and for all*' in one breath, especially at the speed Bela requested.

'That's a little tongue-twister right there,' Lee pointed out. 'That'll fuck you right up. This isn't gonna be "The First Song Of The Day", Bela. It's gonna be the last song of my career!'

The problem was that this German icon hadn't taken into account the fact that Lee was always a slow talker, and these days, now that he was older, he was slower still. Rattling through this at such a pace was nearly too much to ask of him. I began to worry yet again that we might be on course for a tantrum. Whether Lee liked someone or not was irrelevant when he was tested too hard. If things weren't going the way he wanted— no matter who was at fault—he'd lash out at whoever was nearest. I knew this at my own cost: two years earlier, he'd fired me without notice when a migraine had kept me vomiting all night and prevented me from driving him to a radio interview.

'Next time you get sick,' he'd fumed later that day, 'you just come to me. I've got pills for every damned illness you'll ever have.'

He never officially reinstated me, but within a few hours we were carrying on as if nothing had happened.

Back in the studio, Lee was still struggling with the words when he had a brainwave.

'You know what's wrong, Lee?' he muttered to himself.

He plucked his spectacles off the end of his nose.

'If I take off my "fuck you" glasses and put on the ones I see with …'

He swapped them with another set hanging from the neck of his T-shirt, his mood immediately improving.

'Aha! There's a world out there I didn't know existed!'

'What did you call them?' Bela interrupted, twirling his headphone cable in the air and anticipating an entertaining answer. 'Your "fuck you" glasses?'

'When I bought these glasses,' Lee explained, relaxing more now that he had an excuse to take a break from singing, 'everyone fell in love with them, and I wouldn't tell them where I got them in LA. And Jeane said, "Everybody's commenting on your glasses. I think they're kind of, 'Fuck you, I'm not going to tell you where I got them' glasses." So they're my "fuck you" glasses. I ask her, "Have you seen my 'fuck you' glasses?" With children in the house and everything ...'

Bela smiled, genuinely amused, before endeavouring to refocus Lee on the business in hand. Another, harder challenge lay ahead. Lee's half of the tune was in English, with Bela's sung in his own native tongue, but Lee was required to deliver one sentence in German.

'*Bela, genau so denk ich auch,*' he faltered. This was the kind of German whose pronunciation presents a challenge to most non-native speakers, and clearly my efforts to train him earlier had been less than successful: his attempts to deliver the final two words seemed completely oblivious to the idea that they might sound different here to his native English. Outside the booth, those present acknowledged that this was not going to be as easy as they'd hoped. I flashed back to an afternoon we'd spent in Oslo, where Lee had tried to re-record 'Jackson', once the B-side to 'You Only Live Twice', Nancy Sinatra's James Bond theme. While his Eurovision foil that summery day had sped through her parts with ease, Lee had found the entire experience depressingly difficult, and I wondered if a comparable situation was developing.

'Bela,' he offered again, '*Gernowso denk ick owk*'.

'Not bad,' Bela reassured him. 'One more time, maybe? Softer on the *ich*, perhaps? And the *auch*, if that's OK?'

Lee began to worry that he was taking too much time.

'I'm fighting the clock here,' he commented wryly. 'The death clock.'

Finally he offered a solution.

'If you can record me a line at a time, how about I say each word separately and you string them all together? I'm never gonna get all this goddamned German right in a row.'

'We can do that, Mr Hazlewood, sure.'

'OK, then, roll the tape.'

'Gernow. Gernow.' The word was *genau*, but this was close enough.

'So. So.' The word was indeed *so*, but pronounced as *zo*. The instructions from the booth still sounded exasperated.

'Be kind to it: it's old,' Lee warned.

We asked him to try again.

'Goddamn it, Bubba, get me something to drink.'

Bela had presented Lee with a bottle of vodka, so I measured out a shot. To Bela's amusement, I asked for a second glass—he must have thought I was going to match Lee drink for drink—and took that in with me, too. Lee tipped his head back and gargled, spitting the liquid out into the spare glass when he was done. This alcohol was genuinely for medicinal purposes.

'That's better,' he rasped as I cleared up, trying to locate the privilege in carrying a glass of his sputum, and not for the first time. 'Still rolling? Zo. Zo!'

'That's perfect, Mr Hazlewood. Now: *denk* … ?'

'*Denk! Denk!*'

'*Ich*? Like it's from the back of your mouth?'

'Ick. Ick. That'll have to do. I can't do any more of this German phlegmy stuff.'

'OK, last word: *auch*.'

'Thank God. Owck. Owck. Right!' He snatched the headphones off. 'That'll do. Piece it together from that.'

He emerged from the booth and sat back down on the sofa overlooking the mixing desk.

'I love these guys,' he murmured to me, 'but let's try to do something in English next time, Bubba? Fucking German language.'

At the desk, they started pasting together the various takes.

'Bela?' Lee grumbled. 'I think we should just bring the backing girls in a whole lot earlier and forget about it!'

'But Lee,' Bela blushed, 'that would cover up your part.'

'Exactly,' Lee deadpanned.

'You should use that,' someone suggested.

Bela and Lee smiled at one another. With barely another word, they stepped towards the booth to repeat the exchange on tape.

Lee called the song 'a silly little thing' and claimed no real love for it, but he said the same of nearly all the songs he'd written himself, so I knew that deep down he liked it. It reminded him of The Astronauts, he said, one of whose biggest hits was 'Baja', which he'd composed. He even added the track to *Cake Or Death*, and his subsequent request that Claudia join him on a second duet, 'Nothing'—the album's opening tune—confirmed his affection for the team. Before we left, though, he couldn't resist adding one final voiceover to the song's conclusion.

'Let's just hope this song will never be the first song of the day for anybody else ...'

* * *

With the football now underway, guests gradually start to arrive at Lee's home, where they're greeted by the unexpected sight of two unknown faces shouting at the television in German. Fitz, dressed in a smart, pressed white shirt and expensive sunglasses, his hair slick, his tan impressive, sits with a deflated football in his lap that he's pummelled into a bucket so he can fill it with crisps. Bela's put on a similarly expensive ensemble, though once again his keychain hangs rebelliously from his belt. Like Fitz and myself, he's clinging to a cold beer.

It's a Liquorice Allsorts array of people who've been invited. By the breakfast bar stands Marvin Zolt—Lee's octogenarian business manager, who looks uncannily like a bespectacled Mr Magoo—with his wife, a fragrant Florida type in flowery dress, and their daughter. There's Ginger, Jeane's friend, a New York prosecuting attorney who later tries to muscle in on my photo shoot of Lee's most personal possessions—his hat, his bracelet, his ring, his boots—for *Cake Or Death*'s sleeve. Out by the pool sits Dion, Lee's grandson, dressed in a casual hip-hop style with his heavily pregnant girlfriend, and Samantha, Lee's daughter, a fireball of fun and strong opinions who fills every room she enters with a personality that's spookily like Lee's own.

Then there's Tommy Parsons, a lifelong friend of Lee's who sings one of the songs on *Cake Or Death*. He's a ghostly colour with long white hair hanging down in a ponytail, and looks exactly as you'd imagine a man would that used to hang out with bikers in his youth. Lee's bond with him is fierce.

'If you ask Tommy why he never got a tattoo,' Lee says, 'it's because ...' Tommy joins in and they chorus, '... it's just another identifying mark!'

Others in attendance include Richard Barron, who's been mixing Lee's new album; Lasse Samuelson, Lee's Swedish arranger, who's flown in with his wife; and Samantha's fiancé Rob, a tattooed rockabilly who—not entirely unlike me—can't quite comprehend how he's ended up here today. Sam didn't tell him until a few weeks into their relationship who her dad was, and even now he finds the idea somewhat surreal. Others, too, have made the journey: Lee's publisher Bo Goldsen, for instance, and his sister Eileen, a diminutive American with a voice that seems to flutter in the breeze. As a young woman, she had hits with French and German versions of some of Lee's songs, and she still lives in Paris, where she's responsible for administering Lee's European song catalogue. 'She was a cute little thing,' Lee likes to remind me.

One of the last times I saw Eileen was in 2002, as Lee and I endured a taxing, whirlwind tour of European capitals to promote *For Every Solution There's A Problem*, a collection of unreleased demo recordings that drew upon a CD of twenty-one songs he'd sent me two years earlier. Some were vintage Lee, including early versions of tracks he played in London—'Dolly Parton's Guitar' and 'Your Thunder And Your Lightning'—as well as the poignant elegy 'Dirtnap Stories'. But others were disconcertingly less appealing.

After he'd enquired about City Slang releasing them—by then he'd sadly fallen out with Steve Shelley—I'd risked his wrath by insisting that some weren't up to his normal high standards. In particular, the adolescent humour of 'For My Birthday', despite being one of his favourites, seemed undignified rather than irreverent: '*I want a POA or a BJ for my birthday*,' he sang, his joke founded on the idea that a POA meant 'pear or apple' rather than 'piece of ass,' while the BJ, he claimed, referred to a 'Blue Jaguar'. Age, perhaps, had dulled his humour the day he wrote that one. But in the end, after he'd threatened to scrap the entire project or find another label, we found a compromise: I selected the ten songs I found best and hid 'For My Birthday' away at the end as a secret track. 'If those letters keep me out of heaven,' he'd sometimes say, 'then I don't want to spend eternity there anyway.'

In the run-up to its release, we'd made our way hurriedly from city to city, interviews stacked up from dawn 'til dusk, before enjoying a good dinner at the local rep's expense. In France, this meal had stretched out for hours, and by the time we'd finished, Lee was considerably the worse for wear. All the same, he'd declared he wanted a nightcap back at the hotel bar. I'd declined to join him, saying I'd prefer simply to retire to my room with a joint.

'Then bring the damn thing down to mine and keep an old man company,' he'd ordered.

I'd done as he instructed and sat on the end of his bed as he prepared himself for a night's rest, a travel magazine that I'd found on his desk lying on my lap while I rolled. Lee poured himself a drink from the Duty Free he'd brought and then began to get ready for bed, all the time rambling aimlessly about the events of the evening. He wandered into the bathroom, then reappeared in his dressing gown and stood before me, slurring, as he cast a shadow over my work. Finally ready, I looked back up. His penis hung six inches from my nose, swinging like a pendulum, framed by his open bathrobe. Our friendship, I realised, had just reached a new level of intimacy.

This, unfortunately, is the image that comes to mind as I greet Eileen in Las Vegas. Luckily, other distractions swiftly displace it, not least the food. Leafy green salads, chilli so thick it barely drips off the spoon, mountains of bread and tacos, heart-stopping desserts: all of these and more are laid out in the dining room, stacked up so extravagantly between decorative straw hats on miniature bales of hay that I fear the table may collapse under the unfamiliar weight. It looks like a window display in a Southern country diner, and to begin with I steer clear in case the food itself isn't real. Instead I head for the barbecue at the back of the house, where steak after vast steak sizzles on the grill, threatening to buckle the paper plates onto which everyone piles their food.

This is where most people have gathered, clutching red disposable plastic cups as they lounge around a swimming pool whose bottom is swept by an 'aquabot' that trails a pipe behind it like a giant grey, ribbed condom. Swimming from end to end requires only a few strokes, and most guests choose to stay dry, seated instead on the modest terrace, its borders decorated by a few hardy plants and flowers. Their view looks out over undeveloped scrubland and mountains beyond, upon which the sun sets in the evening with brash, bold colours. Coyotes supposedly come out to prowl at night, but I've never actually seen evidence of a single animal, apart from a solitary jackrabbit, amid this wilderness.

Today, my attention is confined to activities within the patio's borders. Once the heat has become too much, I jump into the water to give Phaedra the piggyback rides she craves, before throwing her carefully but dramatically off my shoulders. When I've finally tired of the water, I settle down in the temporary gazebo that Jeane's had erected around the garden furniture, where misting hoses cool us as Lee—proudly wearing a cowboy hat with a colourful beaded headband—tells his stories to Bela and Fitz now the football's over. Planes regularly roar overhead, but otherwise the party remains a quiet, laidback affair, tempered by the average age of those present, and the fact that Lee can no longer drink more than one or two shots of neat vodka a day, or else his organs might give up the ghost.

'I love this kidney too much,' he reminds me, as he declines another offer to get him something to drink. 'It's my best friend.'

Late that afternoon, we gather around a colossal cake to sing 'Happy Birthday' to the man whose life we're celebrating. All of us, I suspect, are quietly aware that this may be the last time we'll do so, and that the next time we assemble it may well be to commemorate Lee's death. As Phaedra helps him blow out the candles, I sense both joy and sadness in the room.

'Do you want the piece that says Grandpa?' Jeane asks, offering the little girl the first slice.

'I want the slice which has the *L*,' Phaedra announces, pointing at the word 'Lee'.

'And what does that stand for?' her devoted grandfather asks.

'Lazy,' she giggles cheekily.

As the sun sinks, the number of guests—like the temperature—declines. Rob retires upstairs to read to Phaedra, having told us to advise him if we need a ride back to the hotel, while Jeane and a couple of friends busy themselves clearing up. Soon only a jetlagged Bela and Fitz—who's drunkenly slumped in a corner, the deflated football now on his head like a helmet—remain with Lee and me. We sit quietly, half-heartedly observing a boxing match that flickers on the TV ahead of us, its volume unusually low. Finally, a little after 8pm, nauseous from the pills he's been taking, and tired from the exertions of so many conversations, Lee makes a dignified exit.

Now that the responsibilities of the party are over, Jeane's restless. She gathers the remaining crew to head off to the Sunset Station, where she wants to play the slots. Recalling that, earlier on, Lee's neighbour had invited me over to sample his homemade mango Margaritas, I tell Jeane I'll swing by his place and walk back to the casino later. She approves; she knows my fondness for a good Margarita outweighs my love for gambling. In truth, however, I simply need to remove myself, if only briefly, from constant reminders that these may have been some of my final hours with Lee.

Having watched the red lights of Jeane's car recede into the dry night, I knock at the neighbour's. He greets me jovially, advising me that he's been living it up a little because his wife is away for a few weeks. I'm surprised to learn he's married. A bong sits on the kitchen counter, and his lounge is exactly how I'd imagine a fortysomething Las Vegas bachelor's to be: open plan, low lighting, brown walls with a sofa to match, plants wrapped in colourful fairy lights, a huge flat-screen plasma TV above a stone hearth.

He sets us up with cocktails before the doorbell rings and he brings back a friend with shoulder-length hair who's dressed like he just returned from the gym. We sit down on stools by the breakfast bar while the two of them catch up. The new arrival, softly spoken and gentle, barely acknowledges my presence, but there's nothing impolite about his behaviour: he's merely unperturbed to find an unknown Englishman sitting in the kitchen. I let them talk, content in my own world. After a while, however, I notice that there have been a number of references to him feeling tired and ill.

'The pills have ruined my appetite,' he says at one stage. 'I lost twenty-four pounds in a week.'

He declines the bong, explaining that he can't smoke weed any more. I decide that, unless I know what's up, I won't be able to take part in the conversation at all, and to do that is probably ruder than asking what's wrong.

'Well …' There's a brief pause. 'I've got pancreatic cancer,' he states coolly, looking me straight on.

'Shit,' I say, struggling to work out what else to add. 'I'm really sorry to hear that.'

My attempts to flee shadows of mortality tonight are proving ineffective.

'That's OK,' he mumbles. 'Shit happens.'

He elaborates on the many side effects of his medicine, and adds that he's getting treatment from the same place Lee is attending, the Mayo Clinic. At no point does he look for sympathy, and he never talks about what it all means, but the unspoken certainty that he's going to die prematurely hangs quietly in the air between us. After half an hour or so, it feels awkward explaining that I have to go to the casino, but though I'm offered another drink, it feels more appropriate to leave these two friends together.

'Bang on the door any time you're back,' my new acquaintance instructs me as he guides me out.

'I will,' I say, stepping into Nevada's muted heat. But I'll never see either of them again.

Above me, the moon is swollen, lighting up the few clouds in the sky that lie between us. I worry that Rob will be offended if I don't accept his earlier offer of a lift, but I need more time to think, and the walk will do me good. Almost five years on, I've barely come to terms with my business partner's suicide. Today, I've spent time with two people who, in a matter of months, could be gone. One of them is little older than me.

The front door's unlocked, so I slip back into Lee's house to collect my stuff. Phaedra now sits in his armchair in front of the TV. Rob, still wearing his hat, is stretched out on the sofa alongside.

'Hello,' I say. Phaedra smiles at me and holds her fingers up to her lips.

'Shhh,' she points out. 'Rob's sleeping.'

'Sorry, Phaedra,' I whisper, relishing the sound of her name. 'I'm going to walk home, OK? Tell Rob I'm fine.'

She nods sweetly at me.

'I'll see you tomorrow. I'll come back in the morning before I go to the airport.'

I lean down to pick up my bag from beside her chair.

'Sleep well,' I add, knowing full well she'll probably stay in front of the television until Jeane returns. I start walking towards the door, but then, instinctively, aware even now that it's a melodramatic thing to do, I tread softly back. I take her little hand in mine and look her in the eyes.

'Look after your granddad, OK?' I say.

She considers this carefully before nodding again sincerely.

'I will,' she says, wise beyond her years. 'I promise.'

As I walk down the street on which Lee lives, I look up at the sky. Lightning lacerates the horizon. The silence that follows is frightening.

CHAPTER SIX

WE ALL MAKE THE LITTLE FLOWERS GROW

It's a little before 9am, exactly eight months later, in Lee's Las Vegas residence. I stand in my bedclothes, bleary eyed, and stare at the body. It lies on its right side facing out of the bed, its left arm outstretched towards the bedside table.

'Please check him, Bubba,' I hear a voice behind me implore. Jeane stands there with her friend Patti, who's visiting for the weekend with her husband, Bob. 'Please check him again, will you?'

Neither of them is really sure what to do. I don't know what to do either. I've never seen a dead body before. I tentatively, squeamishly reach out to take his wrist in my hand, pausing for a moment, concerned that I'm going to wake him up—which, of course, is the one thing we all wish would happen—and then check his pulse. His skin feels cold, and yet I doubt my instincts, altering my position to see if that changes anything. The whole process is deeply unsettling, despite a secondary level of my consciousness kicking in to remind me that this is just a human being. Or perhaps a human *was*. I really ought to be able to tell.

For a moment I feel the faint throb of blood pumping through veins. I nearly wrench my hand back in alarm, about to declare that he's still with us, before I realise it's my own pulse, the pace of my heart actually picking up with the shock of the situation. I loosen my grip slowly, respectfully.

'I'm sorry,' I sigh. 'I think he's gone.'

I stand beside the bed, uselessly. I look at Patti and Jeane, uselessly. I gaze back down at the corpse, uselessly. It's unquestionably pale, but I don't want to stare long, so I can't tell whether its peculiar blue hue is in my mind, a result of the drawn blinds in the bedroom, or genuine. Patti and Jeane start to talk. It's a conversation that will continue for much of the next sixteen hours or so, until we all finally reach a state of exhaustion so great that it forces us to go to bed. The talk, too, will have been useless.

The two women leave and I follow them out, stepping into the room next door, where I've been sleeping. I hover by my bed, utterly at a loss as to what should happen next. Jeane and Patti still stand outside.

'He's in a better place now,' I hear. 'He won't be in pain any longer.'

'I know, I know.'

'At least it was painless,' the voices continue. 'He looks so peaceful.'

I remain immobile. The voices recede. I decide that I can't be useful to anyone if I'm hiding away. Outside, I see Patti and Jeane standing in the dark of Lee's room. He lies motionless as they look down at him, talking quietly. I watch, surreptitiously but nonetheless invasively, from a distance.

Finally, Lee stirs. His growl is even deeper through having not spoken for several hours. He slowly lifts himself up in his bed and mutters something that I can't quite make out.

'Bobby's dead,' says one of the women. 'He died in his sleep.'

There's a long pause while the news sinks in.

'Oh, God,' Lee groans.

My presence feels illegitimate. I tread away quietly, heading for the kitchen to put the kettle on.

For the time it takes the water to boil, I pace around the ground floor, up and down the stairs, in and out of my room. I try to work out how to get the coffee machine to work so I can make everyone a cup, but I'm not much of a coffee drinker, and I soon give up. The fact that I'm doing such banal things seems somehow inappropriate, although if there are alternatives right now I don't know what they are. My head is spinning, but at such a pace that it almost feels like I'm in equilibrium. To anyone observing, I'm certain I'd appear calm and collected, even if I know from experience that this is shock.

Back in the hallway with my tea, I see Lee appear on the landing. He's wrapped in a lightweight blue dressing gown and his baseball cap—the black one he loves so much, the one with a dragon design above the peak—is perched on his head. He looks confused. Jeane and Patti fuss around him, but it's clear he's not quite sure what he should be doing either.

'Well,' I hear him drawl slowly, 'I gotta say, Patti: I'm jealous. When I go, that's how I want to go: quietly, in my sleep. I'd swap that for this goddamn cancer, I'll tell you.'

He pads down the staircase towards me.

'He's a lucky man,' Lee tells me, though his tone inevitably suggests otherwise.

'Bubba,' Jeane asks, leaning over the banisters, 'could you call the police?'

'Sure,' I tell her, smiling sympathetically, so she knows I'm here for anything if she needs me.

I feel momentarily like I'm turning into my father. Having something to do—a role to play—fortifies me. I'm in the midst of an appalling situation, but dealing with it in something approximating the same composed, organised manner that he employs. I've put up a shield that, in the short term, at least, will protect me from the harrowing scene unfolding in the house. I wonder if this is how my father has got through some of the things that he's experienced—whether family crises or events connected to his military work. It's a curious time to realise this, but I'm proud of him. So little seems to leave him flustered, whereas so much seems to agitate me. Still, here I am, taking control, or at least kidding myself convincingly that I am. I wish he could see me now.

Back in the sitting room, I pick up the phone, carrying it into the dining room so I can call in private. It'll be better if no one hears me discussing Patti's loss. It's suitably dark everywhere I go: the curtains are, as ever, drawn throughout the ground floor.

I stand by the dining table and dial 911. They answer within two rings.

'Hi there,' I say. 'Erm … I need to report a death.'

It feels so strange saying this that I nearly hang up, doubting the truth of the statement. What if Bob wakes up? How stupid will I look then?

I find myself answering questions calmly, while also nursing an inexplicable sense of guilt, as though I'm laying myself open to all sorts of speculation if I don't answer the questions correctly. It's the same feeling I've always had when I face authority, from schoolteachers to US Customs: I've broken rules and am about to be found out.

'Is there a defibrillator in the house?'

'I don't know.'

Is it OK not to know?

'What was the deceased's name?'

'Bob.'

'Bob what?'

'I don't know. I'm just a guest here. I only met him two nights ago.'

Is it OK not to know the name of the person who just died in the room next to mine?

The call lasts only a couple of minutes, and once it's done I tell Jeane that police and an ambulance will be here soon. There's also another job I have to attend to right away: the coroner is coming, and the police have instructed me to ensure that the scene isn't disturbed any further. I walk back up the stairs to Bob's room, step inside discreetly, and take one last look at the dead man. It seems strange that he hasn't moved an inch despite all the noise and confusion around him. As I leave, I shut the door gently behind me, nervous of the symbolism this might acquire were Patti to hear it close.

I pick out clothes and get dressed in time for the arrival of the authorities. Jeane answers the door and sadly informs the first medic that his equipment won't be needed. She and Patti are still in their bedclothes. A policewoman—short, chubby, and kind—starts to take information from the two women before they've even had a chance to invite her beyond the hallway. I wander in and out, desperately looking for something to keep me busy, unable to focus on anything for more than a minute or two. I make another tea. I go upstairs to type an email. I tidy up plates in the kitchen. I sit with Lee, who lies on his side on the sitting room sofa.

'I'm trying to remember,' he says quietly, his head tipping up to look at me, his eyes forlorn like an old spaniel's, 'whether I've ever had anyone die in my home before.'

I can hear Jeane and Patti in the hallway, trying to lift each other's mood by cracking jokes: deep, dark jokes. This makes me feel uncomfortable, and looking at the policewoman, it's making her feel a little awkward, too. The forced hilarity is hollow. I understand why they're doing it, however, so when they continue in front of me the next time I walk into the hallway, I try to join in, because no one needs me to tell them that this is not a time for laughter. We all know it only too well.

In the sitting room a short while later, after boiling the kettle yet again for more tea, I find Lee still stretched out on the sofa, exactly where I left him. In the dark, with his hat pulled low over his forehead, I have to look closely to see if his eyes are open. When I ascertain that they're not, it strikes me that he looks unusually static. For a moment, my own heart stops, and I have to suppress a surge of panic. I gingerly take a couple of steps forward and peer more carefully at him. To my relief, I can detect the faint movement of his chest: he's breathing.

Jeane appears and strolls over to the coffee machine.

'Is there anything I can do?' I ask, as Lee stirs beside me.

'No, Bubba,' she sighs deeply. 'Poor Patti.'

She shakes her head. I can already tell the sadness she's experiencing for her friend is only part of what's going on behind the tearstains, but then, softly, she spells it out as I approach her.

'I thought Lee was going to be next …'

So, I suspect, did Lee. Three months ago, Jeane had sent me a message that he'd asked her to prepare. 'These days most of my days are bad,' it read, 'so keep me away from stuff of little importance. Or I will.' The real significance of the message lay in the next sentence, however: 'Jeane can now sign her name MRS. Lee Hazlewood. Did it today at 1600. Ask her about ceremony.'

I'd not had time to do so before she sent me pictures of the happy couple. The nature of the pictures was unexpected: the first blurry shot found them seated in their car, Lee in his best, black, zip-up suede jacket, his grey, thinning hair slicked back from his tired, drawn face. Jeane, dressed in jeans and a low cut grey sweat top, her face free of make-up, was holding a small bunch of flowers. It had clearly been an informal occasion. Another fuzzy image showed Jeane's hand, complete with newly ringed wedding finger, resting on Lee's own, and a third was of flower petals, Jeane's bouquet lying among them on the bonnet of their car. Oddly, the fourth showed a minister leaning out of what looked like a tollbooth window, and it was this that betrayed the haste and truth of the ceremony, even if it couldn't deny the sentiment that provoked it.

On November 26 2006, Lee and Jeane had wed in a 'Drive Up Wedding Chapel' called A Special Memory. Its 'menu' was on display in the fifth and final picture. The cheapest ceremony, the 'Appetizer', cost only $25. This, I speculated, was what they'd booked. It looked like they'd not even been there long enough to take off their seatbelts.

Phaedra was also present. It was as though they'd gone out to buy her ice cream and got waylaid on the way home. Part of me felt sad that they'd got married in such an impromptu fashion, but I realised this had probably been Lee's means of ensuring that Jeane become his legal wife before it was too late and the inevitable quarrels that follow a wealthy man's passing began. He'd known just how little time he had, and this was all the romance he had remaining. It was the only way left to show his love for his 'keeper'.

With her husband asleep on the sofa, Jeane steps out to speak to the neighbours either side of their home. Most are aware of Lee's cancer, and she doesn't want them to see the commotion outside and think it's Lee who's gone. By the time she's back, the coroner has arrived. He's a man who, as Jeane later puts it, looks like he's never missed a meal. A plastic ID tag, attached to a black lanyard, hangs round his neck, confirming that he's from Clark County Coroner's Court. He's brought a trauma counsellor, who sits down with Patti on a sofa in the sitting-room-cum-dining room that last saw use during Lee's birthday party. All things considered, Patti's holding it together well so far, though it's clear from the way she laughs with the counsellor that, under the surface, she's struggling to maintain her composure. When I introduce myself, there's much laughter about my British accent, and Patti tries inopportunely to encourage a bout of flirtation. Our mutual embarrassment underlines that this is something neither of us intends to pursue.

I leave them to their business, lingering in the background in case I'm needed, but trying not to interfere. It's hard to decide whether my presence is obstructive or helpful. The coroner meanwhile continues his work, and I feel like I'm getting in the way just by pacing the corridors. At least Lee's still resting, a movie playing on the huge flat-screen TV before him, its volume as always louder than necessary, so I know he doesn't need me right now. If I go to my room, however, I always feel compelled to return downstairs minutes later, and on the way it's hard not to sneak a look down the hall to where Bob still lies silently, oblivious to all that's happened since he said his gentle farewells and headed to bed some time around midnight.

My dilemma is solved when the doorbell rings. I answer it to two undertakers. I'm impressed by how a single phone call to the police was enough to provoke the necessary formalities. One of the men has a particularly greasy comb-over, and it occurs to me this may be mandatory after a certain time in the job. They head upstairs together to scope out the work ahead, then return to their vehicle to collect a trolley and body bag. The counsellor steers Patti—who's come out to check on the activity—away from the hallway and back into the dining room, so she doesn't see what's happening. I open the other half of the front door to allow the trolley in, and watch as they arrange their tools.

The policewoman approaches me, suggesting I join Patti to ensure that she's occupied while the undertakers collect the body. I explain that I hardly know her, so I'm not too sure how beneficial I can be. Hovering between Patti, the counsellor, and the gurney, I do my best to obscure the view. Again, I feel absolutely useless: small talk seems out of the question, joining Patti and the trauma counsellor seems insensitive, and standing on my own waiting for them to carry Bob down makes me feel like both a voyeur and a coward.

'So if you don't know them,' the policewoman asks finally, rescuing me from my purgatory, 'how come you're here?'

'I actually work for the guy sleeping on the sofa,' I explain.

She scrunches her eyebrows. 'What do you do?'

'I manage him,' I say to her surprise. 'He's a songwriter. He wrote a lot of hits in the 60s, and I look after some of his business these days.'

'Really?' she says, clearly intrigued.

I point at a picture frame that's filled with a collage of record sleeves from his career.

'He's the guy who wrote "These Boots Are Made For Walkin'" for Nancy Sinatra.'

I always feel like I'm short-changing him when I summarise his work with this single sentence.

'Oh, right,' she says nonetheless. 'How cool.'

Before I can elaborate, we hear noises from above, hushed mutters and grunts of exertion. I look around the corner for a moment—long enough to register the body bag emerging from the bedroom. Stepping back, I glance over my shoulder at Patti, who's deep in conversation with the counsellor as they huddle over a booklet detailing the various legal procedures necessary after a death. I continue blocking their view as the undertakers come down the stairs—Bob was a large man, and they're struggling a little—and then hear his body land with a weary thump as they swing him up onto the trolley. It's loud enough to make me wince. There's the sound of zips being adjusted before they step back.

The fan hanging from the ceiling overhead continues turning, as though this is just another day. Beneath, the top of the body bag is pulled back to reveal Bob's ashen, inanimate face. The policewoman takes a couple of paces towards Patti.

'Would you like to say goodbye?' she asks quietly.

Patti, still dressed in her green nightclothes and wrapped in Jeane's bathrobe, stands up from the dining table and moves slowly into the hall. The counsellor accompanies her, holding back the last couple of feet, leaving Patti to step up to her late husband. I'm surprised to notice that the undertakers and coroner are still almost as close to him as she is, like they're standing guard. To compensate, I move back into the shadows and look down at my shoes.

'I love you,' Patti whispers, her voice refusing to crack. I hear the sound of a final kiss.

Looking up, I see the counsellor wipe a tear from her right eye with a finger. She smiles at me, her unforeseen confusion mixed with acknowledgement of the sweet moment I've just tried my best to pretend wasn't happening. Patti turns timidly away from Bob. She walks past the counsellor towards me and, just in time, I hold open my arms to embrace a woman who, less than two days ago, I'd never met. She collapses into me as finally, predictably, she breaks down. She's a small woman, and she buries her face in my chest, the tears at last released and now, inevitably, relentless. I hug her as tightly as I can, rubbing her shoulder and back in a feeble attempt to comfort her.

Bob's pain is over, his diabetes a thing of the past. As the undertakers wheel him outside, the bottles that contained all the drugs he took, emptied by the coroner, stand on the sideboard at the top of the stairs. Patti's trauma counsellor remains out of reach, still coming to terms with the fact that she has to face suffering like this on a daily basis.

Painfully aware—as am I—that it's only a matter of time before she'll go through the same as her friend, Jeane hides away in the artificial light of her office. And, with Lee lying undisturbed in the gloom of the sitting room, still in the same position I last saw him, Patti holds me tightly, like her life depends upon it, her shoulders shaking, her nose sniffing against my sweater. In two days time it will be her sixtieth birthday.

CHAPTER SEVEN

CAKE OR DEATH

Lee lies in the reclining chair to my left, tipped back as far as possible while still enjoying a view of that vast television that dominates the wall above the brick fireplace. A small table separates us, its surface covered in plastic cups containing the various drinks that he's requested over the last hour or two: milk, always with ice cubes, Gatorade, Diet Coke, even a mug of tea. He's taken a shine to the way I make it, despite having shown little interest in it before. He rarely finishes any of his drinks, complaining that the drugs mean they don't taste the way they should, but we keep bringing whatever he requests in the hope it'll keep him content.

Amid the cups stands an ashtray, often overflowing with half-finished butts. We try to keep it empty, but Lee smokes with such monotony, often forgetting that he's only just stubbed one out before lighting the next, that it's hard to keep pace. He sees no purpose in quitting now; it's only a matter of time, and it's the only vice he has left.

Then there's the small wicker basket that holds his medicines. Pill containers, ointments, droppers, syringes, lotions, and tall brown bottles all fight for space, carefully marked by Jeane so that she can ensure there's no room for error. She, however, has secreted herself away in her den, making phone calls, tapping on her computer, answering Lee's regular appeals for aid.

'Jeane,' he'll shout, after pointing the remote control fruitlessly at the screen for a moment or two, 'can you come here?'

And Jeane will trot out patiently and show him again what to do to get the channel he wants.

'Jeane,' he'll yell, minutes later, 'is it time for my next shot? I'm hurting.'

And Jeane, who'll only have just sat down, will rise up again and explain when he can have his next dose, and what measures he's currently allowed to take to ease his pain.

'Jeane,' he'll holler, yet seconds later.

And Jeane will come back once more into the lounge, trying to hide a look of impatience. She doesn't mean it, even if her face responds that way.

'You know I love you, don't you?' he'll croak, his throat parched by the cigarettes.

And Jeane will hurry round to the side of his chair, lean over, and kiss him gently, watching as a smile drifts across his face. This is what keeps her going—the fact that through all of this, through all the distress of watching her husband die, through all the waiting on him hand and foot and answering his every beck and call, just when she wants to throw her hands in the air and scream that she's not his servant and can't he just let her have some peace, that's when Lee will turn to her and melt her heart and remind her why she fell in love with him twelve years ago, the very first time they met in Glendale, Arizona's Pack Saddle Saloon, where they'd both gone to hang out with their favourite bartenders.

It happens over and over again. Lee knows he's wearing her out, but he's got little choice. He refuses to be admitted to hospital—he wants to die with domestic dignity—and Jeane doesn't want to hand over responsibility for his care to complete strangers who don't know his peculiar, stubborn, sometimes short-tempered ways. But he's always been a master of pushing people right to the limit and then winning them back again, invariably getting what he wants before making sure they're rewarded for it. It's hard to decide whether I admire this habit or resent it, especially since I've been on the receiving end. But it works a treat, and when that smile forces the wrinkles up and away from his bright white teeth, and he lets a short, triumphant 'Ha!' slip from his mouth, it's impossible not to love him.

'There seems to be one eternal contradiction with you,' I once gently suggested. 'You're capable of being very tough and also very sentimental …'

'Oh, God, yes,' he said emphatically. 'Now that I confess to. I cry at card tricks. I just love a good old-fashioned, sloppy movie. I think the songs—and I'll probably never confess this again—I think they're all written like 1932 or '33 pulp. I don't think I've ever admitted it before, although the other day I was even talking to Jeane about it and I said, "You know, I think I just write dreck. But it's good dreck. I think I know how to write a song." And I'm terribly sentimental and protective of my family. My mum and dad hugged and kissed, and they hugged and kissed my sister and me. And so I hug and kiss my family. Yeah, I'm sentimental, there's no way to get round it. I'm terribly sentimental.'

My arrival in their home—a week before a party that's been scheduled to celebrate a seventy-eighth birthday that none of us ever expected Lee to see—gives Jeane some respite. She's exhausted, her nerves frazzled from watching over Lee twenty-four hours a day. At night, she tries to unwind with her computer games, but her ears remain alert to the sounds from the bedroom above, in case Lee should call or bang the floor with his cane. When she sleeps, it's usually on the couch, so as not to disturb him, the TV volume turned down so low that Lee's set upstairs often drowns it out.

When I arrive, I know immediately that he hasn't got much time left. I've almost always managed to maintain some sense of immunity to the sight of his physical decline, but now it's unmistakeable. I try to spend as much of each day as I can sitting with him, allowing him to tell me familiar stories, laughing as he shouts at the television about actors that he used to know. Alan Alda, who'd starred in Lee's only shot at Hollywood, 1970's *The Moonshine War*, receives an especially fierce tongue-lashing. Most of the time, though, he talks over the action because he's seen it before anyhow.

He seems almost pitifully happy to have me here, but perhaps he's just overjoyed that he's still alive to see me. He must go to sleep every night not knowing if he'll ever wake up.

* * *

It's Saturday night, and Jeane asks if I'd mind supervising Lee while she heads to the casino. She'll only be an hour or two, she says, and she really needs to get out for some other reason than grocery shopping.

I'm fine with the idea, and Lee's fine with the idea, so she grabs her bag and cigarettes. After a fond farewell to Lee, and a detailed explanation as to what medication I can give him and when, she slips out of the house, driving to the Sunset Station a mile away.

Lee flicks through the onscreen TV guide and spots a boxing match due to start shortly. He offers his take on each fighter's form, recalling the last time he saw one of them compete, and tells me it's going to be a good one. He requests another drink, then asks me to help reposition him in his chair.

'I know you don't want to know this, Bubba,' he smiles ruefully, 'but it's not the goddamn cancer that's killing me tonight. It's the goddamn wind. If I could just get it out …'

He pats his stomach.

'It's right here. I just can't seem to shift it.'

He tries to make himself comfortable before pointing down at his feet.

'Stick some cushions under my legs, will ya?'

I scrabble around the two sofas, and after he's explained how he wants them to be placed, lift his feet, carefully sliding four cushions under his ankles, one at a time, so that his fragile legs point at a forty-five degree angle towards the ceiling. His dressing gown slips open, revealing the fact that he's wearing nothing underneath. He pulls it closed again, unruffled. These things don't matter between friends.

'And, by the way, grab me my blanket, will ya?' he says, gesticulating vaguely at the floor round his chair. I pick up a soft spread and shake it out, then lay it over him, making sure his feet are covered and his arms free. I feel oddly privileged to be able to do this for him.

'Jeane discovered this,' he says. 'If I sit like this it helps ease the gas and lets it out. Sorry if it bothers you.'

'No, of course not,' I laugh, and in truth I never notice a thing.

We settle down and watch the fight. I make judgements at various stages, deciding after three rounds that the favourite looks like he's not handling things well, that the underdog is troubling him with short, stabbing punches that are never returned.

'You've got an instinct, Bubba,' Lee laughs, when the commentators come to the same conclusion a few minutes later. 'Thought you said you didn't watch boxing.'

'I don't,' I laugh. 'But you can tell when someone's losing a fight.'

Lee nods wryly.

The match comes to an end, and Lee congratulates me on calling the result so early. Then he moves his legs so that the cushions slip off the end of the recliner.

'You need any help?' I ask.

'No, no, I'm fine,' he says, as he strains to shift himself up out of his seat. He leans over to his right to release the handle that sets the footrest down, landing his legs on the ground with a little bump. Then he grips the sides of the chair and stiffly pushes himself up. I pass him his walking stick.

'Thank you, Bubba,' he says, so slowly I feel like a small child that's pleased his favourite grandparent.

He shuffles slowly through the room, dressing gown loose around his wasted frame, baseball cap still proudly crowning his head. I gaze mindlessly at the television while I wait for him.

Eventually he returns, his slippers rustling on the thick carpet.

'I know you don't want to hear this, Bubba,' he laughs, 'but I have to tell you: that felt good! I waited a long time for that.'

I smile self-consciously, not knowing quite what to say.

'Sorry to share the troubles of an old man's bowels with you, but that started off well, and it just kept on coming! By God, that was what I wanted!'

He's still laughing as he lowers himself back into his chair, flipping the handle so that his legs are raised. I fuss around him, lifting his feet once more to place the cushions underneath, covering him with his blanket, offering him another drink.

'Thank you,' he says. 'You know what I'd like? I'd like a little sandwich. Where's Jeane?'

'She's at the casino,' I remind him.

'Ask her if she'll come back and make me a sandwich, will you?'

'Sure,' I say. She's been gone a couple of hours, so I figure she'll be back fairly soon anyway, and won't mind if summoned a little prematurely. I dial her number, but she doesn't answer. I hope that Lee won't notice.

'When's it time for my next shot?' he asks. I look up at the clock on the wall.

'You can have the big one now, if you like,' I notify him. He has one serious dose to take, though it mustn't be too early, and there's also a different medication to help him handle the pain if he needs it before then. Tonight he hasn't, and I feel quietly proud that I've kept him distracted well enough to get him through the evening.

'Do you want me to do it?' I ask, picking a syringe up off the breakfast bar. These days his hands shake.

'If you don't mind, sure.'

Luckily, this isn't something that needs to be injected, even if it's in a syringe. He opens his mouth, waiting patiently until I've pushed the plunger down and sprayed the liquid towards the back of his tongue. He grimaces, then, briefly, looks puzzled.

'That's the wrong shit!' he accuses. 'That's the sour stuff. I was meant to take the sweet stuff. That shit tastes nasty.'

My head starts to whirl. *Did I just give him the wrong medicine?* Surely not. I can't have.

'I don't think so,' I say, trying to reassure him, though he doesn't look convinced. 'I'm certain that's what Jeane told me.'

I'd double-checked the procedure with her to make sure. There were only two syringes there. This was definitely the right one.

'Well, you're wrong,' he says.

There's a nasty edge to his voice. I'm not sure whether it's the potential result of giving him the wrong medication or my fear of his possible fury that scares me most. At times like these, I recall an incident after the first

Royal Festival Hall show where, as we'd tried to authenticate the figures for Lee's final payment, I'd been witness to a short but painful row between him and Jeane. His good humour had returned moments later, but this sudden, manic loss of temper had stunned and distressed me then—even though that time I'd not even been the object of his ire—and haunted me ever since.

'Well, not much you can do now,' he grunts. 'Where's Jeane, anyway?'

I remind him that she's still at the casino, and offer to call again. The phone just keeps ringing. It must be on mute.

'Do you want me to make you a sandwich?' I ask. 'It's no trouble.'

'No, Jeane makes the sandwich a special way, and that's the only way I like them.'

Lee has always been picky with his food, but since he got really sick he's chosen from little and eaten even less.

'OK, but I know how to cook, and I'd be more than happy to.'

'Nah, forget it. I'll be fine. Jeane will be back soon. And if she's still out there, it means she's probably having fun. That damned woman is luckier than a pig in shit. She goes and plays the penny machines and walks out with a purse full of gold every time. I don't know how she does it. Maybe she's got an adding machine in her ass. But she'll come back with a smile on her face, and that's a good thing. It's gotta be good for her to get out rather than sit here cooped up with a sick old man like me.'

I laugh. I laugh even more around Lee these days, often because he's funny, and sometimes because I don't know what to say and don't want him to think I'm not listening. Other times it's just because I think it'll make him feel better.

The phone rings. Lee points at the handset and nods at me to answer it.

'Hey,' Jeane says brightly, though I can hear concern in her voice that she's missed two calls. 'What's up?'

'Oh, Lee's a little hungry,' I tell her, feeling a little inadequate.

'Oh, damn it,' she laughs, relieved. 'Can you deal with it? I'm winning good here. He just wants a bacon sandwich. Everything you need is in the fridge. Use the wholegrain bread. Make the bacon crispy, but not too crispy.'

'Actually, he insists you make it. Apparently you're the only one who does it the way he wants it.'

'He'll be fine. I'll be back later, but I don't want to leave yet. You don't mind, do you? You're all right with him, aren't you?'

'Sure,' I say, slightly concerned about how I'm going to break this news to Lee.

'OK, see you later, Bubba. Thanks for taking care of him.'

I put the phone down.

'Was that her?'

'Yep,' I reply cautiously. 'She's on a roll up at the casino, and she wants to hang around a little longer. She suggested I make you a bacon sandwich.'

'No, that's fine,' he says. 'I'll be all right. I don't need to eat. I can wait 'til she gets back.'

He makes an effort to relocate himself in his chair.

'What did I tell you, Bubba? Every time she goes she wins. And by the way, I'm pleased for her. I can wait.'

I settle back in my chair again and we stare at the TV in silence. A crime series is playing and Lee turns the volume up loud.

'You know what,' he says suddenly, silencing the show. 'I will have that sandwich after all. You think you can do it?'

'I think I can cook bacon, yes,' I smile. 'What else do you want in it?'

His instructions for preparation are precise. I fry up some streaky strips then make the sandwich as per his wishes. Before I make a second, I take the first over for his approval.

'Looks good,' he smiles.

I've never paid so much attention to a bacon sandwich, and I watch him try it even more closely. He bites down. I stand nervously by, like a contestant in a cooking competition.

'Not bad, Bubba,' he concedes. 'Not bad at all. Thank you.'

I've passed another test. I can now officially cook for Lee.

* * *

Lee's back in the same seat, reading a newspaper, by the time I come down to breakfast.

'Hey, Bubba,' he says. 'Get yourself some tea and come sit down. There's another story I wanna tell you.'

I'm tired from sitting up late into the night with Jeane after she got back, and I also spent the last hour responding to emails. I know full well that once I've made my appearance for the day there will be little time left for anything but Lee's apparently now vigorous desire to share as many memories as he can. I buy time to adjust to Lee's company, boiling the kettle and fetching myself some cereal—Jeane now buys it in especially for my visits—and only then, once my tea is brewed, do I settle down beside him.

'You ready? Yes? Good. So, Nancy and I were in Nashville,' he begins. 'We'd just finished recording "Jackson", which was the last song on her country album. That's the old word for CD, don't you know? And she said, "Daddy wants us to come to Miami and stay a week. He's doing a film down there in the day and singing at the Fontainebleau Hotel at night. And, since you've never seen him live, I told him yes. And, besides, he wants his plane back before he reports it stolen, since we've had it for some time."'

I'm always impressed by his ability to toss off these jokes within his jokes.

'It was true, you know,' he goes on. 'We'd borrowed Frank's Learjet and just couldn't find the time to return it! And I said, "Did you tell your daddy that I don't have any clothes, just jeans, and they're all dirty?" And she said, "Yes, I did, and he said you could wear your jeans." So I said, "And did you tell daddy that I have work scheduled in LA starting the day after tomorrow?" And she said, "Yes, I did, and he said, 'Cancel it.'"'

'So he was opening the next night, and we left Nashville and arrived in Miami at 4pm, and his limo picked us up and took us to the Fontainebleau Hotel. And no sooner had my little sack full of dirty, dirty jeans hit the floor of my two-bedroom suite than the phone rang. "Daddy wants us to come up. See you there."'

Jeane wanders in from her office, looking over to check that Lee's all right. She waves and smiles before disappearing again.

'Now,' Lee resumes, oblivious, 'if you've been to a football game in the Los Angeles Coliseum, then you'll understand when I say its dimensions are similar to Mr Sinatra's suite in the Fontainebleau Hotel: lots of cheerleaders, players, a bar that seats twenty, a room that stands a hundred, and rows and rows and rows of Chivas, which several folks were trying to thrust on me. And Nancy? Well, she was sitting on her daddy's lap, exclaiming, "Don't you all think my daddy's just the cutest thing in the world?"'

Lee, I notice, is unusually coherent this morning, and his speech is faster than it's been for a while. He went to bed reasonably early, and perhaps the medication hasn't befuddled his mind yet. I wonder if he's been rehearsing this tale in his head all morning, while waiting for me.

'So the players nodded yes,' he continues, 'and the cheerleaders smiled, and "Daddy" handed me a Chivas on the rocks in a glass that was the size of a milk bucket. And he asked me, "You still drinking this stuff?" And I told him, "Only if I'm chained, cursed, and made to speak Latin." And then Frank says, "Nancy said you were strange, Lee." And I just say, "Nancy who?"'

This time he makes me laugh so hard I nearly spit out a mouthful of cereal.

'Anyway … two hours and fourteen seconds later, I was back in my suite and I'd been robbed. My sack of dirty jeans was gone, and my beautiful semi-expensive second pair of boots was missing. And that's when the phone rang. It was Nancy again. "Daddy says we'll meet at 8pm tonight in the …" And I stopped her there and said, "I've been robbed. I can't go. I can't go." And Nancy, she was a cute thing, she said, "Who would steal a sack of dirty jeans?" And then she asked if I'd checked my closet. So I walked the mile and a half to the closet in my bedroom, slammed the doors open and—*Bang! Bang!*—there was my complete wardrobe: clean jeans, clean jackets, shirts, socks, my shorts. They even shined my boots. And, by the way, you could go blind from those boots by the time they'd finished with them.

'So, afterwards, we went to the show. The noise was deafening. There were enough folks there to give a fire marshal migraines for eternity. And there were eight of us seated at a table about ten metres from the stage. The joint was packed, as you'd expect, and I got to see, no less than ten metres away, Frank Sinatra. I'd met him, but I'd never seen him perform live. And he just ripped them another ass. He was tremendous. He just was unbelievable. I've always been cynical about live performances, but everything he did … you know, just a little wave of his hand brought them to their knees.'

Lee adjusts himself in his seat and pulls his dressing gown tighter around his bony ribs. His flamboyant diamond ring twists on a finger that's now too thin.

'Afterwards, he came back and made sure that we liked the show. We sat up at the bar and had a couple of drinks. And then he said, "You'll go out to the yacht with us?" And I said, "Yacht?" And he said, "Yeah, we got a yacht out here." And I said, "Well, I'd better go upstairs and get me some Dramamine, because I get sea sick just from water in a glass." And he tells me, "You won't need any Dramamine."

'So we drove out to the pier. He had a beautiful yacht. I mean, it was big and beautiful. But you couldn't dynamite it away from the pier. It was just a stationary yacht. So we sat out and drank a while, and I went back early. There were a lot of guys I didn't know there, and movie star girls I did know, but I was high from having seen Frank live. People had told me he was the greatest singer in the world, but having seen him, I knew they didn't describe him quite right. He was better than that—better than I'd ever seen! And it was strange. I was ready to find something that I didn't like, but I didn't find a thing. It bothered me. It bothered me a lot.

'And so I asked Nancy the next day if I could go again the next night. She said, "The table's yours. It's there just for us. You can come every night." So I went again on Tuesday night. He was good. He wasn't as good as Monday night, but he was good. And so I went back on Wednesday night. He had some trouble with people making some noise in the back, interrupting, and he was OK. On Thursday night, the joint was packed again, but he was miserable.

I really thought he was miserable. I guess that's from having seen the best. Anybody can have a bad night, and he was having one on Thursday night.

'So I had second thoughts about even going back on Friday night. But I did. It was just me and a couple of guys at the table. And he made Monday night look like Amateur Night. He was so good on Friday night. He was back! And that taught me many things. One is that we all have bad nights. Two is that when you're good, nobody can take it away from you. And three is that if they try to take it away from you and you're strong enough, you'll get it back.

'And they didn't try to take it away. They just came there to drink it up. They drank Sinatra that night. I think he even went a little over time that night and sang a couple of extra songs because he was so high on it. It was just an amazing thing to have seen that at my age and I'd seen, I guess, just about everybody that I wanted to see. And he asked me, "So, how'd ya like the show?" And I said, "There ain't never going to be anything better than that." He said, "Thank you." And I said, "No. Thank *you*."'

Lee turns round, signalling the end of the tale. And then, with a wag of his finger, he winks at me.

'I saw some things, Bubba, I gotta say. I saw some things in my life …'

* * *

Lee rarely speaks about the music on his old records. He'll talk until your smile muscles ache about all sorts of things, but not the contents of the albums that he made. Of course, I've heard countless stories about 'The Sinatra Girl', been told often how many copies 'Boots' has sold, and he's discussed what it cost to record such and such a session musician in such and such a studio on more than a handful of occasions. But he's never been especially interested in talking in depth about the very essence of what earned his reputation. Music has always been commerce to him; a means of paying the bills.

'I was in the business for the money,' he says. 'Everybody else might have done it for glamour, or for nice clothes, or good-looking girls … well, that wasn't a bad reason. It might have been for that. But it was a job. I didn't make houses; I couldn't paint. I could do this, and it was like a job to me. You can ask my children.'

'Boots' and 'Sand' and 'Ladybird' and 'Sugar Town' and 'Some Velvet Morning' were, he insists, merely what enabled him to put those children through the best colleges in the US. He's more interested in numbers than notes, it's always seemed, unless of course they're bank notes. He refers to his songs as garbage—'The way I play guitar has increased piano sales nearly ten percent a year!'—and considers himself little more than 'a redneck Indian cowboy singer'. Nowadays, he betrays little interest in music at all—'The only thing I listen to is my bank account,' he likes to say—and only occasionally stumbles upon something, perhaps on TV, that he'll later ask me about. These are often unexpected targets of his affections: The Corrs, for instance, or a transvestite cabaret act. What they usually have in common is a fondness for covering his compositions.

It's a surprise, therefore, when I find us talking about some of his older recordings. I can't remember how we started, but suddenly he's reminiscing about string arrangements and lyrics and specific musicians with an extraordinary clarity. His eyes shine as he recalls particular episodes in his recording career, but even he's a little doubtful as to which song is on which record. The problem is that Lee has no copies of most of his own albums—especially not the ones that have so far failed to be reissued—and he even gave away all of his gold discs. In fact, only one remains on his wall, curiously for the 1992 multi-million-selling version of 'Boots' by Billy Ray Cyrus. I once asked him why, of all the awards he'd won, he'd kept that.

'Well, royalties have been very kind to me,' he laughed. 'I saved my pennies. That album sold about fourteen million worldwide. I was pretty dead before then. I made good royalties, good performances for radio, but they were just steady. Then, all of a sudden, that album took off. That kind of turned me around a little bit, which I didn't expect at that time of my life. It made me want to write again. It made me want to do other things again.'

It had seemed odd to me that Billy Ray Cyrus, an artist who'd earned universal derision from musical 'connoisseurs', should have awakened Lee's creative instincts. But back then, Lee still had little interest in anything other than commercial success. This presumably explained his sternly negative reaction to the attempt around the same time by the Seattle-based indie label, Sub Pop Records, to compile an album of his songs performed by the likes of Beck and Nirvana—little known acts at the time. This previous attitude, he conceded, was one he regretted.

'I know that Beck is a fan,' he sighed, 'and I know that Kurt Cobain was a fan, too. And I found that out from the guy in Seattle who I crawled all over 'cos he was gonna make a tribute album on me. I wasn't ready. I told him, "No, I don't want it. If you do, I'll sue you." That's awful isn't it? I didn't know anything. I wasn't even listening to radio then. I was living in Florida with my son Mark, and my grandson, and we were having a lot of fun together, and that's all I cared about then.

'But somebody sent me one of the Cobain things, and one day I put it on—and by the way I still didn't know who Nirvana was—and I just wished I would have been near the garage that mess started in. That doesn't prove me smart or dumb or anything else, because, you know, the guy who started that label, I think he would have taken me and married my sister, for Christ's sake! But I wasn't ready to have things put together. I did not know—and it's my stupidity—that anybody in the world cared about anything except the hits. 'Cos the hits is what I was making my money off in those days.'

It's not only the hits he's talking about now, however. I listen to him a while longer, as he summons up memories of long spells in the studio and prolific songwriting sessions, waiting for a chance to announce that I have a little surprise for him.

'Lee,' I finally say, after he's stopped for breath. 'There's something I have to show you. Wait there a moment.'

I race upstairs to my room, where most of my belongings are strewn carelessly over the floor because I've spent almost every waking hour with him or Jeane. In the top of my bag is a collection of ten or so CD-Rs. I swipe them up and carry them downstairs as fast as possible. I don't like leaving him alone for long.

'I thought it might be nice to play these at your party,' I tell him. 'A friend of mine helped me get most of your records digitised, even the ones it's impossible to find.'

'Oh, yeah?' he asks, arching his eyebrows.

'Yup,' I say proudly. 'We've got *Love & Other Crimes*. We've got *A House Safe For Tigers*. We've even got *The 98% American Mom & Apple Pie 1929 Crash Band*!'

'Well, how about that!' he beams. 'Go get that stereo. Let's listen to something now.'

I cross the room and return with one of those Bose CD players advertised in magazines. (Jeane's always had a penchant for brochure purchases.) I plug it into the power board by his chair and turn it on.

'Have you got "It Was A Very Good Year"?' he asks.

'I do,' I reply, with some satisfaction. I shuffle through the collection and place a copy of 1969's *Forty* in the CD player. The song is not one he wrote, but he loved it enough—and inhabited it successfully enough—to have included it on this album, the 1974 live recording *The Stockholm Kid*, and then again on 1977's *Movin' On*.

First we hear the crackle of the vinyl from which the recording was sourced, and then a lone flute slides gently down the scale. There's another brief pause, punctuated by more static, and then Lee's voice fills the room, a maudlin and yet comforting sound. He's sung many different kinds of songs over the years—country, pop, psychedelia, surf, standards—but it's easy to forget that there's far more to him than the subterranean rumble for which his voice is best known. In fact, I've largely overlooked this track myself, precisely because it doesn't conform to one's expectations of his work.

Lee begins to sing, softly and tenderly, briefly *a cappella*:

When I was seventeen …

More flutes appear, followed by a swelling wind and brass arrangement. Here, beside me, his eyes mist over. He drifts off to a distant place, while a piano and double bass fill the empty space. The pace picks up, the arrangement bold, playful, and full of swing, subtle but imaginative. Frank Sinatra covered it, too, though somehow I've never encountered his version, but if it's better than the one we listen to now, as I sit at Lee's feet by the stereo, then there must be a God. I watch a broad smile creep across Lee's face, one that confirms the true warmth of the man beneath the obstinate exterior. It's a smile I know and love, and I've never been happier to have helped provoke it.

The song's lyrics are especially poignant, the aged protagonist looking back at the relationships he's shared over the years, from the '*small town girls*' of his teenage years to the '*city girls*' that he met at twenty-one, and on to the '*blue-blooded girls*' with whom he'd '*drive in limousines*' at the age of thirty-five. Lee played the field when he was younger, no doubt about it, and his eyes glaze over—a sign, I imagine, that he's rolling back the years and recalling the extravagances of his past. I remember a story he told me only yesterday about a dinner Nancy had arranged not long after 'Boots' became a hit.

'She called me up,' he began, 'and said, "Are you doing anything this evening?" And I said, "No. I hope you're doing something so I can get out of the house." And she said, "Would you come and have dinner with me?" And I said, "Sure."'

The gentle way he'd said the word 'sure' wasn't a simple affirmative. It was a purr of pleasure, as though he was savouring the word, remembering his dinners with Nancy and anticipating the pleasure that the memory of that particular occasion would elicit.

'So I went over to her house, and they'd got dinner all ready, and there were three places set. And who should come in the house but a little old girl about the size of Nancy, cussing like hell and wiping the dust off her and everything. She came over to give me a big hug and a kiss, went into the bathroom to clean up, then came over and sat down. It was Barbara Stanwyck! She was one of my favourite movies stars! Humphrey Bogart was my favourite male, and she was my favourite female, because she had this way of … I don't know; they both spoke like they had a speech impediment. I know he got cut in the navy, and she also had some way of saying her words that I really liked. And every place that has gay entertainers, they do Barbara Stanwyck. So I ask her about this, and she says, "What are you doing hanging out in gay bars?"'

He'd broken off to laugh, but it had turned into a cough.

'Just me, Nancy, and Barbara Stanwyck,' he'd concluded once he'd recovered. 'Nancy did sweet things like that.'

It's hard to reconcile such images with the skeletal figure beside me. The forced recollection of his recent decline makes me swallow so hard I fear he might hear me. Only a few years ago, this atrophied body offered a short but muscular presence that added to my already judicious fear of his personality—something furthered by the fact I knew he wasn't afraid of getting stuck in should the occasion merit it. Not long after we'd first met, he'd boasted to me in one of his faxes about how he'd been caught up in a fight with three men in New Orleans. I could picture him with his fists clenched before him, ducking and diving on the street. 'Their combined ages was around seventy,' he'd written, 'and I'll be seventy-two in July, so it seemed like a fair fight to me.'

This wasn't even the last time he'd got into trouble: two years later, he found himself caught up in another brawl. 'I've never been circumcised with an egg beater,' he told me afterwards, 'but I'm sure it's not as painful as a broken rib.'

Lee's just a shadow now, lost in the music, inert apart from a single finger that taps his leg where his hand rests. If the song's making him sad, however, he's hiding it well, and the celebratory quality of the recording—especially when the trumpets burst through—forces the smile that's continued hovering upon his face to widen even further. He leans forward carefully to listen more intently, the music stripped back suddenly to its original, opening arrangement, his hushed, rich voice close to the microphone once again. Gently, tenderly, he sings from the perspective of the old man that he's now become, his life at last recognised as '*vintage wine from fine old kegs, from the brim to the dregs*'. Why this of all songs is the one that he's chosen finally becomes clear.

We sit in silence until the music has played out, then open our eyes and exhale, staring into the darkness. It takes us a while to return to the room itself. Finally Lee speaks, and his words are ones I've waited years to hear.

'You know what, Bubba?' he mutters quietly. 'I quite like me.'

* * *

A few weeks before I flew over for Lee's birthday, I sat with colleagues from Ever Records, engaged in yet another round of demoralising disagreements about how to sell our releases. Much of the music I'd signed had proved to be commercially challenging: a Sámi band from the North of Norway; a trio whose bizarre mixture of metal, punk, jazz, and more had proven baffling to almost everyone who'd heard it; a quartet from Iceland best known as the string section for one of the country's biggest musical exports, Sigur Rós.

The latter group, amiina, specialised in intricate, delicate pieces performed on a number of instruments, some recognisable, like violins, some—including wine glasses and a saw—less established. Their album, *Kurr*, had picked up plaudits from the media, but we were struggling to get their music heard by the wider public. Our budgets were small, touring was expensive, and instrumental music rarely finds its way onto mainstream radio.

The four young women responsible had told me early on that they were dedicated fans of Lee's. As I argued with the team taking care of Ever's releases, I devised an idea that, while unlikely, filled me with excitement. A number of Lee's solo records had featured spoken word introductions to his songs. Sometimes these were eccentric vignettes, while others were rather more personal. All of them, however, were imbued with a sensitivity and warmth that had perhaps been undervalued over the years. What, I wondered, would happen if I were to ask him to write one last piece that could be combined with one of amiina's? Their fragile arrangements left plenty of space for Lee's voice, and maybe, just maybe—even though he'd never really shown much interest in most of the acts with whom I worked—the idea might capture Lee's imagination.

My initial proposal was met with silence. Lee by this time was so sick that it was not unusual for Jeane to need a number of days before she could get him to focus on anything business associated, so I thought little of this. But finally my enthusiasm for the concept got the better of me, and I raised the idea again. Lee's response to my request was straightforward.

'If you come to my birthday party this year,' he said, 'then I'll do your damned Eskimo song.'

Not long afterwards, a message arrived via Jeane that Lee wanted me to track down an old Finnish fairy tale he'd once heard about an island where the snow tasted of sugar. This, he said, was to provide him with the basis for his lyrics. It might already exist in a form that he could simply read for the recording, assuming we could get any permission that might be required, but otherwise he'd need me to adapt it. I sat up late that night, searching relentlessly online for anything that might resemble the story he claimed to recall, but there was nothing out there. I went to bed frustrated, concerned that my failure might be enough to render the entire scheme redundant.

As I lay awake, I began to wonder what the tale might have been about and, after a while, turned the light back on, grabbed a scrap of paper and a pen, and wrote down the following words:

At the top of the world there's an island
A place where the sun never shines.

I put the pen and paper back onto my bedside table and switched the light off. A few minutes later, however, I turned it back on again and wrote another three lines.

But the people don't care
Because the snow over there
Is so bright they nearly go blind.

This time, I kept the lamp on, scribbling down phrases and rhymes that I tried to imagine him reciting, until, around 7am, I finally conceded to sleep.

The next day I read through my fairy tale, pleasantly surprised by what I'd written—words that somehow created a narrative that, before I'd first tried to rest, had never existed at all. I'd tried to adopt a suitably childlike tone but, while it had never been my original intention, I'd smuggled in an ecological theme that in some way held together. I spent a little while tweaking and polishing the verses, put it to one side another night, and then, the following day, dared to send it to Lee with a message explaining that my search for his Finnish fairy tale had proven fruitless, but that I'd been inspired to make up my own.

It was a presumptuous thing to do, I knew, but I felt an unusual sense of pride in what I'd composed. At that time, my writing was largely confined to occasional album reviews for a British magazine, press releases for my record label or anyone else willing to hire me, and, periodically, stories about some of the more curious experiences that my life offered, many of which I shared with friends via email but which never travelled beyond. Lee again took his time to respond, but when he did so his answer was straightforward: I should make sure I was equipped to record him when I came to visit in a few weeks.

Now, in the late morning of his birthday—his party will take place later on in the week—I sit on the floor in front of the reclining chair in his sitting room, holding an expensive radio microphone while my friend Nina perches on the sofa beside me with a minidisc player. She's joined me from Germany, where she works as a freelance journalist, to carry out one last interview with the old man. We first met late last year, when she was sent here by Lee's label to put together a short, filmed documentary intended to promote *Cake Or Death*. It's her microphone, and her minidisc player, upon which I now depend.

Lee's in his dressing gown, as he is so often these days, holding the sheets of paper upon which I've printed the text in huge type so that his eyes aren't tested too hard. He's refused to take his medicine, arguing somewhat heroically that he'd rather have a clear head and endure the pain. The process is a struggle; like Bela before me, I've not always managed to replicate the manner in which he speaks, despite having worked hard to ensure that the cadence of my words matches the rhythm of amiina's music. Lee's not bothered to listen to the music more than once, however, and each sentence is battered around until he's satisfied, irrespective of the context it will soon adopt.

'Take six thousand, four hundred, and eighty,' he says at one point, his frustration getting the better of him, while another time he starts to speak before giving up again, muttering softly, 'Not with these teeth …'

It becomes increasingly hard to tell whether his growing impatience is directed at the little story he's attempting to read or his inability to recite it successfully. His limbs ache, his mouth and throat are dry, and his once canyon-esque voice sometimes cracks like desert mud. I fret that he's altered one or two words without my consent, or refused to re-record a line that doesn't sound quite how I'd hoped. Nonetheless, there are times when he brings my words to life in a way that is almost overwhelming. He finds subtleties in the text that I'd never even imagined, and instils a gentle authority and sentiment in the parts I've deemed most significant that's way beyond anything I anticipated. Seated at his feet, I feel like a youngster listening to a tale told by a charismatic elder who heard it himself as a kid. Though my arm aches from holding the microphone close to his face, I can barely move a muscle, spellbound as I am by his voice. I can't help but speculate whether it will do the same for others, assuming this recording really comes off.

Eventually, the exertion proves too great. Lee calls out for Jeane, who hurries over and offers him the drugs from which he's so far abstained. He's lasted around twenty minutes, and although I have no idea whether I've got what we need—he's been through each line at least a couple of times—I raise myself off the floor to thank him. Whatever comes of this, even to have had him attempt it is something I'm never going to forget. That he considers my poem worthy of such efforts is perhaps the greatest compliment he's given me. Furthermore, I realise later, it may be the first time he's ever worked for free.

* * *

The day of the party arrives. Nina and I have spent the preceding forty-eight hours in Los Angeles, where she's been interviewing a German photographer and I've visited family I rarely see. Now we need to get back to Vegas. There's no point leaving LA early through the morning traffic, so we set off at 9am, giving us five hours to make it from Venice Beach, across California and through the Mojave desert, before the party starts. We're cutting it fine, but I figure that no one will mind if we arrive a little after the official start time of 2pm. My phone soon starts to ring, however. There are complications at the house, and they need me there as soon as possible.

Nina and I are both tired, and the temperature in the desert is overpowering. I'm wary of speeding, but I drive as fast as I dare, and as the phone calls continue, I start to put my foot down harder. By the time we reach the outskirts of Vegas, we ought to have just enough time to check into the hotel—with other guests in town, there's no room for me at the house, so I've offered to keep Nina company at the Sunset Station rather than leave her stranded for her stay. But a wrong turn off the freeway proves a problem. We end up lost, scuttling through suburban streets with only the planes rising from the airport as a landmark around which we can orientate ourselves.

The calls from the house keep coming, and by the time we've checked in, we have only a few minutes to dump our belongings, put on a fresh change of clothes, and squeal out of the parking lot to make it to Lee's by 3pm. The party is underway as Nina and I nervously enter the lobby, but whatever was happening earlier seems fortunately to have passed. Lee's seated in the lounge in his favourite chair, dressed in his finest trousers, his T-shirt this year proudly proclaiming, 'I'm not dead yet.' Around him is gathered another curious selection of friends, among them family, business associates, his landlady and her husband, Shelley King—the writer of a song on 2004's neglected *Nancy & Lee 3*, who until today he'd never met—and, at his feet, Nancy Sinatra, who wears a conspicuous straw hat. She gazes up at him fondly and listens as he rattles off anecdotes. He's clearly happy to be the centre of attention one last time.

As I grab a beer, Lee calls me over.

'Tell Nina to film everything,' he instructs me. This is unanticipated:

a few days before, he'd banned any filming at all, because the cancer made him look so haggard.

'Are you sure?' I ask him, surprised.

'Yes, I'm sure. Tell her to get her camera and record it all for me. I want this for the family. And the world, if anyone gives a damn.'

I pass the message on, then mingle. It's an intimate party, smaller than last year's, but one thing that's plainly evident is that everyone here loves Lee dearly. In fact, most of them—myself included—are in awe of him. This becomes even more apparent when the stereo upstairs, whose speakers are filling the house with the music I brought, plays Shelley's song. At this point, Lee and Nancy are for some reason in the hall, and as an audience gathers around them, they begin to dance, Lee unsteady on his feet but held up when necessary by his partner. Like paparazzi, we all reach for our cameras, and soon flashes strobe the small vestibule. It feels like we're interrupting a private moment—there's something definitely impolite about the way we're trying to record it—but they continue until the song ends, posing for more pictures afterwards and inviting Shelley to join them.

It is, of course, a historic moment, whether or not it's a private one. Nancy and Lee are unlikely ever to be united again, and though this remains unspoken, most of us know this is the last time we'll see him. When people walk out of the house in a few hours time, they'll be saying goodbye forever. No wonder everyone wants something to remember him by.

Not long after, we prepare for the presentation of the cake, although nothing, Lee's adamant, can begin until Nina is ready with her camera. She hurries off to find Sam, whom she wants to film lighting the candles out of Lee's sight, and then—as everyone sings 'Happy Birthday' to the accompaniment of Lee's best surviving friend, Tommy Parsons, who strums the chords on a guitar—Sam carries the cake towards her father. He sits patiently, waiting for its delivery, his head resting against his chair as though he barely has energy to keep it upright. He's still got his shades on, despite the fact that the curtains are almost drawn. The darkness fails to hide the fact he looks gaunt, however, his black shirt and the T-shirt beneath it hanging off him like a cloth draped over a crucifix. His 'turkey neck', as he still disparagingly calls it, is more evident than ever.

There's applause as the cake reaches its destination.

'No, goddamn it!' Lee cries out, abruptly. 'That ain't right! You're gonna have to do it again. That's not what I wanted. Nina? Where are you?!'

Nina makes herself visible by his side.

'You're supposed to film the cake!'

Nina looks baffled. There's an embarrassed silence throughout the room. As far as we're aware, that's exactly what Nina's just done. But Lee denies this, so she and Sam return the cake to the table, its candles now out. Preparing everything again takes so long that premature attempts to re-sing 'Happy Birthday' have to move to a second verse.

'You bastard, you bastard,' Tommy intones affectionately, his voice weakened by his own health battles, 'Happy birthday to you …'

Once again, though, Lee's not satisfied.

'No, goddamn it!' he yells, a desperate fury to his voice. 'How many times do I have to tell you?'

He tries to explain again what it is he has in mind, conducting the entire episode as though it were one of his studio sessions. As so often in the past, I become concerned that this is all going to go very, very wrong. I slip away to check Nina's all right. She's panicking, her hands shaking as she fiddles with her camera.

'I've run out of film!' she whispers urgently. 'Where's my bag? I need another memory card!'

I sweep through the house, desperately trying to find her stuff. I can't see it anywhere, but I can hear the song begin a third time. I return to the room hastily, relieved to discover that Lee now seems happy with what's happened, though Nina hasn't even filmed it.

'I'm so sorry,' I say, taking her to one side. 'Are you OK?'

'That,' she replies, trying to laugh it off, but still quivering, 'was absolutely horrible.'

After the cake has been devoured, Nancy joins her former mentor, seating herself on the edge of his chair, her arm draped uncomfortably over the back as though she wants to put it round Lee's shoulders but daren't. Everyone crowds around them, eavesdropping as though they're offering an audience, and perhaps because of this, their conversation dries up.

In the end, Tommy breaks the ice. He strums the chords to their hit 'Jackson', and Lee and Nancy start singing, floundering over the words from time to time, their voices sometimes failing as we watch. With his upper lip occasionally sticking to dry teeth, Lee looks almost like he's grimacing, while Nancy seems curiously emotionless. That all changes with the third verse's final line.

'*I'm going to Jackson*,' she sings, her voice cracking as she joins in with what should have been Lee's line. '*Goodbye, that's all she wrote.*'

'That's it,' Lee says, interrupting her quietly. 'I can't do anymore.'

There's a moment of disappointed silence. Lee and Nancy smile bashfully at one another. The rest of us know there'll be no encore, so we soon start to clap. The applause lasts a while. Lee quietly drinks it up.

'We did that in three takes in Nashville,' he announces proudly, turning back to Nancy with a laughing face. 'It's because I didn't want to spend anything on overtime. I was cheap even with your dad's money.'

* * *

The last time I see Lee, he's lying on his sofa in his dressing gown, his legs spilling out from underneath the same blanket I threw over him a week ago while we watched the boxing. Nina and I have spent the afternoon at his house, ready to record him and Tommy perform songs that they want to write spontaneously in front of the camera. But Lee's been in too much discomfort, and it also seems that his mind might be starting to go. To some it's most likely imperceptible, but I know it all the same. He's unfocussed, he's restless, and his mood swings rapidly from soft to sharp and back again.

Nina has another interview to do in the city that night. I'm also flying out early the next day, and have promised her dinner as thanks for her help with the reading a few days earlier. When Lee finally concedes that he and

Tommy aren't going to be able to work, I spend one last hour with him while Tommy dozes nearby and Nina works in another room. We sit quietly together, watching television, occasionally interrupting the show to discuss an item of business that I fear will never be accomplished, or for Lee to tell me another of his long, rambling, and now frequently muddled stories. Finally—grudgingly, guiltily, gloomily—I gather my stuff together.

'I have to go, Lee,' I say, as I walk towards his resting place.

Lee tilts his head at me, slowly reaching out his right arm. The skin hangs from his biceps, the muscle gone. I take his hand and he grips mine weakly.

I want to hug him goodbye more than ever. I know I'll never have another chance. But I don't want to disturb him by making him stand up. Later, I'll claim that I embraced him, but the truth is I merely wish I did.

It's not the emotional farewell I'd have preferred. I want to tell him what he means to me, how fortunate I feel to have known him these eight years, how much his music still speaks to me, how I'm going to miss him; how, no matter what bad tempered words he's said to me over the years, I forgive him everything, absolutely everything. I love him, I long to tell him. You're like a father to me.

Instead, I hold his hand and shake it solemnly, lost for words.

'Goodbye, Bubba,' he says, his eyes full of the life he's lived. 'Have a safe journey.'

He smiles broadly at me one last time.

'You too,' I say instinctively, immediately aghast at the ambiguity, before making a promise that I know even faster is never going to be fulfilled. 'I'll see you soon.'

I let go of his hand reluctantly.

'Goodbye,' I say.

'Goodbye, Bubba.'

* * *

Just over three weeks later, at 6:22am on Sunday, August 5 2007, my phone rings. For the last few days, I've been tour-managing one of Ever

Records' bands, and I'm lying in bed in a shabby Travelodge somewhere on the outskirts of Oxford. I pick up my mobile and carry it quickly into the bathroom, so as not to wake the musician with whom I'm sharing a room.

The call is from Lee's home. I know the moment I see the number what it's about.

'Lee's gone,' Jeane croaks. I can tell she's fighting back tears. 'He died about four hours ago.'

'Oh, Jeane,' I stutter, staring blankly at my reflection in an ugly bathroom mirror. 'I'm so, so sorry.'

I don't know what else to say.

'It was so peaceful,' Jeane says. 'He was lying in bed.'

'I'm so, so sorry,' I say again.

'I'm sorry too, Bubba.'

There's a silence that I feel has to be filled, but I'm too sleepy to know how. I can hear Jeane sniffing at the other end of the line.

'I can't talk any more, Bubba,' she finally says. 'I've been calling people for hours. I'm sorry.'

I tell her not to apologise, and that I'll be in touch later that day. We hang up, and I look down at my phone, as though this will tell me what to do next. Then, hesitantly, I turn off the bathroom light, make my way back to my bed, and climb back in. I lie there taking deep breaths for a while before pulling the blankets around me and curling up in a ball. Sleep takes its time, but comes in the end, blessedly.

CHAPTER EIGHT

I'LL LIVE
YESTERDAYS

Phoenix seems like a nice enough place. Its conservative, low key charm, clean streets, and surprisingly thriving vegetation distract from the fact that it lies in the middle of a bone-dry desert under a hospital blanket of smog.

My short taste of the lifestyle here hasn't been too shabby either: last night, for the first time in over six years, I met up with my old friend Meg, who moved here with her husband, Wez, some time ago. He proudly unveiled his 1964 Chevrolet to take us for fine Mexican food and ten-pin bowling before we topped things off with a liberal number of cold beers outside the adobe bar where Meg once worked as a waitress. These aren't things I do every day.

This morning's drive to the hotel, however, has revealed that there's far more to Phoenix, and that it's not all so quaint. A vast plume of bitter black smoke rises from a warehouse fire, endless anonymous shopping malls border a road so hot you can smell the tyre rubber as you drive, and the closer we get to our destination, the more ramshackle the houses seem, their yards increasingly full of decaying cars, bikes, and toys, their exteriors incongruous among nearby factories and storage facilities. When Meg finally pulls off the highway into the car park of the North Phoenix Embassy Suites, it strikes me as an odd choice to celebrate the passing of a legend.

It's also an incredibly warm choice. These are record-breaking temperatures, I've been told, and no one spends any part of the day fully dressed outdoors unless they have to. I build up a fine sweat in just the fifteen-metre walk to the air-conditioned lobby, where I impatiently check in. I'm eager to unload my two suitcases, one an especially large one donated by Jeane after she'd encouraged me to go through Lee's wardrobe during an earlier leg of my trip, a visit to help her sort out his possessions in Las Vegas.

'If there's anything you want, take it,' she'd said, pulling open the mirrored sliding doors in the bedroom they once shared. 'I'd far rather you found a use for something, but anything left is going to the Salvation Army.'

This felt uncomfortable for many reasons: for starters, I wasn't a relative, and I wasn't sure I merited the opportunity to take clothes from Lee's cupboards. Second, I was far from convinced that any of Lee's clothes would either fit or suit me. He was significantly shorter than I am, and towards the end of his life, without wishing to sound impertinent, I wouldn't have called him a snappy dresser. Third, I felt awkward removing clothes from his closet knowing that they might otherwise benefit Lee's favourite charity, the Globe branch of Arizona's Salvation Army, to whom he had made many donations since they paid special attention to local Native American children. He took great pride in his ancestral ties to his land's original inhabitants, and he loved the fact that by helping them he could reduce his payments to the Federal Tax authorities.

It was hard, then, not to think of myself as the kind of person who goes through the bins of Hollywood stars in search of tawdry souvenirs. There was also something terribly sad about rooting around among a dead man's clothes, a sensation emphasised further when I stumbled upon an unopened but punched packet of Marlboro cigarettes in one of Lee's jacket pockets. Every item was an unfinished story.

Jeane was persuasive, so much so that I took clothes that weren't my style at all rather than risk offending her enthusiasm. She understood how close Lee and I had become, and she wanted me to know that. But once she'd thrown in one of his dressing gowns and his 'duster'—the coat he'd worn in Berlin that made him look like a High Plains drifter—I was forced to ask if she had an extra suitcase that I could borrow to take it all home.

I'd actually spotted a set of luggage embroidered with Lee's initials.

These were a little more distinguished than the only thing of his that I'd 'inherited': his ring, the conspicuous, chunky diamond set in gold whose receipt Jeane also passed on to me, proving that neither element was quite what it seemed. Its price was of little interest; for a while, I'd put it on simply to provoke stories about Lee. But the suitcase somehow seemed more suited to the elegance with which I wished to associate him.

The luggage set was not to be separated. Jeane instead offered a case she no longer needed from her own closet. I felt embarrassed to have even thought about taking something I wasn't offered, and thanked her for her generosity. It's heavy, however, and doesn't have wheels, so I'm a little less grateful when the receptionist at the Embassy Suites advises me that my room is at the furthest end of their grounds. She gives me instructions how to get to there in a manner that suggests she's never walked so far herself.

I gather my belongings and trudge round the hotel perimeter to the furthest block of rooms. Drenched in sweat, I unlock my door and haul the cases in behind me. I resent the fact that I seem to be so far from the action, until I emerge a few minutes later and realise how civilised the setting is. Stretching back towards the main body of the hotel are well-watered lawns, lush palm trees providing regular shadow from the unrelenting heat, a couple of tennis courts, and a functional albeit less attractive pagoda that sadly obscures the view of the swimming pool in whose direction I now head.

Lee chose this place himself as the venue for his Memorial Party in the months before he died. He spent much of his early career in Phoenix in the mid 50s, and he returned regularly during his cancer treatment at the nearby Mayo Clinic, where the staff had handled him with notable respect. Phoenix also provided a home for two of his best friends, Al Casey—who sadly passed away a year ago, leaving Lee significantly more lonely—and Tommy Parsons, who missed being at Lee's bedside when he died by mere minutes. It's a location that's reflective of Lee's later, more modest lifestyle rather than the glamour around which he once circled, but at least offers some sense of closure. In addition, by the time he got sick, Lee had moved around so much that his friends were scattered across the globe. Though these may not be prestigious surroundings to celebrate the passing of a legend, they're probably as good as any.

* * *

At one end of the reception lobby stands a noticeboard confirming the adjoining room as the location for tonight's events. It displays a photograph of Lee's boots and cane taken by Jakob Axelman, Torbjörn's son and Kalle's brother.

'In Memory Of Lee Hazlewood,' the poster reads. 'July 9 1929– August 4 2007.' Underneath this runs the legend, 'The World's Greatest Songwriter.' If the superlative is overenthusiastic, I welcome it anyway. It wasn't my decision.

Inside, I find Lee's son-in-law Marty bent over a laptop, trying to plug in a cable that will allow him to project pictures and films onto a large screen in the far corner. Around him, burly, tattooed, shaggy-haired men are setting up a PA, carrying in equipment through a fire door that everyone keeps closing in order to keep out the heat. Hotel staff scuffle around circular dining tables that take up much of the space, laying down tablecloths, vacuum cleaning a red carpeted floor, preparing a bar that for some reason they've set up right by the door. It's nonetheless hard to shake off the impression that this conference room was probably used the day before by short-sleeved businessmen with PowerPoint presentations.

'Hey, Marty,' I say, holding out my hand. 'How are you?'

He turns round from the computer and glances up.

'It's Bubba,' I add, in case he doesn't recognise me. 'Wyndham.'

We've only met once before, and in truth he doesn't look as I remember him. Thanks to his name, the shiny pate buried beneath his baseball cap, and his salt-and-pepper beard, I instead think of Marty DiBergi, Rob Reiner's alter ego as the director of *This Is Spinal Tap*, so much so that I expect him to announce, 'But hey! Enough of my yakkin'. Whaddaya say? Let's boogie!'

But he doesn't. It's not his style. We shake hands instead, and I tell him I have the pictures that Jeane would like displayed during the course of the evening. He says he's almost got the rig set up, and I start to gather together the snaps of Lee that I've amassed over the years, many of them from his last two birthday parties. He rarely enjoyed the presence of cameras, so consequently the collection is bulked out with the promotional shots with which I've worked, as well as others downloaded from websites, and a selection that Deana Martin, Dean Martin's daughter, emailed over to Jeane earlier in the week.

Outside, a black van pulls up. Its occupants clamber out and excitedly stretch their legs. I recognise Joey Burns from the band Calexico and excuse myself so I can say hello. I'd worked with them at City Slang for many years, and they'd met Lee during the label's tenth anniversary celebrations in 2000. Lee had no formal connection to the company at that stage, but I'd made a tentative attempt to persuade him to make a guest appearance with the group. The fee he'd demanded was ruled too large. No way would Lee work cheap.

I never figured out why he still joined us that festive weekend. He wasn't especially excited by the bands playing, and it certainly seemed a little rash to think his presence might be anything so simple as a gesture of support. I put it down to restlessness. Sometimes, he'd told me, he liked to 'play phantom,' slipping out of the house unannounced and not returning for days. When he'd come to visit me in Berlin to record with Bela B., he'd suggested I find a bigger apartment so that he could contribute to the rent and have a room at his disposal any time he needed to escape.

For two nights, I'd enjoyed the presence of this reclusive figure up in the box of the Royal Festival Hall, as well as the sight of him backstage with my parents, teasing my father for being the kind of officer who might send soldiers into battle on the front line while sheltering miles behind in his bunker. This was one of the only times I ever heard him talk about his time in the army. It was no secret that he'd been called up to work as an Armed Forces Radio DJ in Japan, having left home at the age of eighteen to go to university, but his active service afterwards in Korea remained undiscussed. In fact, he made clear to me, it would always remain so. He wouldn't ever say why, but I asked as often as I dared. The most he'd ever reveal was that 'Korea taught me two things: how to run and how to cry'.

Lee had decided not only to attend the two celebratory shows at London's South Bank, but also to travel on to Berlin, where the label had lined up an event in a former postal warehouse that had been taken over for a long Sunday night. The Flaming Lips, who'd worked with City Slang in their early years, were headlining the party. They were an almost big enough draw to fill the venue singlehandedly, and the other acts performing—Calexico again among them—ensured that this was going to be a popular night. But it soon became clear that the massive, makeshift venue hadn't been suitably prepared to handle the huge crowd that had bought tickets. For starters, the bars couldn't handle the numbers, with queues extending so far that it could take the best part of half an hour to get a drink. More worrying was the slowly dawning awareness that the room's electricians had failed to set things up safely.

The first warning signs emerged early on, during a set by Lee's one-time 'favourite' band, Built To Spill, as amplifiers buzzed, stuttered, and eventually gave up the ghost, forcing the band to leave the stage. Despite this, I was relieved and entertained to learn that Lee had actually liked what he'd seen. The next band suffered comparable problems, and worse was about to happen. We were watching Yo La Tengo, another act from City Slang's early days, when halfway through their set, one of them, Ira, stepped up to his microphone and was thrown violently backwards towards the drum kit.

'What the hell?' Lee asked sharply. 'Did you see that?'

I did. I was pretty sure I knew what had happened, and shared my suspicions with Lee. Ira confirmed it a moment later, putting down his instrument and staggering off stage in a painful daze. He'd been electrocuted.

'Damn it!' Lee muttered in my ear. 'I didn't expect to see The Flaming Lips until later.'

By the time the real Flaming Lips appeared—in the small hours of the morning, thanks to the time it took to resolve these technical difficulties—Lee had gone back to his hotel. It was definitely for the best: he'd taken greedy advantage of the Chivas Regal that had been provided for him backstage, and at one stage tripped over a cable with such clumsiness that he'd nearly landed head first in a speaker. As the festive mood disintegrated, and the headline act's trademark balloons fell from the ceiling onto a half-empty auditorium, I was glad he wasn't there; the whole affair, with its high expectations and terrible disappointments, was painfully reminiscent of Lee's Fanclub show in Stockholm. We all have off nights, but no one wants to be reminded of them.

Lee and I had joined the label's staff in the boss' garden the following evening, each of us desperate to dismiss memories of the previous night's disarray. A barbecue had been arranged, and we all tried hard to ignore the sense of anticlimax we were feeling. Lee, who evidently felt himself to be above recent events, didn't help; he patronisingly referred to the record company as a 'little label' and offered unwelcome advice from the chair he commanded on the lawn, oiling his already vocal opinions with yet more whisky. This time his anecdotes weren't appreciated in the slightest. One individual was even moved to stand behind Lee's seat, firing imaginary arrows at his head. Lee failed to notice any of this, rambling through his catalogue of tales as though the party were in his honour. I was forced to concede that, on occasions, he could be embarrassing.

'You dug him up,' one of my colleagues reminded me, as I gritted my teeth. 'He's your Frankenstein.'

It was Jeane who recalled that Lee had enjoyed Calexico, and since the band lived in nearby Tucson, she suggested they attend his Memorial. I passed her invitation on, adding that they'd be welcome to play a few of Lee's songs if they felt so inclined. It was a suggestion to which the singer, Joey, a big fan, responded positively.

Joey and I embrace at the reception desk, but however excited he seems to be here, I can't shake off the sense that I've lured him and his musicians here on false premises. I apologise unnecessarily about the small space, and the smaller stage, and that there are no real stars in attendance. Duane Eddy, who's uncomfortable with flying at the best of times, is busy recording; Dean Martin's daughter is trapped in Chicago by bad weather; Sanford

Clark is sick. In fact, Joey himself had informed me at the beginning of the week that, due to surgery, Nancy wouldn't be coming, either: he'd found out when he approached her to sing with them, since they'd recorded together a few years back.

I wanted a more dazzling send-off. '*When you're born in Mannford, Oklahoma,*' Lee had once sung of his birthplace, '*There ain't no up in your cup, there's just down.*' Yet he'd survived the Great Depression to find himself, within four decades, moving among some of the most notable cultural names of the twentieth century. Today's final farewell seems almost as unbecoming as the fate that befell Mannford itself, now no more than a ghost town, much of it underwater, after its inhabitants relocated in the 60s to allow the building of the Keystone Dam. Having circulated among silver-spooned heiresses and earned countless gold discs, having lived comfortably off the proceeds of his multifaceted genius for years, and having finally returned to the public arena to claim his dues, Lee surely deserves better than a buffet in the convention room of a nondescript chain hotel off a busy Arizona freeway.

* * *

Lee discussed plans for his wake almost as long as I knew him. Initially, his schemes were outlandish; he talked of sizeable assets put aside exclusively to provide for the party, and on one occasion claimed it would take place on a boat that would keep sailing until the money ran out. Additional funds, he added, would be set aside to get everyone home from wherever it was they ended up.

Another time, when we were sitting together in the kitchen of my Brixton flat, he told me he wanted to be cremated, and that his remains would be mixed with marijuana so everyone could get 'stoned on my bones'. Since he said he'd rarely taken drugs, this seemed a little bizarre, and as the party approached, I was grateful Lee hadn't been reminded of this particular concept by Keith Richards' recent revelation that he'd snorted his father's ashes like cocaine.

Over the years, as death became an increasingly imminent reality,

Lee's plans—which he never kept secret—had inevitably transformed into something more modest and conventional. During the promotion of *Cake Or Death*, he regularly talked about how he didn't want people to mourn his passing but instead to celebrate his life, adding that Jeane had a set of instructions as to how he wanted this to transpire. Journalists emerged from interviews in which he'd revealed these details thinking that they'd just achieved the most intimate and candid interview of his and their careers. But this was just because few people talked about death with such honesty and humour as Lee.

For these reasons, I arrive at the party determined to have fun. But I also wish to pay my respects. This is no place for formal attire—Lee only ever dressed up once while Jeane knew him, she reminded me a few days earlier: for Sam's wedding, when he'd pulled his tie and blazer off the moment the formalities were over—but nonetheless I'm wearing one of my favourite summer suits. So as not to appear too stiff, however, underneath my jacket I'm wearing an old promotional T-shirt adorned with a portrait of Lee's suave, moustachioed, fortysomething face. I immediately start fielding questions from others keen to get their hands on one. I look, I'm told, like a colonial Reservoir Dog.

Soon I locate Thomas Levy, a French documentary-maker who's been following Lee on and off for the last two years of his life, and who's again on hand with his camera. Lee took the project so seriously that he actually asked Thomas to film his passing, even trying to persuade him to stage a mock bedside death scene in case he should miss the real moment.

'You know what Lee was like,' Jeane explained. 'He told Thomas to record him throwing up in a bucket, and then he wanted to kiss me, lean back on the bed, and close his eyes.'

The scene was never filmed. Instead, Lee passed away quietly while Thomas was on his way to the airport to collect Tommy Parsons.

Tommy's here now, albeit with his own increasingly troubling health issues: in fact, he's wandering around in another popular T-shirt, the one Lee wore for his final birthday with the slogan, 'I'm not dead yet.' Later, someone bleakly jokes that they hope they never inherit the shirt: it'll most likely mean they're up next.

Sam, Debbie, and Mark—Lee's three children—are also here, as are members of their extended family, alongside other loyal members of Lee's circle, including publisher Bo and venerable accountant Marvin. Kalle Axelman, too, is hovering around with his camera; he now controls his father's archives, and always tried to document any meetings he had with Lee. There are further faces I don't recognise, some of whom I meet later; they include Nancy Sinatra's daughter A.J., people with whom Lee worked in Phoenix's studios, artists Lee produced, a local archivist who claims to have unreleased music, and a studio engineer whose honesty would have amused Lee as much as it might have insulted him.

'I worked with him in the 50s,' he tells me. 'Never did like the man, actually. He was hard. Great music, though. Great music!'

I'm less shocked by this indiscretion than I might have been, having had lunch with Duane Eddy a few days earlier in Nashville, where he'd related a story about one of their early sessions.

'Lee was unhappy with the way we were playing,' he'd mumbled—as Lee said Duane always did—over buffalo burgers at Ted Turner's Montana Grill. 'There were three of us, and eventually Lee shouts down the foldback into the studio, "For Christ's sake, guitarist number three! Get it together!" And guitarist three couldn't believe it. He was completely shocked. "Is he talking to me?" he said. And that's 'cos his name was Ry Cooder.'

Like Duane, everyone today is promoting their opinion of Lee as honestly as they can, so there's as much censure as praise. But each comment, whether positive or negative, is laced with a deep affection for the man's achievements. It's as though we all concede that his refusal to compromise at any price was sometimes painful, but also something to admire. We laugh at his frailties and screw-ups as they relate to us, and at times it seems he's just missing, not gone …

Since I'm here—at least partially—in my official capacity as 'Manager (Europe)', I feel obliged to circulate with the guests, but the truth is that, beneath my cheerful exterior, I'm a little jittery. Tucked away in my jacket pocket is a sheaf of papers that represents a speech I'll soon be making. I have no idea when Jeane wants me to deliver it, nor have I had any time during the day to prepare it to the degree I'd hoped, but in a strange way I'm revelling in my nerves. They're not an indication that I think I'm incapable of fulfilling my duty. They're a sign I know how important the job is.

When Jeane first asked me if I'd make an address, I felt honoured. She'd argued she wouldn't be able to stand up in front of the crowd and maintain her composure, and that I'd be the most appropriate person to take her place. I was flattered—delighted, even—although I questioned whether it was really my role to do so. I'm more than aware, after all, that I'm not family, even if Lee sometimes suggested otherwise: shortly before his death he had, in my presence, shocked Samantha—and indeed me—by claiming he had four children. When she'd confronted him with his mistake, he explained that I was the fourth—something that seemed to have troubled her even as it secretly gratified me. I'd been reminded of a questionnaire that Lee had filled out some months earlier to promote *Cake Or Death*. Asked for the names of his three best friends, 'Bubba' was third on the list.

I'd sat up into the small hours the evening Jeane had made her request, and when we next spoke I told her proudly that I'd prepared something, but that I'd like to check it was what she had in mind before spending any more time polishing it.

'I just want something to welcome everyone,' she replied breezily, 'and to tell them about the buffet.'

I paused. This wasn't exactly what I'd written.

'Do you want anything more than that?'

'What do you mean? Do you think we need it?'

I hadn't been sure what to answer. Of course I felt Lee merited more, but wasn't sure it was my place to tell his recently bereaved wife.

'What,' she then asked, 'is it about?'

'Oh, it's about ten minutes long,' I replied, trying to steal one of Lee's oldest gags. She hadn't noticed.

'Well, it's up to you,' she said. This wasn't so helpful. Whatever I did, I wanted it to please her.

So I sent her the speech. She never responded. The next time we spoke, she couldn't remember whether she'd read it or the two eulogies I'd provided for magazines. I decided to take responsibility for the content myself. I actually appreciated the opportunity, I realised: I wanted to share some of the things that I'd learned from him, and some of the adventures we'd enjoyed. I don't believe in an afterlife, but I somehow hoped he might hear, as though it would make up for my feeble farewell at his home.

Now the buffet has arrived, and people are mingling, moving from table to table, watching as Tommy Parsons plays, talking loudly to be heard, embracing, reminiscing, smiling. I no longer know whether a speech is even suitable, so casual is the entire affair. I loiter by the fire exit, smoking a cigarette, holding short conversations with anyone who passes, moving on as fast as I can. I have a growing sensation that I'm at the wrong party. If I stand up before these people, few will know who I am. It was Lee who ensured I belong here, and he's already been gone too long.

In the end, it's Phaedra, in a sophisticated brown dress, her hair perfectly arranged, who breaks the ice and begins the formalities. Samantha leads her to the stage, announcing that Lee's granddaughter has something she'd like to read. With that, Phaedra takes the microphone, provoking sentimental applause over a short minute before Sam hustles her away, giving her a big hug. I decide this is probably the best time for me to address the guests, and move discreetly forward.

Tommy, who's taken on a temporary role as compere, has other ideas. An introduction is made on behalf of a gentleman called Joe Cannon, a rugged blonde-haired all-American cowboy who recorded a soundtrack for *Smoke*, one of Lee's Swedish films. He runs onto the stage like a seasoned professional and introduces himself, his guitar slung over his back. I casually step to one side, as though I'd never meant to go anywhere else. Tommy joins me as Joe begins to sing. I whisper that I have a speech to make, worrying that Tommy might think I'm gatecrashing, hurriedly adding that Jeane invited me to talk.

Tommy in turn looks mortified, as though this was something he should have known. Lee was right: he's always had a good heart.

Joe digs out old songs that he and Lee once worked on, telling stories and trying to involve the crowd. He seems to be fighting a losing battle for their attention—some are even debating whether it really is Burt Reynolds up there—but eventually his attempts to persuade the audience to participate pay off. By the time he plays his final song, they're singing and clapping along.

'I think we've got a special guest in here tonight,' he concludes, as the applause dies down, having presumably spotted me loitering nearby. 'He's one of Lee's best buddies, who's handling all the business affairs.'

This isn't strictly true, so I'm not entirely certain he's referring to me. But when no one else moves forward, I step up to the stage.

'Give a warm hand to Wyndham, all the way from Berlin, Germany!' Joe declares, much as a faded tent-show host would introduce an elderly, exotic cabaret dancer: with enthusiasm that doesn't quite seem matched by conviction. I step up and look around the room. I'm surprisingly relaxed. I'm going to make Lee proud.

'On Jeane's behalf,' I begin, after a short exchange with Joe and a few brief words of introduction, 'I'd like to welcome you all to this celebration of one of my all time heroes, long before I met him: an extraordinary man.'

I take a deep breath and then forge ahead.

'I'm never going to forget the first time Lee wrote to me. I'd just been asked to be his UK publicist and faxed him to introduce myself. His response was typical. He wrote back to me and he said:

Dear Wyndham Wallace,

If I had a name like Wyndham Wallace I would not associate or correspond with anyone with a simple name like mine.

'This probably explains why he started to call me Bubba.'

There's a satisfying, welcoming round of laughter.

'Over the next eight years I progressed from being Lee's UK publicist to being his so-called manager, though I think I was mainly there to protect him from the music industry buffoons for whom he had so little tolerance. I also progressed, far faster than I ever could have believed, to calling him my friend. I think he called me his friend, too, though I never quite worked out why, and he certainly called me "asshole" from time to time, too.'

Everyone breaks up, recognising the truth in this.

'But, then again, he called a lot of people "asshole", so I could live with that!'

They roar louder this time, recognising a still-greater truth.

'I even started to enjoy his legendary "hate faxes", especially the one that culminated with him declaring, "I'm surrounded by assassins!"'

Lee's son Mark cackles particularly noisily at the back.

'I'm probably in the minority here in that I was first of all a fan of the man and only later his friend. Some people remember where they were when Princess Diana died, or when John Lennon was shot, but I can remember where I was the first time I ever saw a picture of Lee. I can remember the first time I ever heard *Cowboy In Sweden*. And I remember these things because Lee's music made such an enormous impression on me. I feel deeply proud to have been able to call Lee my friend. I think we all do. He was a remarkable man who touched us all. They don't make them like Lee any more. They probably never made many like Lee in the first place.'

Off-mic, I mumble, 'I kind of hope not,' but immediately I regret it. I know I don't mean it, and it's not even funny.

'He was a true maverick, a one-off,' I continue, recovering fast. 'But he was far more than that, and he had a whole life outside of the music industry, which is why most of you are here. He was a husband—a provocative but loving husband—who over the last twelve years brought Jeane enviable happiness, as she also did for him.'

Jeane fights back tears as the guests applaud her.

'He was a father to three children, all of whom he talked of incessantly whenever I visited, often when I was on the phone, and especially when I was paying for the call.'

Mark's laugh is again the loudest.

'And he was a grandfather, too, without doubt one of the proudest grandfathers I ever met. I can see why.'

Behind me, images of Lee light up the screen: shots of him in the studio with stars; pictures of him at home with his family.

'Some weeks before Lee passed, I asked him if he would be interested in recording a spoken-word performance as a collaboration with an Icelandic band that I also work with called amiina. He didn't answer my message. I assumed it was because he was going through a tough time with the cancer. A week or so later, though, I received an invitation to his birthday party, and this presented me with a real dilemma: I was meant to be in London that day, meeting my latest signings to the record label I also work with.'

I pause a moment, all at once nervous about what now lies ahead.

'Lee called it a piece-of-shit label, incidentally,' I smile, going off the cuff. 'He was probably right!'

'He was!' a voice in the audience calls out. I have to assume it's friendly. At least it raises a smile.

'Anyway, I replied that I might have problems attending the party, and again I didn't hear back, so I thought that was it. Finally, though, Lee agreed to record the spoken-word performance for me on two conditions: that I attended his birthday party, and that I wrote the text. This was typical of Lee. In one fell swoop he'd given me a very reasonable excuse to pass on to the band who I was meant to be meeting, and managed to secure my attendance at his party, which was great news as far as I was concerned. He'd also made the Icelandic girls, who were huge fans of his, very happy indeed, and he'd indulged my desire to write. As always, he knew exactly what he was doing.

'Just before I left Europe to come here, the band finished mixing the song for which Lee recorded my text. Every time I hear it, it makes me think of him more fondly than I can sometimes bear. The sound of that voice, and the sentimentality with which he managed to deliver my childish words, and the gravity that he gave them, and the power and dignity which he maintained right up to the end: they're all in this song.'

Indeed, the first time I'd heard it, only days after he died, I'd dropped to my knees in front of the stereo and wept, especially when the brass— which had been missing from the original version of the song and recorded especially for this new one—burst forth out of the speakers like paint powder thrown into water.

'Because,' I continue, getting a little caught up in my own theatre, 'when Lee's autumn done come, he treated it exactly as he treated his spring and his summer: like he owned it. Like he wasn't afraid of it. Like there was nothing he couldn't do.'

I particularly emphasise these last words. They seem enormously true to me.

'It's therefore only right that I should actually leave Lee to have the last word tonight. This is the last song he ever recorded. It's called "Hilli (At The Top Of The World)", and you are pretty much the first people ever to hear this. It was finished last week. Maybe, for the next three minutes, as this song plays, we can all reflect for a moment on what an extraordinary man he was and … well … how much we're all going to miss him.'

I take my beer from the table and raise it high in the air. As I take a swig in Lee's honour, guests whistle and cheer.

I feel elated: less because people enjoyed the speech, more because I'm certain I've not let Lee down. I may have worried about stealing the spotlight, but instead I've shone it upon him. He avoided it as much as he could, his mixture of arrogance and insecurity forcing him to protect himself, but now I've shown him he could take it. It's something I can do only because he showed me how. Every dog has its day.

Over to my right, Marty clicks his MacBook, and Lee at last joins us, his voice rumbling from the PA.

At the top of the world there's an island
A place where the sun never shines
But the people don't care
Because the snow over there
Is so bright they nearly go blind.

Guests sit in contemplative silence, some looking up at the huge projections of Lee, others with their heads bowed. I spot Jeane's friend Theresa at the bar, her face stricken with grief. At the back—as the gentle instrumental sounds give way to the band's cherubic voices, cushioning Lee's sometimes parched speech and simultaneously masking the only mistake we'd had to include—I can see Nancy's daughter, her head cupped in one hand, visibly moved. To my right, Phaedra hugs Jeane tightly, and Sam, her eyes red and swollen, her shoulders shuddering uncontrollably, puts her arms round them both, stroking Jeane's hair.

> *The flakes as they fall look like candy*
> *Children rush out when it snows for a treat*
> *Then they open their mouths*
> *And gulp down the flakes*
> *Because nothing on earth tastes so sweet.*

Here a Theremin swoops in, casting a shadow over the song's mood with a ghostly vibrato, before a swell of brass fanfares and deep bass. It gives me goosebumps to hear this, even if part of me feels exploitative for having recorded Lee at such a critical stage in his illness, and perhaps also for tugging unnecessarily at people's heartstrings tonight. But it's definitely a privilege to be able to unveil the track, today of all days. So far I've only played it to Jeane.

There's another thing, too. Years after giving up on teenage dreams of fronting a band, I'm now enjoying the sound of my lyrics being delivered by one of the finest songwriters I've ever encountered. To have Lee read my words—so beautifully, too—and to have amiina work with his raw material and make something so special out of his halting but determined efforts, is the kind of validation I've always sought, something I'm not foolish enough to fail to recognise.

I'm not so proud, though, that I don't care what others think. Fortunately, everyone is listening intently, and I can tell they're thinking of Lee. They can hear the resilient strength in his voice, the invincibility with which it appears he recited the text. He's filled the room with his presence, just as he always did. It may be atypical of his work, but even if I say so myself, it's quite a swansong.

As the track continues, it takes a dark turn. The island's snow begins melting under the heat of the sun, causing the waters to rise. In so doing, it carries a warning to other lands of the damage they're doing to the world.

> *As they started to cry*
> *Their tears filled the sky*
> *And black storm clouds gathered above*
> *And then the heavens opened*
> *And the rain came to show them*
> *That the world needs a little more love.*

Tonight, even I—someone who's now heard the song countless times— fight to keep my composure. Not once has Lee failed to bring tears to my eyes when I hear him pronounce that last phrase with his wry, self-conscious sentimentality. But now, in the face of others around me who have far greater cause to let go, I bite my stiff upper lip and sit quietly until the song comes to a hushed conclusion, like a music box slowly winding down.

> *At the top of the world there's an island*
> *A place where the sun never shines*
> *But the people don't care*
> *Because the snow over there*
> *Is so bright that the sun's in their mind.*

The entire room sits in silence as the final chord fades. Finally, after a long moment of respectful reverie, the party breaks into applause, punctuated by shouts of approval. I lean over to hug Jeane, who's seated nearby.

'I love you, Bubba,' she whispers.

The room falls quiet again, no one quite sure what's happening next. I notice Marty cueing up the other surprise I'd arranged but which, caught up in the song, I'd forgotten all about. I hurry back to the stage to explain the origins of the short film I'm about to show, something edited together by Nina.

'There's something else I want to share,' I announce. 'There are some people who might be a little surprised to see this, because obviously Lee was very ill when it was made. But I hope that you'll enjoy this as a tribute that documents his last party.'

Marty starts the video, and I sit back down again as one of my favourite songs from his final album—'It's Nothing To Me'—plays beneath extracts of Lee's last ever interview. With Sam delivering the cake, Nancy sits at his feet, while others gather around his frail figure, and we watch the famed duo singing together as Tommy strums his guitar. Apart from his friends singing 'Happy Birthday', we only hear Lee: his music and his voice.

'There's nothing in my life I would want to change very much,' he affirms, somehow summing up much of his personality in a few, short seconds, 'unless I hurt someone really bad. If I hurt someone I didn't like, then I don't care. If I hurt someone I like, that would bother me a lot.'

The grandiose strings from 'T.O.M. (The Old Man)', *Cake Or Death*'s closing track, rise in the background.

'People,' he continues, turning to the subject of the very party we're attending, 'are going to fly in—I hope—from all over the world and sit around and tell bad stories on me, I guess, for a couple of hours, and that will be my whole funeral thing, because I'm being cremated. So it will be a nice time: sit around and have a few thousand drinks and tell Lee Hazlewood stories, which I can't … which I'll be … I think I'll be glad I'm dead then, because I don't want to hear all those damned old stories!'

The film finds Nancy and Lee in his hallway, then swings round to family and friends, myself included, all grinning, cameras in hand, one last picture show as he stands in his 'I'm not dead yet' T-shirt. As the lyrics play out, his shy, beautiful smile spreads across his face like mist.

And his tongue, his tongue tastes forever
And his mind wonders what forever will bring
In this place they call forever
Will there be any songs to sing?

This is what happens when you meet your heroes. It always ends in tears.

* * *

Much, much later, Jeane corners me quietly.

'Bubba,' she says. 'There's something I've been meaning to tell you.'

I turn to her expectantly. She looks tired, the emotion of the day having caught up with her, but she has a wicked grin on her face all the same.

'What's that, Jeane?' I ask playfully, in my most polite British accent. It always seemed to charm them.

'It's about your song,' she says, giggling. 'I should have told you before, but somehow I forgot.'

Her smile spreads further. She's relishing this moment. Soon I will, too.

'There was no Finnish fairy tale,' she confides at last. 'You know he made that up? Lee just wanted you to write.'

* * *

May your house be safe from tigers
May you never need to die
May your house be safe from tigers
May you never need to cry
May all your times be good ones
May they never end
May your house be safe from tigers
May you always be my friend …

DIRTNAP
STORIES

There are almost 200 million people in the United States, and the other day one of them asked, 'Who is Lee Hazlewood?' Well, there wasn't no one else around, and since I am Lee Hazlewood, I said, 'There ain't no one else around and, since I am Lee Hazlewood, I'll answer that, friend …'

—'The Lee Hazlewood Biography',
Mercury Records promotional seven-inch single, 1963

A great deal of the dialogue in this book is accurately recorded, but may not have taken place quite when I say it did. The rest is less accurately related, but took place just when I claim. You can't get it all right unless you live with a camera.

Fortunately, that's part of the reason so much of what Lee Hazlewood said to me here is faithfully relayed. In London, Stockholm, and Gotland in 1999, as well as at Lee's Memorial Party in 2007, my friend Kalle Axelman was present filming, and since then he's been kind enough to share relevant portions of his archive in order to ensure at least the partial accuracy of this book. In Berlin and Las Vegas in 2006, furthermore, I was lucky enough to be accompanied by Thomas Levy, whom Lee had allowed to document his life as it came to an end. Thomas, too, gave me access to the footage he had of Lee and me together. Additionally, Nina Fingskes was sweet enough to provide me with the raw tapes of the last interview that Lee carried out, as well as footage of his final birthday party. I am enormously grateful to them all.

Lee, Myself & I also makes significant use of extended interviews I did with Lee before the release his album of demos, *For Every Solution There's A Problem*, and the tribute album I produced, *Total Lee!*

There are many other portions of this book that call upon taped conversations: not long before Lee died, we spent several hours together while he told me stories of some of the celebrities and personalities he had met. These were to make up a small collection he wanted me to put together under the title *Famous People I Have Met. Most Of Them Are Dead. It Wasn't My Fault.* Sadly, by that stage his memory was declining, just as his physical health was—from the treatments he was receiving as much as the cancer itself—and he often struggled to tell his anecdotes as well as he once did. I was therefore forced a few times to amend these so they better reflect the facts—as best as I know them from other times he shared them—but in so doing I've attempted to remain true to his voice.

And by the way, as Lee used to say … Lee may not have chosen to be my subject, but I like to think he would have approved of what he's inspired. It was, arguably, his idea that I write, and sometimes he would tell me things before adding, with a grin, 'and don't put that in your damned book!' He might not have remembered everything quite the way I do, of course, but then again, I suspect plenty of the stories he told himself never took place quite as he claimed. This rarely seemed to bother him—or indeed anyone else—so I hope it won't bother people now.

Navigating your way through Lee Hazlewood's solo and duet catalogue isn't easy for a number of reasons. Records have gone in and out of print, songs are duplicated or re-recorded on various releases, and while even the best albums may have weaknesses, the less perfect ones—with almost no exceptions—have their strengths. The list below compiles what is considered by most people to be Lee's primary commercially (and legally) released catalogue. In one way or another, it includes most of his singles, thanks largely to Light In The Attic's ongoing reissue programme, which has made them available as album bonus tracks, on compilations, or on the priceless boxed set included at the end of this list. While not all of these releases are currently available, the vast majority are, or soon will be. The rest are out there somewhere.

SOLO AND DUET RELEASES
1963: *Trouble Is A Lonesome Town*
Lee's remarkable solo debut was originally recorded as a demo, but it's hard to imagine anyone else singing these songs. (Having said that, producer Charles Normal tried to make exactly that happen in 2013 with his own version of the record, featuring a variety of his friends, among them Frank Black from the Pixies and Isaac Brock of Modest Mouse.) With spoken-word vignettes between each track that sound like they were delivered by some gravel-voiced, psychedelic Garrison Keillor, *Trouble* sketches a picture of a colourful, eccentric America, drawing upon Lee's own experiences, especially from his childhood growing up in the 1930s. It includes one

of the most cheerful songs ever written about death, 'We All Make The Flowers Grow', and 'Run, Boy, Run', most likely familiar to some from a 2011 commercial for the Kia Sportage.

1963: The Shacklefords, *Until You've Heard The Shacklefords You Ain't Heard Nothing Yet*

Named after Naomi Shackleford, Lee's first wife, The Shacklefords were only represented in public by cartoon figures, but in fact featured Lee, his friend Marty Cooper, Albert Stone, and Jack Nitschze's wife, Gracia. The public were confused, but amid these country and folk tracks there are gems, including a touching interpretation of Lee's lullaby-esque 'Our Little Boy Blue', which would be resurrected for *A House Safe For Tigers*.

1964: *The N.S.V.I.P.'s*

Lee's second solo album is especially notable for the offbeat humour of his spoken introductions, delivered in an exaggerated Southern drawl about subjects as diverse as alcoholic dragons and a man who thinks he's a goose. The song titles, which include 'Have You Made Any Bombs Today' and 'Save Your Vote For Clarence Mudd', are similarly quirky. The tracks themselves, however, are stripped back to little more than voice and guitar, their content as moving as their context is amusing.

1965: *Friday's Child*

If you're looking for grander arrangements, and country pop is more to your tastes, then *Friday's Child* is worth tracking down. It lacks the blunt lyrical wit of Lee's first two albums—though there are still smiles to be had in, for instance, 'A Real Live Fool' or the darker 'Me And Charlie'—but it's a wonderful curio that boasts many production traits that later became characteristic Hazlewoodisms.

1966: *The Very Special World Of Lee Hazlewood*

Though it's perhaps best known for Lee's solo version of 'Boots'—complete with a running commentary about the song's more famous incarnation—there's much else to recommend this, not least the astonishing 'My Autumn's Done Come', the doomed romance of 'Bugles In The Afternoon', and the windswept 'For One Moment', all of which owe a debt to legendary arranger Billy Strange. 'Not The Lovin' Kind', meanwhile, betrays Lee's love for the kind of songs that would make up *Farmisht Flatulence* some thirty years later. As good an illustration as any of the peculiar middle ground between pop, country, and what-the-hell-was-that which Lee inhabited.

1966: The Shacklefords, *The Shacklefords Sing*
Lee's cartoon band return for a second time, giving a couple more Hazlewood classics a new sheen, including 'The City Never Sleeps', which Nancy covered for the B-side of 'Boots'. There's also a memorable, increasingly frantic take on Johnny Cash's 'Five Feet High And Risin''. 'That Ole Freight Train', meanwhile, has Lee hitting notes so low they can hardly be heard.

1967: *Lee Hazlewood Presents The 98%: American Mom & Apple Pie 1929 CRASH Band*
Quite what Lee had in mind when this was recorded is hard to say, but unless you have a hankering to hear his songs performed on honky-tonk piano and kazoo, among other things, this collection of covers of some of his biggest hits may be better left to one side. There are uncredited stars like Duane Eddy—here billed as Duane Goldfarb, King of the Pluckers—lying in the shadows of these tracks, but one of the better things that can be said of this novelty album is that it's only twenty-one minutes long.

1967: *Lee Hazlewoodism, Its Cause And Cure*
With Billy Strange onboard once again, classic Hazlewood is assured, and it's present here in the boozy 'After Six' and the hilarious 'Dark In My Heart': *Woke up Sunday morning and I thought that I could sing / But I can't / No I can't*. There's also the moodier 'I Am A Part', the nostalgia of 'The Old Man And His Guitar', the bubblegum pop of 'Paris Girls'—who apparently sing

La la la la la la Lee—and the mariachi inflected story of 'Jose': *He lived for one thing and nothing more / He had to be the very best matador …*

1968: *Love & Other Crimes*
Aside perhaps from the bluesy interlude provided by 'Rosacoke Street' and 'She's Funny That Way', this collection, recorded in Paris, is vintage Lee. Its sound is vast, its tone is often intimately melancholic, and Lee's voice is as rich as it would perhaps ever be, especially on 'Pour Man'. The album was only half an hour long, but the sixty-four-second title track, the haunting 'This House', and the sensational 'Morning Dew' more than compensate.

1968: *Something Special*
Unreleased for twenty years but recorded at the height of his fame, *Something Special* is an eccentric collection, not least for the bizarre scat singing evident on a jazzy version of 'This Town' and the late-night bar-room vibes of 'Stone Cold Blues'. There are also some choice little nuggets on offer, including the autobiographical 'Mannford, Oklahoma' and the tongue-in-cheek 'Them Girls', with yet more scat singing courtesy of producer and arranger Billy Strange.

1968: *Nancy & Lee*
Lee's 'reward' for a job well done with Nancy's solo work, *Nancy & Lee* was their first album together, and it's packed with grandeur and humour in equal measures. Even if you've never knowingly heard them sing together, much of this will be familiar, not least 'Summer Wine', 'Jackson', and the indelible 'Some Velvet Morning'. In a nutshell, this is a master class in duet singing.

1969: *Forty*
More heavily orchestrated than most of his albums, *Forty* is an oft-overlooked release, and unfairly so: though it lacks many of his own compositions, versions of songs like 'The Bed', 'The Night Before', 'Mary', and 'Paris Bells' find Lee on fine vocal form. There's also a version of 'Let's Burn Down The

Cornfield'—one of two Randy Newman covers here—while the undeniable standout is a stunningly arranged 'It Was A Very Good Year'.

1969: *The Cowboy & The Lady*

Some people find Lee's collaboration with actress Ann-Margret a little over-egged, and it's true that she was never going to win awards for subtlety here. There's still plenty to enjoy, however, and even if the chemistry between Lee and his newfound foil isn't quite as combustible as it was with Nancy, they both sound like they're having one hell of a time. Ann-Margret vamps it up, while Lee lets his crooner out to play, but, like *Forty*, the album may well have benefitted from a few Hazlewood originals. The 2000 reissue—care of Smells Like Records—boasts four bonus tracks, three of which were penned by Lee: 'Sleep In The Grass', in particular, is outstanding, like 'Some Velvet Morning' reflected in a fairground mirror.

1970: *Cowboy In Sweden*

The first album Lee recorded in Sweden was also the first to be rereleased by Smells Like Records in 1999, and there couldn't have been a finer way to reintroduce people to his idiosyncratic style. Quite apart from the weirdness of hearing Lee translate co-vocalist Nina Lizell's Swedish on 'Vem Kan Segla', the compelling manner with which he seems to have transferred his cowboy stylings to a Scandinavian landscape makes this sound familiar and yet utterly unlike anything else. A soundtrack to a curious TV special of the same name, it's truly one of Lee's classics, with barely a step out of place, except when—as was sometimes his wont—he meant it to be that way.

1971: *Requiem For An Almost Lady*

One of the harshest, most candid break-up albums ever made, *Requiem* again finds Lee delivering little monologues between songs, this time about a painful romantic split. Often said to be about Suzi Jane Hokum—the girlfriend he'd had who had produced Gram Parsons' album with The International Submarine Band, *Safe At Home*, for Lee's LHI label—Lee insisted it instead featured a composite subject that drew upon more than just one relationship. Either way, it's brooding and heartbreaking, but, thanks to Lee's inimitable sense of humour, never self-piteous. 'Come On Home To Me', meanwhile, remains one of his masterpieces.

1972: *Did You Ever* aka *Nancy & Lee Again*

Though it lacks the big hitters of their first album together, Lee's reunion with Nancy Sinatra benefits from its comparative obscurity: the relative freshness of the songs make it arguably a more playful, joyful record. That's most evident on the charming 'Tippy Toes'—an ode to parenthood—and the throwaway closer, 'Got It Together', as well as the flirtatious 'Did You Ever', which gave the record its original name. (It was re-released in 1973 as … *Again*.) Light-hearted it may be, but it's still something special.

1972: *13*

From the opening fanfare of 'You Look Like A Lady'—one of many contributions provided by Larry Marks, a musical arranger on children's cartoons—you know *13* isn't going to be your average Hazlewood collection. In fact, this finds Lee getting all showman, its songs seemingly suited for both the big stage and the dance floor, sometimes at the same time. 'Tulsa Sunday' is sexy and sluggish; 'I Move Around' demands a spotlight, a tuxedo, and a pencil microphone; and both the aforementioned brassy first track and the closing 'Hej, Me I'm Riding' find him working up a funky, slick sweat. A contrast to the previous year's sombre *Requiem*, and one of two records he released this year, it's a curveball in Lee's career, but a fine one, nevertheless.

1973: *Poet, Fool Or Bum*

Best known, especially by Lee, for having been reviewed by a British critic with one word—'Bum'—*Poet, Fool Or Bum* is most notable for 'The Performer''s droll wit, the dreamlike 'Kari', and the grandiose 'Come Spend The Morning'. Though it lacks the impact of the work immediately preceding it, it's fair to say that critics might have done better to focus on its poetic nature.

1974: *The Stockholm Kid*

A noteworthy record of a live performance in Sweden that, these days, is almost impossible to track down. Lee himself was feverish that night, but he's so cool you'd never know. Sadly only thirty-eight minutes long, *The Stockholm Kid* offers a wonderful version of 'The Performer', a sophisticated version of 'It Was A Very Good Year', an inevitable canter through his back catalogue with a five-minute medley of his hits, and some typically high-class patter.

1975: *A House Safe For Tigers*

For a long time, this was the Holy Grail for Hazlewood addicks. The soundtrack to an obscure art-house film made in Sweden, copies were once exchanged by collectors for foolish sums of money. Much of this was provoked by the outstanding six-and-a-half minute opening song, 'Souls Island': with its huge orchestral arrangement, it remains one of the most dramatic recordings Lee ever undertook. Elsewhere there are variations on the album's main melodic theme, as well as curios like 'Sand Hill Anna And The Russian Mouse' and a version of 'Little Boy Blue' (also recorded by Lee's shortlived group The Shacklefords), while Lee reminds us of his Native American blood on 'The Nights'.

1977: *Back On The Street Again*

This barely made it past the borders of producer Bobby Bobcine's native Germany, and also has a cover that looks like a dirty floor tile, but it still contains the fabulously lugubrious 'Rider On A White Horse', the tongue-in-cheek 'Dolly Parton's Guitar', and an unforgettably smooth take on Kenneth Ancell and A.J. Spezell's 'New Box Of People'.

1977: *Movin' On*

The beginning of the wilderness years, and often it shows: you'll find songs previously released on better albums—'It Was A Very Good Year', 'Come On Home To Me'—while elsewhere Lee sounds like he's treading water.

'Mother Country Music' and 'I've Got To Be Movin'' are disappointingly reflective of the bland, mainstream country-pop sound prevalent in the 1970s—something also underlined by the cover, which would be better suited to a truck stop compilation—and, throughout, the production suggests Lee was tired of the very things that had made him so distinctive. Move on; there's nothing to see here.

1993: *Gypsies & Indians*
This collaboration with Finland's Anna Hanski may have been released as interest in Lee's work was first beginning to reawaken, but it was never going to be the record to inspire his resurrection. Bombastic and dated—even at the time of its release—it would really be better if one didn't mention this at all. That's especially true if you don't wish to desecrate the memory of some of his finest songs, like 'Some Velvet Morning', 'Sand', and 'Ladybird', which all make an appearance here.

1999: *Farmisht Flatulence, Origami, ARF!!! & Me*
OK, no one ever asked Lee to record a collection of standards, and at the time of its release this wasn't quite the comeback that anyone wanted. Get past the album cover, however, and the presence of his old friend Al Casey on guitar helps confirm that Lee was born to sing these songs, if only for a small audience. Jazzy and sophisticated—if not innovative—it deserves to be taken as seriously as Lee meant it, not least for 'She's Funny That Way', the song that Lee dedicated to his future wife, Jeane, at his first Royal Festival Hall show.

2002: *For Every Solution There's A Problem*
Compiled from a CD of twenty-one demos that Lee sent me, this provided an opportunity for his fans to delve further into his 'missing' catalogue following the Smells Like Records reissues. It also gave Lee the chance to head out across Europe on what would turn out to be his final tour. Some songs will now be familiar, in their non-demo states, from other

releases which, at the time, were out of print. But there are also tracks—the mournful 'Dirtnap Stories' and the hidden track 'For My Birthday'—that have never seen the light in any studio-recorded form elsewhere.

2002: *Bootleg Dreams And Counterfeit Demos*
This album contains the ten songs that didn't make *For Every Solution*. Among them were the original demos for tracks that ended up on 1993's *Gypsies & Indians*, and a drinking song—Lee called it an 'Oom Pah Pah song'—entitled 'Drinking Kölsch In Cologne'. Its official release was limited to Sweden, and on this occasion that wasn't a bad thing.

2003: *The Lycanthrope Tour*
Recorded live, this is a faithful account of the shows Lee performed on his 2002 European tour, the last concerts he would undertake (apart from one final Royal Festival Hall appearance in 2004). A band made up largely of members of The High Llamas and Stereolab—led by the former's Jon Fell—provided simple arrangements of Lee's songs, drawing from across his career, including the two recent demos albums. There's plenty of evidence of his between-song chatter, and you'll also hear Al Casey on a few numbers. (Sadly, Al got ill after five shows and had to head home.) Perhaps the loveliest thing about it, however, is hearing the affection in which Lee is held by his audience.

2004: *Nancy & Lee 3*
Better overlooked, which it was easy to do until recently, since it was only ever released in Australia.

2006: *Cake Or Death*
While other veterans seek celebrity producers to reinforce their comebacks, Lee went it alone, another signal of his abiding insistence upon doing things his own way. 'Baghdad Knights' addresses the Iraq conflict with blasts of brass and a kick-ass riff, while the satirical 'White People Thing' reminds

one of his more caustic side. There's also a version of 'Boots', with Duane Eddy on guitar, that returns to the song's original, previously unheard melody. Closing tune 'T.O.M. (The Old Man)'—Lee signed many of his messages towards the end of his life with 'T.O.M.'—provides an agreeably schmaltzy but eloquently affecting way for ole Barton to leave the building or, to employ an expression he was especially fond of, to 'buy the farm'.

THE SWANSONG SINGLE
2007: 'Hilli (At The Top Of The World)'

Released as a seven-inch and download shortly after his death, Lee's final recording—which featured him reciting a text over music by amiina, Sigur Rós' former string section—was backed by a beautiful instrumental cover of 'Leather & Lace', performed on, among other instruments, a saw. I'm not an entirely impartial critic, I concede.

COMPILATIONS
1989: *Fairy Tales & Fantasies*

For a long time, this compilation was the only way to hear Lee on a legitimate release, and it was a wonderful introduction. It includes not only the most commercially successful of Lee and Nancy's duets, but also some of their more eccentric collaborations, including the stormy 'Arkansas Coal (Suite)' and their version of The Righteous Brothers' 'You've Lost That Lovin' Feelin''.

2002: *Total Lee: The Songs Of Lee Hazlewood*

A tribute album that I put together over two years, *Total Lee* isn't quite the record it could have been. PJ Harvey recorded a track with Vincent Gallo that she then decided wasn't up to par, and there were other artists, including Beck, whose schedules wouldn't allow them to participate. It nonetheless boasts some wonderful interpretations of both prominent and more obscure Lee compositions, my personal favourites including Stephen Jones (aka Baby Bird) and Luke Scott's 'We All Make The Flowers Grow', Kathryn Williams' 'Easy & Me', Erlend Øye (of Kings Of Convenience)'s 'No Train To Stockholm', Lambchop's 'I'm Glad I Never', and Kid Loco featuring Tim Keegan's 'If It's Monday Morning'. Also present, among others, are Jarvis Cocker & Richard Hawley, St Etienne, Tindersticks, Calexico, and Evan Dando (of The Lemonheads). The liner notes, meanwhile, document the increasingly drunken evening I spent playing the album to Lee for the very first time.

2012: *The LHI Years: Singles, Nudes & Backsides (1968–71)*

A compilation that draws upon the singles Lee released on his own label, LHI, in the years following his success with Nancy Sinatra up to, and including releases from, the time of his relocation to Sweden. A succinct primer, it also features images—including the cover—from one of his most striking, formerly 'lost' photo shoots, and liner notes by, well, me.

2013: *There's A Dream I've Been Saving: Lee Hazlewood Industries 1966–71*

Despite the extraordinary wealth of audio material here—107 tracks, 4 CDs … and that's excluding the data discs, which include a mass of other archive material recorded by Lee and other acts signed to his LHI label—the true highlight of this boxed set is a lovingly compiled, LP-sized book. Full of rare pictures, interviews, and much more, this is perhaps overwhelming for a newcomer, but it is without doubt one of the grandest, most impressive tributes to the cult of Lee Hazlewood one could ever wish for, and entirely worthy of its Grammy nomination. You'll also get a DVD of Lee's first Swedish film, *Cowboy In Sweden*. Beg, buy, or borrow.

AUTHOR'S THANKS

I would first like to thank the following individuals—in a fairly random order—for helping to support me in one way or another during the prolonged genesis of *Lee, Myself & I*: Kalle Axelman, Thomas Levy, Ela Hund-Göschel, Meret Frey, Paul Sullivan, Arezu Weitholz, Erling Ramskell, Anita Overelv, Irma Gißrau, Tariq Goddard, Stephen Dalton, Torbjörn Axelman, Nathan Beazer, Nina Fingskes, Christian Obermaier, Keith Nealy, Perry Serpa, Ewan Pearson, Sondre Sommerfelt, Bo Goldsen, Dean Wareham, Gerrit Sievert, The Ådland family, Ed Harcourt, Fabian Schmidt, Matt Henderson, John Doran, Luke Turner, Eva Liedtke, Christof Ellinghaus, Richard Barron, Vera Arntsen, Tim Burgess, Teri and Ben Olins, Tom Reiss, James Johnston, Nicola Borradaile, Owain Bennallack, Melissa Taylor, Matt Sullivan, Kate Bomphrey, Mark Pickerel, Drew Pearce, Dahlia Schweitzer, Matt Sullivan, Sharmaine Lovegrove, Thomas Hess, Chris Sharp, Lena Obara, Chad Foltz, Simon Benham, and of course anyone else I may have carelessly omitted. I'm sorry, too, that Tommy Parsons, who died days before I finished editing this book, never got to read it. Rest In Peace.

Particular gratitude goes to my agent, Matthew Hamilton, at Aitken Alexander, for his belief, commitment, and advice, and to Tom Seabrook, of Jawbone Press, for much the same, as well as his wise editing.

I'm also deeply indebted to the four women of amiina—Hildur Ársælsdóttir, Edda Rún Ólafsdóttir, Maria Huld Markan Sigfúsdóttir, and Sólrún Sumarliðadóttir—for the magic of 'Hilli'. You brought a fairy tale to 'Eskimo' life.

Thanks, too, to Steve Shelley, for enabling me to meet Lee in the first place, and to Bela B., Claudia Stülpner, and Fitz Braum, for helping to make the last adventure I shared with him so unforgettable.

I must also express thanks to Stefan Kassel, for the wonderful cover he designed, and to Stewart Lee, for responding so gracefully to my initial overtures, and writing such an elegant foreword.

Parts of the chapter 'My Autumn's Done Come' were originally written, in a slightly different form, for the liner notes to Light In The Attic's reissue of Lee's *A House Safe For Tigers* album. I'm grateful to them for allowing me to reuse the work.

Additionally, I'd like to thank Simon Long, who has always offered me invaluable legal advice and shown great faith in me.

Naturally, I would also like to thank my parents, as is only appropriate on these occasions. At no point have they ever questioned the wisdom of me devoting great chunks of my time to writing a book instead of earning a decent living. Their encouragement has been a great gift. It doesn't matter how old one gets: one always wants one's parents to approve.

I would also like to thank my sister, Suzannah, first of all for helping transcribe some of the interviews I did with Lee, but mainly for putting up with me all her life. No one else has, or will.

Finally, I would like to offer gratitude to Marvin Zolt, and especially to Jeane Hazlewood, without whose kindness, generosity, and hospitality I may never have been able to get to know Lee as well as I did. *She's funny that way …*

Photo credits

The photographs used in this book come from the following sources, to whom I am very grateful. If you feel there has been a misplaced attribution, please contact the publisher. **1** Jakob Axelman **2–3** Kevin Cummins **121** Mark Pickerel (3) **122** author's collection (2), Jeane Hazlewood **123** author's collection **124** author's collection (2), Kalle Axelman **125** Simon Leigh **126–7** Steve Double **128–9** author's collection (4) **130–1** Franziska Stünkel **132–3** Jakob Axelman (3) **134** Kevin Cummins **135** author's collection **136** author's collection (3).

Song credits

'Pray Them Bars Away': Words & Music by Lee Hazlewood © Copyright 1970 Lee Hazlewood Music Limited. Carlin Music Corporation for UK & EIRE. Universal Music Publishing Limited for World excluding UK & EIRE. All Rights Reserved. International Copyright Secured.

'Leather & Lace': Words & Music by Lee Hazlewood © Copyright 1970 Lee Hazlewood Music Limited. Carlin Music Corporation for UK & EIRE. Universal Music Publishing Limited for World excluding UK & EIRE. All Rights Reserved. International Copyright Secured.

'After Six': Words & Music by Lee Hazlewood © Copyright 1967 Criterion Music Corporation. Universal Music Publishing Limited. All Rights Reserved. International Copyright Secured.

'Come On Home To Me': Words & Music by Lee Hazlewood © Copyright 1971 Lee Hazlewood Music Limited. Carlin Music Corporation for UK & EIRE.

Universal Music Publishing Limited for World excluding UK & EIRE. All Rights Reserved. International Copyright Secured.

'For One Moment': Words & Music by Lee Hazlewood © Copyright 1966 Criterion Music Corporation. Universal Music Publishing Limited. All Rights Reserved. International Copyright Secured.

'Hutchinson Jail': Words & Music by Lee Hazlewood © Copyright 1966 Criterion Music Corporation. Universal Music Publishing Limited. All Rights Reserved. International Copyright Secured.

'Houston': Words & Music by Lee Hazlewood © Copyright 1965 Criterion Music Corporation. Universal Music Publishing Limited. All Rights Reserved. International Copyright Secured.

'Trouble Is A Lonesome Town': Words & Music by Lee Hazlewood © Copyright 1963 Guitar Music Corporation. Carlin Music Corporation for UK & EIRE. Universal Music Publishing Limited for World excluding UK & EIRE. All Rights Reserved. International Copyright Secured.

'My Autumn's Done Come': Words & Music by Lee Hazlewood © Copyright 1966 Criterion Music Corporation. Universal Music Publishing Limited. All Rights Reserved. International Copyright Secured.

'These Boots Are Made For Walkin'': Words & Music by Lee Hazlewood © Copyright 1965 & 1966 Criterion Music Corporation. Universal Music Publishing Limited. All Rights Reserved. International Copyright Secured.

LEE HAZLEWOOD DELUXE EDITIONS
from Light In The Attic Records

V/A
There's A Dream I've Been Saving:
Lee Hazlewood Industries 1966–1971
(8xLP + Deluxe CD Box Set + Book)
LITA 109

LEE HAZLEWOOD
Trouble Is A Lonesome Town
(CD, 2xLP)
LITA 096

V/A
You Turned My Head Around:
Lee Hazlewood Industries 1967–1970
(11 x 7" Box Set + book)
LITA 094

LEE HAZLEWOOD
A House Safe For Tigers
(CD, LP)
LITA 087

LEE HAZLEWOOD
The LHI Years:
Singles, Nudes, & Backsides (1968–71)
(CD, 2xLP)
LITA 084